NEW GUINEA IMPATIENS

A Ball Guide

Edited by
Warren Banner and Michael Klopmeyer

Ball Publishing

Batavia, Illinois USA

Ball Publishing
335 North River Street
Batavia, Illinois 60510 USA
708/208-9080

Library of Congress Cataloging-in-Publication Data
New Guinea impatiens : a Ball guide / edited by Warren Banner and
   Michael Klopmeyer.
         p.   cm.
   Includes bibliographical references and index.
     ISBN 1-883052-07-6 (pbk.)
     1. New Guinea impatiens.   I. Banner, Warren, 1955-
   II. Klopmeyer, Michael, 1957-   .
   SB413.N48N47 1995
   635.9'33216—dc20   95-6865
                                                              CIP

Front cover: Celebration Raspberry Rose New Guinea impatiens from Ball FloraPlant,
         West Chicago, Illinois.

TABLE OF CONTENTS

PREFACE

New Guinea impatiens have experienced explosive growth in the last five years in North America, Europe, Japan, and Australia. This crop represents the most significant new and improved product to enter the floriculture market since bedding impatiens. With worldwide consumption of over 100 million cuttings annually, New Guinea impatiens are a major spring bedding and pot plant. The North American market consumes 30 to 40 million plants while Europe consumes two to three times this quantity.

Why has this crop found its way into gardens, windowsills, and hanging baskets worldwide? Consumers routinely comment on the large, showy flowers, aesthetic foliage, and lack of pests and diseases. They also love the wide assortment of colors. New Guinea impatiens can take the heavy rains encountered in the summers without succumbing to Botrytis and provide a continuous display of color. Requiring partial sun, New Guinea impatiens are ideal for many settings around the house that do not have full sun or shade. The bottom line is that the New Guinea impatiens is an ornamental plant for today's consumer, providing the value and beauty in demand.

We would, however, be remiss to tout New Guinea impatiens as the perfect ornamental plant. It is a thirsty plant with a poor water conserving ability. New breeding has increased its tolerance to sun, but it still requires some shading in most parts of North America. Growers also recognize New Guinea impatiens as less than simple to grow since it has a unique set of cultural requirements.

New Guinea impatiens have been commercially grown since the early 1970s. However, in the past 20 to 25 years there have been no comprehensive publications on this crop. Many authors in this book have previously published articles and papers on specific culture, diseases, marketing, or uses of New Guinea impatiens, but nowhere could one find in one single publication a thorough review of New Guinea impatiens as a commercial crop.

This *Guide to New Guinea Impatiens* presents the most current knowledge on how to grow beautiful plants; understanding and preventing diseases and pests, including TSWV and thrips; and uses and valuable ideas on how to market finished crops. We have also included a chapter written by prominent growers (Chapter 9) from different parts of the United States outlining their recipes for successful finishing.

The commercial development of New Guinea impatiens is a fascinating and exciting story. Marc Cathey, author of the History of Commercialization (Chapter 2), illustrates the winding path of their development including expeditions to the island of New Guinea in search of the original "parents" of the varieties commercially available today. At one time, Marc had all the original collections from New Guinea in the trunk of his car.

It is almost unbelievable how fast this crop has evolved in the hands of breeders and marketers. The varieties with highly variegated foliage have diminished, and the small flowers have grown from 1 inch in diameter to 3 inches in diameter. Scott Trees has compiled an interesting set of interviews in Chapter 21 with important breeders around the world to capture where we have been and what the future holds.

The foresight that Harold Winters, Joseph Higgins, Toru Arisumi, and Claude Hope had in traveling around the world to search for new ornamental crops is now apparent. New Guinea impatiens are an important ornamental crop providing beauty and livelihoods for millions. The future of this crop is extremely bright. Think of what has happened in the past five years and imagine the spectrum of color, habits, and tolerances to environmental stresses that will occur by the beginning of the 21st century.

ACKNOWLEDGMENTS

The idea for this book originated with John Guenther, Senior Vice President of Geo. J. Ball, Inc. He realized the need, by growers and retailers, for a comprehensive source of culture and uses of New Guinea impatiens required to be routinely successful with the crop.

We would like to thank all of the authors for their knowledge and their generous commitment of time required for each of their chapters. The authors have shown great patience in the long process of producing this book.

The breeders of New Guinea impatiens—Ball FloraPlant, Mikkelsens, Kientzler Jungpflanzen (Paul Ecke Ranch), Dan Flower Farm, and Gartenbau Norbert Bull—were very supportive of this effort and willingly contributed in many ways.

There were several people who have provided invaluable input on the subject matter and content including Vic Ball, Editor-in-chief of Ball Publishing, Marvin N. Miller, Market Research Manager, Geo. J. Ball, Inc., and John Guenther. Carole Hanson of Ball FloraPlant helped provide photography.

The staff at Ball Publishing provided strong professional editorial direction, resulting in a top-quality book. We particularly wish to thank John Martens, President of Ball Publishing; Diane McCarthy, Production Editor; Liza Sutherland, Book Editor; and Kate Barauski, former Associate Publisher.

Janet Cool of Ball FloraPlant did a wonderful job of coordinating manuscripts with authors and keeping us on schedule.

AUTHORS

Chapter	Title	Author
1	Status of the Industry	
	North America	Dr. Roy A. Larson Department of Horticultural Science North Carolina State University Raleigh, North Carolina
	Europe	Garry Grueber Kientzler Jungpflanzen Gensingen, Germany
2	History of Commercialization	Dr. H. Marc Cathey American Horticultural Society Alexandria, Virginia
3	Media	Dr. William Healy Ball Seed Company West Chicago, Illinois
4	Feeding and Watering	Dr. David E. Hartley Paul Ecke Ranch Encinitas, California
5	Light and Temperature	Dr. John Erwin Department of Horticultural Science University of Minnesota St. Paul, Minnesota
6	Certified Stock	Dr. Michael J. Klopmeyer Ball FloraPlant West Chicago, Illinois
7	Stock Plant Production	Pamela Ruis Paul Ecke Ranch Encinitas, California
		Jack E. Williams Paul Ecke Ranch Encinitas, California
8	Rooting	Dr. Edward P. Mikkelsen Mikkelsens, Inc. Ashtabula, Ohio

James A. Bethke
Department of Entomology
University of California -
Riverside
Riverside, California

Edwin A. Shearin
Department of Entomology
North Carolina State University
Raleigh, North Carolina

CHAPTER 1

Status of the Industry

North America

Roy A. Larson

Only a very few floricultural crops have been introduced to the floriculture industry in the last 25 years that can compare with the success of the New Guinea impatiens. At first, the New Guinea impatiens was regarded primarily as a bedding plant. Applauded for its ability to withstand more sunshine than other impatiens, it was suggested that these impatiens be protected from the hot afternoon sun, particularly in the South (fig. 1.1). The need for adequate water and good drainage was emphasized, and one of the pioneer New Guinea impatiens propagators told growers to advise their customers to water the plants daily for the first 10 days and then water them as they would any other bedding plant.

Fig. 1.1. *The original concept was that plants could take full sun. Photo taken in Raleigh, North Carolina, in mid-October, when plants had revived.*

1

Fig. 1.2. *New Guinea impatiens is no longer solely regarded as a bedding plant.*

Twelve years ago it was predicted that New Guinea impatiens would replace many geraniums in the landscape, and a prominent geneticist suggested that New Guinea impatiens would compete favorably with the petunia as a bedding plant.

Growers participating in the 1988 Census of Horticultural Specialties reported that New Guinea impatiens accounted for 1.8% of their total sales. Other impatiens were responsible for 7.6% of total sales, petunias accounted for 6.5%, and vegetatively propagated geraniums were 12.6% of the total [1].

The crop no longer is confined to a bedding plant classification (fig. 1.2). Growers quickly realized that it could be used as a flowering potted plant in containers ranging from 4-inch pots to 10-inch hanging baskets. It can be used as an attractive interior plant, if light intensity is adequate, or it can be a beautiful focal point on the patio.

One propagator listed these uses for New Guinea impatiens: "Hanging baskets for spring flowering sales; combination pots and baskets of two or more cultivars; outdoor plantings; annual flower beds and borders; patio containers, outdoor planters and urns; mass plantings in parks, shopping centers, and industrial developments."

Breeders' ingenuity: the key to success
Much of this crop's success can be attributed to the ingenuity of plant breeders. They took a plant native to the New Guinea tropics, improved its beauty, and adapted it for more temperate regions. Prettier, larger flowers, better growth habit, foliage of several descriptions have resulted from these breeding programs. Several companies have contributed

to these striking changes and improvements. The original list of commercial cultivars was a short one, but perusal of the 1994-95 cultivar list revealed the following numbers in the various series:

Mikkel Sunshine	12	Lasting Impressions	15
Pure Beauty	21	Paradise	20
Celebration	16	Bull	9
Danziger	12		

These numbers add up to a large array of cultivars for a crop with a relatively short history.

New Guinea impatiens are not surveyed every year by the U.S. Department of Agriculture Statistical Service so there is no accurate way to know who and how many people are growing New Guinea impatiens commercially. Propagators probably are most informed about this unique crop's status but not all of them reveal their figures to competitors.

Estimate 15 percent increase per year

Ed Mikkelsen, president of Mikkelsens, has estimated that 30,000,000 to 40,000,000 cuttings are propagated annually in the United States, but he acknowledges that such statistics are not firmly based. He also has estimated a 15% annual increase in New Guinea impatiens for several years. Statistics from individual firms won't be reported here, but hopefully the crop will become a separate unit in future crop surveys so its value at state and national levels will be known.

New Guinea impatiens statistics were obtained from growers in the 1987 survey and listed in the Bedding/Garden Plants section of the *Census of Horticultural Specialties* (1988). The information was not widely distributed, however, and production by states was not given. In 1987 there were 2,175 businesses involved in New Guinea impatiens production compared to 5,509 establishments that sold zonal gerani-

▰▰▰▰▰▰ **TABLE 1.1** ▰▰▰▰▰▰

Production figures for four floriculture crops, 1987 [a]

Bedding/garden plants	Number of firms	Sales (x $1,000)	Number of pots Less than 5-inch	5-inch plus	Hanging baskets
New Guinea impatiens	2,175	16,425	4,367	830	953
Geraniums, zonal	5,509	112,775	53,961	8,394	1,412
Geraniums, seed	3,207	60,256	39,488	3,359	159
Chrysanthemums, hardy/garden	2,869	38,390	9,640	13,173	201

[a] Based on *1988 Census of Horticultural Specialties*.

ums, 3,207 growers producing seedling geraniums, and 2,869 firms growing hardy/garden chrysanthemums (table 1.1).

Monetary value and numbers sold in three size categories show that New Guinea impatiens are not close to seedling and zonal geranium production levels. They also don't compete yet with hardy/garden chrysanthemums, which generally are sold only in late summer or early fall. In 1992 bedding plant growers were polled to determine how many planned to increase production of various species in 1993. Some 53% planned to increase the more common form of impatiens and 9% were going to increase New Guinea impatiens production. Also in 1992, growers were asked to select the best selling plants. New Guinea impatiens rated eighth over all other bedding plants, while pansies and tomato plants were ninth and tenth, respectively.

The 1988 report did not provide information about the status of growers who produced New Guinea impatiens in 1987, but it did show that of 2,175 firms producing the crop, 1,105 were wholesale growers. Calculations show that 51% of the New Guinea impatiens growers sold wholesale, compared to 70% for potted chrysanthemums, 68% for hydrangeas, 67% for poinsettias and gloxinias, 65% for cyclamen, 62% for florist azaleas, 61% for Easter lilies and 56% for spring-flowering bulbs. We can assume that the remaining production occurred in retail greenhouse establishments.

Size of establishment is not a distinguishing feature of New Guinea impatiens production. It's a crop that is suitable for mass market, garden center or even retail florist shop sales. The marketing channel will determine if the plants are sold in flats, packs, small or large pots or hanging baskets. Some markets may have all items in their inventory, while a retail florist shop might only offer flowering plants in 6-inch pots.

Major breeders/suppliers

The New Guinea impatiens plants that plant explorers from Longwood Gardens (affiliated with the USDA) sent back to the United States did not exactly resemble the plants that are available now. The original introductions had smaller flowers with a limited range of colors, leaves were often sparse, and plant habit was not ideal. Talented geneticists and plant breeders, employed by commercial companies, have made major advancements in the crop's beauty. Early contributions also were made by Dr. Toru Arisumi, a geneticist at the USDA facility in Beltsville, Maryland, who used the original 14 selections in his breeding program.

The California-Florida Plant Corporation of Fremont, California, introduced a series named after North American Indian tribes. Plant breeders at Mikkelsens Inc. in Ashtabula, Ohio, developed several cultivars in the Sunshine series and gave them names such as Sundazzle, Sunfire and Sunglow because they performed well under high light conditions. Mikkelsens has continued to develop new cultivars now placed in the Lasting Impressions series.

Improvements haven't been confined to the United States. Claude Hope in Costa Rica made some major contributions when he was affiliated with PanAmerican Seed Co. (see Color Plate section, CP 1.1). The Ball FloraPlant Celebration series is known for its large flowers and attractive foliage. Ludwig Kientzler, a German plant breeder, introduced many new cultivars in the Pure Beauty series and the Paradise series. The Kientzler cultivars are distributed by the Paul Ecke Ranch, Encinitas, California.

Dan Flower of Israel was the plant breeder who developed the Danziger series, distributed by Fischer, which also distributes the Bull series to North American growers.

Not all companies have had the same breeding objectives. Mikkelsen cultivars often were characterized by bicolor flowers and variegated foliage. However, their new series, Lasting Impressions, has solid color leaves with bright, single color flowers. Variegation in leaves is lost in countries with low light intensity, so European breeders such as Kientzler have also developed cultivars with bright, single color flowers and solid green foliage (see color plates of varieties).

Plant breeders don't confine their efforts to improving flowers and foliage. Disease and drought resistance are two goals that would greatly enhance New Guinea impatiens for commercial growers and for people who utilize the plants.

Limitations of New Guinea impatiens

Some early purchasers of New Guinea impatiens undoubtedly were surprised and disappointed that the plants fared about as poorly in full sun as did other impatiens. Water was required on almost a daily basis. Customers might also have been disappointed when a plant covered with flower buds failed to bloom after placing it in low light, indoors or outside.

New Guinea impatiens seemed to have unlimited potential with no reason to expect a decline in numbers or economic value. Then tomato spotted wilt virus emerged as its vector, western flower thrips, was disseminated on a world-wide scale. Losses to some growers were so instantaneous and serious that the future of the New Guinea impatiens seemed clouded. Screening out the thrips from the production area, purchasing insect and disease-free cuttings, and some effective pesticides have alleviated the situation, but growers are aware that a danger exists.

Novice New Guinea impatiens growers frequently are perplexed when newly planted cuttings start off so slowly after transplanting. This slow start can't be corrected by applying water and fertilizer more generously, and the condition will worsen if these attempts are made. Most other crops respond positively to water and fertilizer, so growers might think they are wasting time and greenhouse space with New Guinea impatiens. This attitude could limit a grower's eagerness to grow more plants next year unless he's told in advance that the crop makes little apparent progress in its first month.

The future of New Guinea impatiens

New Guinea impatiens sales don't have to be confined to the bedding plant season. Outstanding flowering plants have been timed for GrowerExpo held in Chicago in early January. Short days and low light intensity are the climatic conditions in northern Illinois in the fall, and yet plants were of very high quality. New Guinea impatiens, in combination with poinsettias or cyclamen, can be very attractive color pots for Christmas sales. Other combinations could be made for other holidays. Their extended flowering season enables growers to have a more continuous sales item.

The almost iridescent flowers, borne so abundantly on every plant, capture the customers' admiration and attention and often even that of the growers who sometimes become calloused to the beauty of the products they grow and sell. New Guinea impatiens don't require pinching, lighting, pulling black cloth, or disbudding. This gives an economic advantage to producing New Guinea impatiens over some crops that require all those steps, at some times of the year. Old flowers, however, should be removed as they don't readily fall off, and their continued presence may adversely affect new flower production.

Garden magazines have generously featured New Guinea impatiens. Such good publicity almost always has a positive effect on sales but a grower's failure to have high quality flowering plants available nullifies the no-effort, low-cost promotion. It might also compel a customer to seek satisfaction in a competitor's salesroom.

Improvements undoubtedly will continue on traits as diverse as the flower keeping quality and tomato spotted wilt virus resistance. Water stress and high light intensity tolerance are current goals of some highly respected plant geneticists.

References ————————————————————

[1]   Voigt, A.O. 1992. Mix of bedding plants, official. *Flower Marketing Information.* June.

Europe

Garry Grueber

In the past the European bedding plant market has been dominated by such well-known staples as vegetatively propagated geraniums, fuchsias, wax begonias, marigolds, and verbenas. Both the grower and the consumer have been quite reluctant to try anything dramatically new. It seems as if the multitude of European cultures, steeped in centuries of tradition and customs, stubbornly lived up to their reputation as being slow to change the way things have been done in the past. A German proverb puts it well: "If the farmer isn't familiar with something, he won't eat it."

The introduction of New Guinea impatiens to the European market and their unprecedented success in this part of the world, prove that the European mentality today is not nearly as stoic and conservative as widely regarded. Indeed, due to the successful introduction of new crops such as New Guinea impatiens, brachycome, scaevola and Surfinia petunias, to name a few, the European floriculture market has developed an insatiable craving for new products. These new crops are creating additional market niches, but much of their success is at the expense of other standard crops such as geraniums.

Looking back, it's hard to imagine that the first New Guinea impatiens were introduced to the European market only a decade or so ago. The very first cultivars, Cheyenne, Violet Velvet and others, made their way from the United States to England; from there, they seeped into Germany, Holland, and other central European countries. These first varieties, however, did not make much of an impact—they were seen mainly as curious novelties. Indeed, with their small flowers, strongly variegated foliage, long internodes, and poor branching, they were a far cry from today's streamlined, modern cultivars.

Major breakthrough with Sunshine series

The real breakthrough came about 10 years ago with the introduction of Mikkelsens Sunshine series, which set the standard for many years in flower size, color range, and floriferousness. The eye-catching leaf variegation and the bright flower colors created a spontaneous demand for the new product line. The Sunshine varieties were introduced to the European market through the Kientzler company in Germany, who, in turn, successfully pressed to add this new crop to the list of species covered by plant variety rights legislation in the most important European countries.

After a time, however, it became apparent that some of the Sunshine series characteristics didn't quite fit the European taste. Besides an aversion by many Europeans to variegated foliage, it was found that excessive foliar variegation would often burn under Europe's climate. Also, the first cultivars introduced to Europe were still quite heterogeneous in their growth and flowering characteristics. Tall, leggy varieties such as Gemini contrasted sharply to extremely compact varieties such as Sunregal.

There was much room for improvement, so breeding companies such as Kientzler, followed by Bull, Dummen, and Klemm, started their own breeding programs and introduced their cultivars to the German market. Danziger in Israel also started their own breeding program. These cultivars, custom-bred for the needs and tastes of the European market, were very successful and the American-bred varieties quickly lost ground.

Europe's quantity increases

The quantities of New Guinea impatiens produced in Europe began to increase dramatically from year to year. New Guinea impatiens were suddenly no longer a novelty crop grown in small quantities by the corner mom and pop operation; they became a mass crop grown in large quantities for the spring market. The actual production has been steadily shifting from smaller retail growers to the large-scale, highly mechanized nurseries catering to the mass market and auctions. As with all crops, increased production also meant that prices were under more pressure than before. Growers became more and more demanding with regard to a cultivar's performance and characteristics. Growers demanded a uniform line of New Guinea impatiens varieties that were compact and bushy, minus leaf variegation, quick to flower, and in a full color range.

Ludwig Kientzler eventually developed the Paradise series, a group of compact, floriferous, and early-flowering varieties, which were introduced to the European market in 1991. The response far exceeded anyone's expectations and the Paradise line now dominates the European market. This line allows large-scale nurseries to grow quantities of impatiens on a weekly schedule, have a maximum number of plants per square meter, and to market all varieties simultaneously with a minimum crop time.

Given this impetus, the New Guinea impatiens' market has continued to increase substantially from year to year, with no slow-down in sight. Reliable statistics for the number of New Guinea impatiens produced and marketed in Europe are impossible to obtain since New Guinea impatiens are usually grouped together with seed-grown *Impatiens wallerana* in the official statistics. It is estimated, however, that approximately 25 to 30 million New Guinea impatiens pots are produced and sold annually in Germany alone with an annual growth rate of about 20%. Production numbers are also high in the Netherlands, Italy, and France, followed by Switzerland, Belgium, Denmark, Scandinavia, and the United Kingdom.

Impatiens used in many different ways

Europe is a microcosm of various cultures, traditions, and climates. So it doesn't surprise one to learn that New Guinea impatiens are used in many different ways in different parts of Europe. In Germany, Switzerland, and Austria, countries with the highest per-capita consumption of floricultural products, New Guinea impatiens are mainly used as traditional bedding and balcony plants. Window boxes are extremely popular in these countries and New Guinea impatiens are ideally suited for mixed window-box plantings with geraniums, petunias, fillers and some of the new balcony plants. Due to their versatility, New Guinea impatiens perform well under different conditions, providing they are watered consistently. The term "bedding and balcony" also encompasses hanging baskets and planters, for which New Guinea impatiens are also extensively used in these countries.

In the German-speaking countries, New Guinea impatiens are rarely used as bedding plants in flower borders; this is usually the domain of seed-grown annuals and herbaceous perennials. Nevertheless, millions of New Guinea impatiens are used each year as a modified form of cemetery bedding plantings. In these countries, cemetery plots are traditionally planted as rectangular flower beds in front of the gravestone. In this protected, lightly shaded environment, New Guinea impatiens perform extremely well and have become a favorite plant for this purpose.

In France and Italy, New Guinea impatiens are also used in window boxes, hanging baskets, and planters, however, the emphasis is definitely on planters. Due to the hotter and drier conditions in the Mediterranean regions, larger plants (and pots) are preferred, and the majority of plant material is robust, dark-leaved, heat-tolerant varieties with intense, fluorescent flower colors.

Impatiens used as indoor plants

The situation is quite different in the Netherlands, Belgium, northern Germany, Denmark and the Scandinavian countries. Although New Guinea impatiens are also used as bedding plants in these countries, the climate is often too cool and rainy for them to perform well. The consumption of flowering indoor pot plants is much higher in these countries due to the shorter summer. New Guinea impatiens are grown and used extensively in these countries as indoor pot plants on a year-round basis. Winter and early spring crops are usually grown under HID sodium lights to maintain quality and reduce crop time. The introduction of compact, quick-to-flower varieties with good indoor keeping qualities has supported this trend.

Although Denmark and the Netherlands are traditionally export-oriented countries with regard to floricultural crops, few of the New Guinea impatiens produced there are exported to other countries, but are used exclusively for the local market—mainly due to the fact that New Guinea impatiens don't ship well. The plants are extremely ethylene sensitive and one or two days in transport quickly result in all flowers and buds being dropped. Silver thiosulphate treatments somewhat reduce this problem, but not enough to allow for long distance shipping. However, this fact has helped keep New Guinea impatiens a financially viable crop in all the different parts of Europe.

TSWV not a major threat yet

Although tomato spotted wilt virus (TSWV) wreaked havoc with New Guinea impatiens in the United States only a few years ago, this disease has not yet become a serious problem in Europe. Many other crops have been more severely damaged in Europe in the past few years. European growers and propagators had an advanced warning through the reports from North America and had sufficient time to set up stringent clean-stock programs for New Guinea impatiens, which prevented diseased cuttings from being disseminated throughout Europe.

Given the modern European production, marketing and distribution facilities, the high per-capita consumption of floriculture products, the traditional love of flowers, the zeal with which breeders are always improving this crop's beauty and performance, and New Guinea impatiens' overall versatility, the future continues to be very bright. With the advent of a border-free Europe and the opening of Eastern Europe, long deprived of such beautiful crops as New Guinea impatiens behind the Iron Curtain, there's no doubt whatsoever that the European success story of New Guinea impatiens has only just begun.

CHAPTER 2

History of Commercialization

H. Marc Cathey

A totally new type of familiar garden plant seldom exceeds the one already firmly established in the consumer's mind. New plants have to be so spectacular for display or so environmentally superb that the consumer is willing to relearn how to landscape with them [18]. The New Guinea impatiens in the 1990s will surpass the value (return to the grower) of the Sultana impatiens (*I. wallerana*). The story of the discovery, great popularity, loss from insect infestation, and reintroduction in the 1970s is a model for exploring other parts of the world for new plants to expand the agricultural crop market [16, 17].

USDA, Longwood Gardens joint project

My contact with New Guinea impatiens began in 1971 when I was chief of the Florist and Nursery Crops Laboratory, Agricultural Research Service, U.S. Department of Agriculture, Beltsville, Maryland. I drove over to the USDA's Plant Introduction Station at Glenn Dale, Maryland, to pick up a collection of 30 impatiens plants from Dr. Harold F. Winters and brought them back to a cytogeneticist working in my laboratory.

I had asked Dr. Toru Arisumi to study why the plants brought back by Dr. Harold F. Winters, research horticulturist, and Dr. Joseph J. Higgins, research plant physiologist—New Crops Research Branch, USDA, did not set seed [45, 48]. The plants had been collected by a joint project between USDA and the Longwood Foundation [14].

The plants in my car, however, looked entirely different than any impatiens that I had ever seen. First, the flowers were much larger and rounder than the ones I knew. The plants were also much taller, with many foliage shapes—some of the foliage was variegated with colors as varied as a croton's in shades of pink, peach, red, orange, cream, purple, and bronze. The colors were solid or mixed with or without a green base.

Most of the selected plant's foliage wilted during the 18-mile trip. We learned later to grow these impatiens in a shaded greenhouse, to water the growing medium, to syringe the foliage several times a day, and to add high levels of water-soluble, complete fertilizer every time we watered them. From this highly varied, but unruly lot, has come what we now call the New Guinea impatiens.

Early history of New Guinea impatiens

The first impatiens received at Kew Gardens in 1884 [1, 20] was from Dr. Schomburgk, curator of the Adelaide Botanical Garden in Australia [37]. This herbarium specimen was collected by Lieutenant Hawker, R.N., as being from the South Sea Islands [22]. William Bull, a London florist, introduced it in 1886 as *Impatiens hawkeri* in his *Catalog of New, Beautiful, and Rare Plants.* By 1901, Lieutenant Hawker's discovery was identified as being from the Sunda Islands. *Curtis's Botanical Magazine* in 1909 published a more complete description and suggested that the plant was a native of New Guinea and was "first raised in Adelaide and thence transmitted to Mr. Bull, of Chelsea" [23].

Illustrations and descriptions of *Impatiens hawkeri* appeared in publications in Belgium, Germany, Holland, and Italy, and it became a popular plant to grow in warm greenhouses [21]. The plant, however, had a fatal problem—it "suffered so frequently from attacks of the Begonia mite (Tarsonymus) that it went almost entirely out of cultivation" [22].

In the early 1900s, botanists from Germany, England, and the Netherlands explored the parts of the Sunda Islands over which they claimed sovereignty [32, 44]. By 1915, nine New Guinea impatiens species were identified in the German-controlled area: *I. dahlii, I. herzogii, I. laxterbachii, I. linearifolia, I. mooreana, I. polyphylla, I. rodatzii, I. schlechteri,* and *I. trichura* [31, 33, 34].

Taxonomically the collections were confusing and were considered by Von R. Schlecter to be habitat-variations of *I. herzogii* rather than new species. Expeditions by botanists from the United States, Australia, France, and Switzerland also searched Papua and New Guinea for new impatiens species [31, 32, 42, 43].

Native influence

New Guinea natives also had an influence on the New Guinea impatiens development. Natives selected, collected, traded, and identified unique forms in the wild, brought them back to their villages, and planted them in their gardens and along paths. They tended to select forms with large, brightly colored flowers and those with reddish, purple, or variegated leaves [19]. Collectors often could not travel into the wild landscape because of the lack of roads and transportation through the rugged terrain. Thus, the natives' collected forms often were the plants selected for introduction into gardening.

Recent history of New Guinea impatiens
The trip to New Guinea to collect ornamental plants was the 12th of 13 plant explorations sponsored by Longwood Gardens, Longwood, Pennsylvania, and the USDA's Agricultural Research Service, Horticultural Crops Research Branch in Beltsville. Beginning in 1956, Longwood funded the exploration, while ARS provided entry to foreign countries, professionals, quarantine expertise, and botanical knowledge [38].

1970 trip
The 1970 trip to New Guinea was selected by Dr. John Creech (ARS) and Dr. Russell Seibert (Longwood) to collect tropical rhododendrons from areas threatened by land development. The area had not been collected from for many years because of the treacherous terrain and the hostile natives [49].

During World War II, Australian and American troops had built roads and airstrips to battle the Japanese troops thus making it possible to travel deeper into New Guinea than ever before. Following World War II, the Australian government set up educational programs to stop cannibalism and to provide adequate health care for the natives.

As the population increased, more roads and airstrips were built, opening the land to more farming higher in the mountains [36]. Increased development of lumbering, livestock, and farming threatened to destroy many plants' habitats.

Interested parties were to submit their requests for collection to John Creech. Although rhododendrons were the main focus of the trip, requests for fireflies and fruits were also considered. Claude Hope, a former ARS employee and presently a plant breeder in Costa Rica with many ties to world gardening, suggested that impatiens should be added to the list of plants to be collected. Harold Winters found references to the New Guinea impatiens collected by K.M. Schumann [34], Karl Lauterbach [34], H.N. Ridley, and R. Schlechter [31] from 1866 to 1915.

In 1970, New Guinea's eastern half was governed by Australia. The Forestry Department and Botanical Garden staff in Lae, New Guinea, supplied the technical support to help Winters and Higgins penetrate the terrain, identify collections, prepare specimens, and fumigate prior to shipment back to the United States [45].

Concerned that some of the species would become extinct because of lumbering and farming, the Lae Botanical Garden staff collected specimens in the mountains of the central and western highlands, the Huon Peninsula, a rain forest area south of Lae, and a savannah region near Port Moresby. Although they travelled in the dry season and at lower elevation sites, temperatures reached 65F (18C) while at 2,500 feet, and the weather was cool and moist with a constant drizzle.

Amazing variety

The New Guinea natives were paid 10 cents or 1 shilling for a good New Guinea impatiens specimen. Considering that over 700 different tribes occupy New Guinea's eastern half and represent over 700 different languages, the variety of forms available was truly amazing [46, 47]. Getting the plants, seeds, or cuttings back to the quarantine houses at Glenn Dale, Maryland, was just as demanding, even in the age of polyethylene packing materials and airplanes.

Impatiens' stems and leaves are succulent—they wilt or rot easily. Ripe seeds burst from their pods and disappear into space. Only 25 of 50 New Guinea impatiens collections survived the trip to Maryland. Even with replacements, Winters and Higgins were unable to transfer all of the forms available in New Guinea to the United States. They brought back 840 live collections of aroids, citrus relatives, ferns, gesneriads, gingers, grasses, hoyas, impatiens, and rhododendrons [24].

Winters and Higgins [48] gave names associated with New Guinea to the original impatiens set. All were named in Pidgin English to refer to places or people and it was hoped the plants would go directly into commercial production. Although one producer did release the original plant directly to the public, most growers realized that further research on breeding, propagation, and production technologies was needed for a commercial success. Descriptions of the varieties collected in the 1970 expedition are listed in Appendix I.

Research needed to solve problems___

The introduction of New Guinea impatiens required years of research to consider and solve the following problems:
- Taxonomic classification
- Breeding: fertility
- Cultivars: diversity for performance
- Propagation: pest-free cuttings
- Culture: light, heat, nutrition

Taxonomic classification

Few botanists in the 20th century have worked on the complex problem of identifying impatiens species. Professor O. Warburg revised the classification in German New Guinea in 1905 and proposed seven new species. Sir Joseph Hooker published two works on impatiens of British India in 1874-75 and in 1904-06. The most recent work is by Dr. Chris Grey-Wilson at Kew Gardens [19]. He suggested that New Guinea impatiens "belong to a single hugely variable species." He identified 15 groups, but felt there was more or less continuous variation. He proposed that "each clone...be given a clear and distinctive cultivar name under *I. hawkeri*" [25, 26, 27].

At the end of their collecting trip in April 1970, Winters and Higgins visited Tjibodas, Java, and there added *I. platypetala*. (There will be more about this species later.)

Breeding: fertility

I asked Dr. Toru Arisumi to work on impatiens cytogenetics. His skills had already been involved with ulmus, hemerocallis, and saintpaulia. He knew how to count chromosomes, how to double the number of chromosomes in a plant, and how to perform the ovule rescue procedure. Our laboratory was mandated by USDA to create fertile breeding lines of impatiens from which the commercial "green industry" could select their cultivars for introduction.

Dr. Arisumi found that most New Guinea impatiens had the same number of chromosomes and could be easily intercrossed with other forms [2, 3, 4, 5, 6, 7, 8, 9]. When selfed, the vigor dropped, and the fertility of the plants was so low that the plants died. Thus seed-grown plants, which are much cheaper than vegetatively propagated, were a major obstacle for successful plant production. Dr. Arisumi made thousands of crosses attempting to solve the loss of vigor. These plants could only be propagated by softwood cuttings.

His first series was called the Rainbow series with such names as Flame, Arabesque, Cheers, Sprite (1974), and later Aloha and Pele (1975) [40], and much later Pee Gee, Pink Cascade, and Pink Lady (1977) [41]. He continued to add new species of impatiens from East Africa, Madagascar, India, Malaya, and the Celebes Islands.

He found the New Guinea impatiens could cross with the species from Java and the Celebes Islands. The hybrids were sterile because New Guinea impatiens were 2N=32, Java 2N=16, and Celebes 2N=8. The hybrids were made fertile with colchicine treatments to double the chromosome numbers. The fertile plant that produced seed was introduced as Sweet Sue (1976), named for Dr. Arisumi's wife.

At the same time at Longwood Gardens, Dr. Robert Armstrong made crosses of all New Guinea impatiens in every possible combination [11,

12, 13, 14, 15]. Some of the initial seedlings from these crosses were so superior to their parents that they were selected for release as vegetatively-propagated plants.

The first set of 10 plants was called the Circus series for their gaudy flowers and foliage. They included Bozo, Carousel, Cotton Candy, Harlequin, Lollipop, Big Top, Charmer, Orange Crush, Painted Lady, Stoplight (1974), Calliope, Cannonball, Fortune Teller, Chariot, Juggler, Magician, Ringmaster, Roustabout, Showboat, Trapeze (1977), Carnival, Headliner, Majorette, Roller Coaster, Ringmaster Improved, and Skyrocket.

Neither USDA nor Longwood cultivars were patented when released, and growers were free to use them to breed for any desired form. All the subsequent introductions came from these three sources: the first New Guinea collection brought to the United States by Winters and Higgins in 1970 [39], Arisumi's series developed at USDA in 1974, 1975 and 1977, and Armstrong's Longwood Gardens cultivars from 1974, 1977 and 1979. The records of which forms were used for which breeding lines have been lost in the hundreds of thousands of cultivars subsequently grown around the world.

Cultivars: diversity for performance

Over 100 universities, botanic gardens, and commercial plant breeders received cuttings of the New Guinea impatiens in spring 1972. Some of the researchers who developed breeding and introduction programs are shown in table 2.1.

Propagation: pest-free cuttings

New Guinea impatiens must be grown in total isolation to prevent the introduction and spread of spider mites, two-spotted mites, and cyclamen mites, as well as the appearance of the western flower thrips which carries tomato spotted wilt virus (TSWV) [29]. TSWV causes infected plants to develop black ringspots or dead areas. In time the plants become stunted and may die. There is no cure; the infected plants must be destroyed to prevent the disease's spread. Fine screens, airlocks, and reversed ventilation must be installed, and all visitors and workers must disinfect their hands and shoes prior to entering the stock production area. Propagators use tissue culture and virus indexing to ensure virus-free stock.

Culture: light, heat, nutrition

The limp, gangly, poor-flowering New Guinea impatiens hybrids have been transformed by **breeding** (compact, flower open and round, pedicel that holds flowers well above the foliage), **culture** (high nutrient

TABLE 2.1

Commercial development of New Guinea impatiens

Year	Variety/ Series name	No. of varieties	Breeder	Institution/ Company
1972	Circus series I	11	Dr. R.J. Armstrong	Longwood Gardens
1974– 1989	Cyclone hybrids	20	Jack Weigle, A.R. Beck	Iowa State University
Year unknown	Orange Gem, Pink Doll, Super Fuchsia	3	Wiley Hinson	Norfolk Botanical Garden
1976	American Heritage series	10	Jim Mikkelsen, Cornelius Van den Berg,	Mikkelsens, Inc.
Year unknown	Series abandoned	Unknown	Walter Jessel	Yoder Brothers Inc.
1978	Sunshine series	43	Jim Mikkelsen, Cornelius Van den Berg, Dr. Lyndon Drewlow	Mikkelsens, Inc.
1978	American Indian series	32	John Ryan	California-Florida Plant Corporation
1984	Vista series		Claude Hope	Linda Vista, S.A.
1980s	Tangeglow (Impatiens Aiyura x Celebes Island impatiens Tangerine)	1	Claude Hope	Linda Vista, S.A.
1980s	Tango	1	Alfonso Parada	Linda Vista, S.A.
1987	Pure Beauty series	21	Ludwig Kientzler	Kientzler Jungpflanzen Paul Ecke Ranch
1989	Danziger series	12	Klara Dehan	Danziger Flower Farm, Israel
1990	Bull series	7	Norbert Bull	Bull/Fischer
1990	Spectra series	6 shades	Alfonso Parada, Mario Guillen	Linda Vista, S.A.
1990	Lasting Impressions	15	Dr. Lyndon Drewlow	Mikkelsens, Inc.
1991	Celebration series	16	Mario Guillen Dr. Scott Trees	Linda Vista, S.A. Ball FloraPlant
1992	Paradise series	20	Ludwig Kientzler	Kientzler Jungpflanzen Paul Ecke Ranch
1992	Twice as Nice	6	Dr. Lyndon Drewlow	Mikkelsens, Inc.

Source: Cathey H.M., and M. Strefeler.

pulse at the beginning of growth, direct sunlight immediately to form sun tolerant leaves), and **pest-free plants** (virus indexing) [10, 28]. European breeders are selecting cultivars with more pigment in their foliage than U.S. breeders and will develop plants with an even more compact growth habit.

Future

New Guinea impatiens have the potential to be successfully produced for bedding, container, and hanging baskets for outdoor and indoor use [35]. The full potential of leaf form (strap to wrinkled), leaf color (endless variations), flower form (hooded to rounded), spurs (tiny to showy), markings (monochrome to great variations), habit (swollen nodes/long internodes to compact stems), and heat and light stress (acclimatization) still haven't been fully achieved in the cultivars available in the early 1990s [30].

I always wonder what kinds of impatiens lurk on the mountains of New Guinea. We have only half the forms collected by Winters and Higgins from the eastern side in the 1970s. There is still New Guinea's whole western side which, because of the lack of roads and landing strips, has never been fully explored.

References

[1]   Arc. 1886. Impatiens Hawkeri. *Sempervirens* 23 (4 June):178.
[2]   Arisumi, Toru. 1973. Morphology and breeding behavior of colchine-induced polypoid *Impatiens* spp. L. *J. Amer. Soc. Hort. Sci.* 98, no. 6 (November):599-601.
[3]   ———. 1973. Chromosome numbers and interspecific hybrids among New Guinea impatiens species. *The Journal of Heredity* 64:77-79.
[4]   ———. 1974. Chromosome numbers and breeding behavior of hybrids among Celebes, Java and New Guinea species of *Impatiens* L. *HortScience* 9, no. 5 (October):478-479.
[5]   ———. 1975. Phenotypic analysis of progenies of artificial and natural amphiploid cultivars of New Guinea and Indonesian species of *Impatiens* L. *J. Amer. Soc. Hort. Sci.* 100, no. 4 (July):381-383.
[6]   ———. 1978. Hybridization among diploid and tetraploid forms of New Guinea, Java, and Celebes *Impatiens* spp. *J. Amer. Soc. Hort. Sci.* 103, no. 3 (May):355-361.
[7]   ———. 1980. Chromosomes numbers and comparative breeding behavior of certain impatiens from Africa, India, and New Guinea. *J. Amer. Soc. Hort. Sci.* 105, no. 1 (January):99-102.
[8]   ———. 1985. Rescuing abortive impatiens hybrids through aseptic culture of ovules. *J. Amer. Soc. Hort. Sci.* 110, no. 2 (March):273-276.
[9]   ———. 1987. Cytology and morphology of ovule culture-derived interspecific impatiens hybrids. *J. Amer. Soc. Hort. Sci.* 112, no. 6 (November):1026-1031.
[10] Arisumi, Toru, and H.M. Cathey. 1976. About our cover, the New Guinea impatiens. *HortSci.* 11, no. 1 (February).
[11] Armstrong, Robert J. 1974. An impatiens circus, the Longwood New Guinea hybrid impatiens. *American Horticulturist* 53, no. 1 (Spring):14-18.
[12] ———. 1975. New Guinea impatiens hybrid response to daylength, temperature and light level. *HortSci.* 10, no. 3 (June):340.

[13] ———. 1975. New Guinea impatiens hybrid response to fertility level and container size. *HortSci.* 10, no. 3 (June):340.
[14] ———. 1976. Introduction and breeding of the New Guinea impatiens. *AABGA Bulletin* 10, no. 2 (April):36-38.
[15] ———. 1977. The New Guinea impatiens, impatiens of tomorrow! *The Bulletin, Pacific Tropical Botanical Garden* 7, no. 3 (July):49-52.
[16] Benjamin, Joan Marie. 1990. The history and development of New Guinea impatiens. Thesis, University of Delaware.
[17] Creech, John L. 1968. The ARS-Longwood plant explorations. *Plants & Gardens* 23, no. 3:50-55, 86.
[18] Fisher, Kathleen. 1993. The incidental ornamental. *American Horticulturist* 72, no. 10:32-39.
[19] Grey-Wilson, C. 1980. Impatiens in Papuasia. Studies in Balsaminaceae: I. *Kew Bulletin* 34, no. 4.
[20] Harrow, W. 1888. Plant Notes. *The Gardener's Chronicle* 3rd series, 4, no. 100 (24 November):602.
[21] Hogg, Robert, ed. 1887. Impatiens Hawkeri. *Journal of Horticulture, Cottage Gardener, and Home Farmer* 3rd series, 13 (18 January):92.
[22] Hooker, J.D. 1909. Tab. 8247 Impatiens Hawkeri. *Curtis's Botanical Magazine* 4th series, 5.
[23] ———. 1911. Tab. 8396 Impatiens Herzogii. *Curtis's Botanical Magazine* 4th series, 7.
[24] Hyland, Howard. 1972. *Plant Inventory No. 178*. Washington, D.C.: United States Department of Agriculture. (August):76, 79, 82, 211, 217-219, 245-246.
[25] 1887. Impatiens Hawkeri. *Ill. Gartenzeit Stuttgart* 31, no. 18:122.
[26] 1888. Impatiens Hookeriana. *The Gardener's Chronicle* (15 December):696.
[27] Jones, Keith, and J.B. Smith. 1966. The cytogeography of Impatiens L., (Balsaminaceae). *Kew Bulletin* 20, no. 1: 63-72.
[28] Mikkelsen, Jim. 1976. New Guinea hybrid impatiens. *Ohio Florists' Association Bulletin*, no. 555 (January):2.
[29] Miller, Russell. 1989. Identifying the most serious problem we face today—TSWV. *GrowerTalks* (July):100-106.
[30] Murphy, Wendy B. 1978. Taming the wild impatiens. *The Time-Life Gardening Yearbook*, 70-75. Morristown, New Jersey: Time-Life Books, Inc.
[31] Schlecter, R. 1915. Impatiens mooreanan schltr., sine neue, wertvolle gewachshauspflauze. *Die Gartenwelt* 19, no. 2 and 3.
[32] ———. 1917. Die Balsaminaceae Papuasiens. *Botanische Jahrbucher fur Systematik, Planzengeschichte und Planzengeographie. Beitrage zur Flora Von Papuasien.* 114-120.
[33] Schumann, K. 1888. Die flora des deutschen ost—Asiatischen Schutzbebietes. *Botanische Jahrbucher fur Systematik, Planzengeschichte und Planzengeographie.* 204.
[34] Schumann, K.M., and Karl Lauterbach. 1905. *Nachtrage zur Flora der Deutschen Schutzgetiete in der Sudsee*:311-313.
[35] Seager, J.C.R. 1980. Evaluation of New Guinea impatiens cultivars. *Irish Journal of Agricultural Research* 19:111-118.
[36] Smith, Robin, and Keith Willey. 1969. *New Guinea, A journey through 10,000 years.* Melbourne, Australia: Lansdowne Press PTY LTD.
[37] Stafleu, Frans. A., and Richard S. Sowan. 1976. *Taxonomic Literature* 2nd ed. Utrecht: Bohn, Scheltemsa & Holkema.
[38] Tschanz, Eric Nathan. 1977. A history: The U.S.D.A.— Longwood ornamental plant exploration program. Thesis, University of Delaware.

[39] *Notice to plant breeders and nurserymen relative to the release of 23 impatiens introductions.* 1972. Beltsville, Maryland: U.S. Department of Agriculture, Agriculture Research Division, Plant Science Research Division (23 February).

[40] *Notice to cooperators among florists and nurserymen of the release of two new seedling cultivars of the Rainbow impatiens series.* 1975. Washington, D.C.: U.S. Department of Agriculture, Agricultural Research Service.

[41] *Notice to cooperators among florists and nurserymen of the release of three new seedling cultivars of the Painted impatiens series.* 1977. Washington, D.C.: U.S. Department of Agriculture, Agricultural Research Service.

[42] Van Steenis, Dr. G.G.J. 1950. *Flora Malesiana.* Djakarta: Noordhoff-Kolff N.V.

[43] Van Steenis-Kruseman. 1950. Malaysian plant collectors and collections. *Flora Malesiana.* Djakarta: Noordhoff-Kolff N.V.

[44] Warburg, Prof. Dr. O. 1905. *Nachtrage zur Flora der Deutschen Schutzgetiete in der Sudsee.* 311-313.

[45] Winters, Harold. 1973. New impatiens from New Guinea. *American Horticulturist* 52:16-22.

[46] ———. 1977. Flower longevity in New Guinea impatiens. *HortSci.* 12, no. 3:261-263.

[47] ———. 1982. Branched pedicels in New Guinea impatiens. *HortSci.* 17, no. 3:340-341.

[48] Winters, Harold, and Joseph Higgins. 1970. *Foreign Travel Report.* U.S. Department of Agriculture: Agricultural Research Service, Crops Research Division.

[49] Womersley, J.S. 1953. A brief history of botanical exploration of Papua and New Guinea. *The Papua and New Guinea Agricultural Gazette* 8, no. 2.

Media

William Healy

Which soil mix to use is a difficult decision for many growers. The "best" soil mix for New Guinea impatiens may not be the best for the other crops in production. Growers currently use a wide range of soil mixes for finishing New Guinea impatiens with the majority using a peat or bark based mix. Specialty growers of New Guinea impatiens may customize the mix for the New Guinea impatiens crop, but in most cases this is not economically feasible. When changing a cultural practice, it's critical to understand how the new cultural practice interacts with the soil. Before making any changes in the soil mix, complete an adequate soil test to ensure an accurate picture of the chemical and physical properties of the old and new soil mix.

New Guinea impatiens have specific nutrient and moisture requirements that many growers compromise by using the wrong soil mix. Growers need to consider the cultural requirements of New Guinea impatiens when deciding on the soil mix. It's important that the soil mix work with environmental conditions to enhance plant growth and that the soil's physical and chemical properties work with, not against, a grower's production program.

Physical properties of soil mixes

The physical properties of a soil mix include water holding capacity, bulk density (weight) and air porosity (table 3.1). Watering practices, temperature and relative humidity interact with the soil mix and its physical properties to produce a specific crop quality. A thorough understanding of how the environment interacts with the physical properties of a soil mix is critical for understanding how to manage an ever-changing environment.

21

TABLE 3.1

Primary benefits of soil mix components for New Guinea impatiens production

Component	Water holding capacity	Aeration	Bulk density	CEC
Sphagnum peat	x			x
Hypnum peat		x		x
Cocofiber	x			x
Rockwool hydrophobic		x		
Rockwool hydrophilic	x			
Composted bark	x		x	x
Noncomposted bark	x			
Vermiculite	x	x		x
Rice hulls		x		
Sand		x	x	
Scoria		x	x	
Calcine clay		x	x	x
Perlite		x		
Polystyrene		x		
Ashed bark		x		
Loam soil			x	x
Clay soil			x	x

Water holding capacity. A soil mix's water holding capacity must compliment the grower's watering practices—usually either "wet" or "dry." "Wet" growers believe a crop should never wilt, while "dry" growers believe that plants should wilt before watering. A "wet" grower tends to have a tall New Guinea impatiens crop and a lack of flowers. To compensate for increased stretch caused by keeping the crop moist, the "wet" grower may use more growth regulators. A "dry" grower will find that his New Guinea impatiens crop is very compact and flowers rapidly. Matching the water holding capacity of the soil mix to a "wet or "dry" grower allows the grower to optimize growth.

The amount of air in the soil mix is essential for strong root development. When plants are grown in anaerobic conditions (water-saturated soil), root death occurs due to soil borne diseases. "Wet" growers should carefully select a soil mix that maximizes aeration, since frequent irrigation can easily create anaerobic conditions. "Dry" growers, on the other hand, are not as concerned with having sufficient aeration in the soil mix because their reduced watering frequency ensures greater aeration.

Relative humidity is a key factor when determining a soil mix's water holding capacity. Evapotranspiration (evaporation from the soil + transpiration from the leaf) dictates how quickly the soil will dry out. Under high relative humidity conditions, soil and plants tend to dry slowly. As the temperature increases, the humidity will drop if no additional moisture is added to the environment. Conversely, as the temperature is lowered to slow down the crop, the humidity increases and the evapotranspiration declines dramatically.

To understand the speed at which a soil mix will dry, you need to understand the relationship between temperature and relative humidity. A soil mix with a low water holding capacity is ideal in the early spring when evapotranspiration is low. The same mix during late spring, when the evapotranspiration is high due to increased temperatures, will dry out very rapidly. In production areas with very low outdoor relative humidity (<40%), the evapotranspiration rate is much higher than in areas with high relative humidity. In low relative humidity environments, it's critical to have a soil mix with a higher water holding capacity that minimizes the need for frequent irrigation.

The soil mix's water holding capacity is dependent on the ratio of components that retain water (hydrophilic) and components that repel water (hydrophobic). Examples of strong hydrophilic materials are peat moss, cocofiber and certain rockwools; slightly hydrophilic materials include bark, vermiculite, rice hulls, loam and clay soils; and weak hydrophilic materials include sand, scoria, perlite and calcine clay. Some hydrophobic materials include polystyrene beads and certain rockwools. By selecting a soil mix with a combination of various components, you can optimize the mix's water holding capacity for specific growing conditions.

A "wet" grower may want to increase the amount of slightly hydrophobic materials in the soil mix especially during the early spring. Several commercial soil mixes contain a combination of materials that gives the soil quick drying characteristics when watered frequently, while other soil mixes tend to hold water and stay wet longer. Growers should supply sufficient hydrophilic components so that the soil mix won't dry out in a retail environment.

Bulk density. Bulk density is defined as the soil mix's weight per unit of volume. Figure 3.1 shows the bulk density of various components for a 4-inch (10 cm) container. Sand or gravel added to a mix can increase the bulk density, which will prevent the plant from tipping over. Conversely, adding perlite or vermiculite will decrease bulk density and make the plant more likely to tip over. As growers add components to

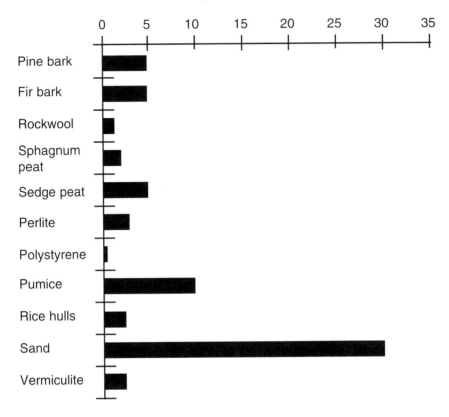

Fig. 3.1. *Bulk density of soil mix components commonly found in New Guinea impatiens soil mixes.*

change bulk density, the mix's porosity also changes. Growers should trial the soil mix thoroughly under normal growing conditions to determine whether a bulk density change is warranted.

Growers can unintentionally increase bulk density by excessive soil mixing, packing soil into containers or stacking containers, which compresses the soil. As container size decreases in volume, growers must avoid increasing the bulk density by compaction because porosity is reduced.

When using mechanical equipment to mix and handle soil mixes, make sure that the soil is not handled excessively. The continuous recycling of the soil mix on conveyor belts can grind the soil into smaller particles, which decreases porosity and increases bulk density. Excessive grinding is worse when sand or other aggregates are added to the mix.

Porosity. Soil porosity is a measure of the soil mix's gas and water exchange. Most growers consider porosity and water holding capacity as opposing soil characteristics and technically, a soil's water holding and porosity properties are different. Increasing porosity will decrease the soil's water holding capacity. A New Guinea impatiens soil mix requires air porosities between 5% and 15% by volume for optimum growth. The ideal soil mix should contain a combination of macropores and micropores—macropores are air filled pores and micropores are water filled pores. Coarse soil mixes tend to have many macropores and fine soil mixes tend to have a larger percentage of micropores. Growers should select a soil mix with a variety of particle sizes that creates a ratio of macropores and micropores for optimal root growth.

Chemical properties of soil mixes

The chemical properties of a soil mix interact with water and fertilizer to provide a nutrient charge that is available to the plant. Because of the number of possible fertilizers, mix components and water sources available to growers, a large number of possible interactions exists for growers to manage. Most growers don't realize how these interactions affect crop quality until they have changed one of the factors. By modifying a mix's components and additives, growers can change the cation exchange capacity, soluble salt level, nutrient availability and balance response to their water and fertilizer solution.

Cation exchange capacity. A soil mix's cation exchange capacity (CEC) is dependent on the mix components. As the ratio between components with high and low CEC changes, the soil mix CEC changes proportionally. Peat moss, vermiculite and clay soil all have high CEC. When these high CEC components are mixed with low CEC components (perlite, sand, loam soils) the resulting soil will have a low CEC.

Think of the exchange sites on a high CEC soil particle as the fuzz on a tennis ball. A low CEC soil is similar to a ping-pong ball (no fuzz). As the ratio of tennis balls and ping-pong balls changes in the soil mix, the number of sites (fuzz) where cations can attach also changes. Growers should select a soil that has a balance between high and low CEC to produce a final mix within the desired CEC range.

Even with an optimum soil mix CEC, plants can show nutrient deficiencies because the soil was not adequately charged with nutrients. Until the soil is saturated with the desired nutrients, the exchange sites may contain undesirable nutrients (sodium, aluminum) or unbalanced combinations of nutrients. Successful New Guinea impatiens production is dependent on maintaining a balanced nutrient charge because New Guinea impatiens are very susceptible to nutrient excess. If a grower provides a heavy feed (300+ parts per million per week), then a low CEC soil is best since very few excess nutrients will accumulate in the soil. Conversely, growers who provide a light feed (100 to 200 ppm per week) need to use a soil with a high CEC to ensure adequate nutrients for the crop.

Soil pH. The mix's pH dramatically affects a soil mix's CEC since the CEC measures the cations (positively charged ions) in the soil mix. As the pH decreases, there are more hydrogen ions (positively charged hydrogen ions) in the soil solution. As the pH drops, the hydrogen becomes attached to the exchange sites, which reduces the amount of the more desirable nutrients that are attached to the soil particles. When using low alkalinity water or very acidic reacting fertilizers, growers must monitor the pH carefully to avoid a declining soil pH.

As the soil pH declines, the availability of desirable nutrients changes in the soil even if there's no change in the soil's CEC. To counteract the soil's changing pH, growers add limestone to the mix. The limestone acts as a buffering agent (like an antacid) that prevents the soil from becoming too acidic or alkaline.

The type and size of the limestone used will significantly modify the buffering capacity. Limestone (calcium carbonate) is more readily available than dolomitic limestone (calcium carbonate + magnesium carbonate). As the limestone particle size decreases, the limestone's initial buffering capacity increases. Limestone type, size and amount added to a specific mix depends on the water quality and the fertilizer program.

Water quality. Water quality dictates which soil mix and additives are most effective for growing a New Guinea impatiens crop. When the water quality is very poor (high salts, excess sodium), then a soil mix with a low CEC may be preferable since undesirable salts won't accumulate. If the water quality is unbalanced in nutrient content (calcium versus magnesium), then soil additives should be modified. This imbalance commonly occurs with high alkalinity water where the calcium to magnesium ratio is 1:1 versus the desired ratio of 3:1. Growers can adjust the water imbalance by increasing calcium additives through limestone (low alkalinity water) or gypsum (high alkalinity water).

If the bicarbonates (sometimes expressed as alkalinity) are high (250+ ppm) then a high CEC soil mix and low limestone charge is recommended. High water alkalinity will raise a soil solution's pH over a short period of time. If growers use a low CEC soil mix, then the pH will climb very rapidly and won't stabilize. Adding very fine limestone (200+ mesh) or excess quantities (3+ pounds/cubic yard) (1.8 kg/m^3) of limestone will drive up the pH when high alkalinity water is used. Using low alkalinity water (<60 ppm) without sufficient limestone will result in a declining pH over time. A low alkalinity water supply is either from naturally low alkalinity water sources or from excessive acidification of high alkalinity water.

Growers can compensate for low alkalinity water by adding either coarse limestone or dolomitic limestone (150+ mesh) or by increasing the amount of lime added to the mix. Adequate trials are critical to determine whether sufficient limestone has been added to stabilize the soil mix. If the water quality changes, then adjust the limestone rates accordingly.

Soluble salts. The soluble salts measurement is a reading of what's left in the soil mix after the plant has extracted the ions necessary for its growth. If the soil mix's soluble salts levels increase over time, then the plant has stopped taking up the available salts. If the soluble salts levels are declining, then the plant is absorbing more than is being applied. Growers must apply sufficient fertilizer to sustain plant growth for successful New Guinea impatiens production although New Guinea impatiens have a very low nutrient requirement compared to other species.

Soil mix starter charges should be relatively low compared to other crops. For New Guinea impatiens, add half the normal rate of a starter charger in the soil mix. Monitor soluble salts levels on a regular basis and apply fertilizers in response to the readings.

Test the soil prior to planting when preparing a soil mix for New Guinea impatiens. If soluble salts levels are high (table 3.2), then the soil mix should be leached prior to planting. Growers who mix their own soil should test each of the components prior to mixing to determine if a component might contribute to a soluble salts problem. For example, there are certain peat mosses and sands that have very high soluble salts. Monitoring the soil components prior to mixing will prevent plant losses.

Nutrient availability and balance. New Guinea impatiens require moderate amounts of nutrients for optimum growth at the time of planting. Many growers fail to fertilize their crops adequately for several weeks after planting. Most commercial soil mixes have an adequate nutrient charge to supply the nutrient requirements of New Guinea impatiens for at least three weeks. When mixing your own soil, incorporate sufficient phosphorus, potassium, nitrate, magnesium and minor nutrients. The soil nutrients at the time of planting should be in the low range specified by a soil testing service.

Most soil components don't supply any nutrients to the soil mix. Vermiculite can supply a variable amount of potassium and magnesium depending on the ore source. Peat mosses used for soil mixes are

TABLE 3.2

Soluble salts readings using different extraction procedures [a]

Total soluble salts	Saturated paste	2 water:1 soil	5 water:1 soil
Low	0.7-1.5	0.3-0.6	0.1-0.3
Desirable	1.5-3.0	0.6-1.0	0.3-0.5
Moderately high	3.0-4.5	1.0-1.5	0.5-0.7
High	4.5-5.5	1.5-2.0	0.7-1.0

Note: These readings are for all plants, not just for New Guinea impatiens.
Modified from: Bunt, A.C. 1988. Media and mixes for container-grown plants. Unwin Hyman Ltd.; Warnecke, D.D. and D.M. Krauskopf. 1983. Greenhouse growth media: testing and nutrition guidelines. Cooperative Extension Service, Michigan State University.
[a] Readings are in mmolhes/cm.

highly variable in nutrient content. Most peats have very low nutrient levels, while other peats may contain high ammonia, calcium or sodium levels. Test the soil component prior to mixing to determine the nutrient additive adjustment needed for proper nutrient balance. Failure to adjust the additives will result in a soil mix with insufficient or excessive nutrient levels.

Rooting systems for New Guinea impatiens

Growers have used a wide range of rooting systems during the last 10 years with various levels of success. Rooting systems are as simple as benches of peat plus perlite, rolls of Jiffy-7s, Oasis strips and wedges to flats with various inserts or special extrusions filled with special media blends. If there were a perfect system, then everyone would use it! Unfortunately each rooting system has some advantages and disadvantages (table 3.3). Consider these factors when evaluating a rooting system:

Rooting performance
A rooting system shouldn't inhibit callus formation, root growth or shoot growth once roots are formed. The rooting medium's pH should be easily managed by using water or fertilizer. The water holding capacity must be managed so that the medium can be kept wet during part of the rooting process and then dried down during other periods. Some cation exchange capacity is desirable. Cuttings should root uniformly in the medium. Over the years, rooting in peat moss seems to

TABLE 3.3

Performance rating of various rooting systems

Rooting system	Wetting	Drying	Water holding	Buffering capacity	Cation exchange	Handling Setting out	Handling Grading	Planting Rootball integrity	Planting Interface	Planting Rooting out
Solid matrix										
Oasis wedge	1	1	3	4	3	3	4	1	1	1
Oasis rootcube	1	2	3	4	3	2	4	1	3	2
Oasis strip	1	2	3	4	3	2	4	1	4	2
Rockwool	3	2	2	4	5	2	4	1	4	2
Jiffy-7	2	3	1	1	1	3	1	1	1	1
Media matrix										
Net pots	V	V	V	V	V	4	4	4	2	2
Pod pack	V	V	V	V	V	2	4	4	2	2
Pro-tray	V	V	V	V	V	1	4	4	2	2
Cell-pak	V	V	V	V	V	1	4	4	2	2
Fabric pot	V	V	V	V	V	2	1	1	1	1

Rating scale: 1=good, 5=poor; V=variable depending on the medium used to fill the flat.

produce the fastest, most uniform rooting performance. However, other factors must be considered when determining the optimum rooting system.

Handling ease

Moving the rooting medium and cuttings around the greenhouse is a major expense in a propagation program. Shipping rooted cuttings requires an efficient handling system that also minimizes weight. The crop handling system in a majority of the North American greenhouse industry is designed around handling a 1020 bedding plant flat, and the rooting system must fit into this system to remain viable.

Growers must be able to quickly and easily place a large number of "cells" on the bench. The more cells a grower can place on the bench at one time, the more cost-effective the rooting system. Rooting cuttings in beds of peat moss is excellent—except it's impossible to ship the cuttings cost effectively.

Density

New Guinea impatiens cuttings can be stuck at a high density (60 to 100 per square foot/6 to 11 per 100 cm²) without any problems.

Although using a fixed tray makes handling easier, the lack of flexibility in planting density limits its usefulness.

Cost

The cost of most rooting materials is comparable within a few cents per cutting. Total cost is much higher when handling costs for the various rooting methods is calculated. The cost per rooted cutting goes up substantially when the rooting system is a single unit that is placed on the bench by hand. When evaluating costs, consider the total picture carefully.

Market acceptance

There are some markets that will not accept liners rooted in anything other than a Jiffy-7 (or oasis wedges or rockwool blocks or pod packs or...). Each market has a special requirement based on a grower's beliefs. Therefore while there may be a rooting system that is vastly superior, it won't be used because of market pressure.

CHAPTER 4

Feeding and Watering

David E. Hartley

Irrigation

Good water management is crucial for the success of New Guinea impatiens culture. Once established, these plants require large amounts of water, but overwatering of newly planted rooted cuttings is a common problem [17]. Thus, meeting the water requirements of New Guinea impatiens is somewhat exacting—not to overwater in the beginning and to supply generous amounts of water later.

Selecting a growing medium for New Guinea impatiens is the first step in good water management (see Chapter 3, Media). The most frequent recommendation is to use a fast draining growing medium with good water retention [1, 2, 13, 19, 20]. Or use a fast draining medium with enough peat moss for good water retention [15]. Peat-lite mixes containing perlite or bark usually provide the needed drainage and aeration. Sphagnum peat moss, alone or mixed with styrofoam, retains too much water and is difficult to re-wet when dry [3, 4, 17].

New Guinea impatiens transpire large quantities of water, but don't grow well in water-logged media [15]. Growing media containing about 50% sphagnum peat moss should give the desired aeration and water holding capacity [17]. Several commercially prepared growing media meet these criteria.

Planting rooted cuttings

Plant rooted cuttings or plugs in a moistened growing medium so the top of the rooting medium is flush with the growing medium surface [2, 3, 4]. Water around the plants so the moist medium makes good contact with the roots. Take special care not to overwater or keep the grow-

Fig. 4.1. *Drip tube irrigation is an efficient uniform way to water New Guinea impatiens in hanging baskets. Plant quality is often better than with hand watering.*

ing medium too wet for the first two to three weeks. The roots become established more quickly when the growing medium dries slightly between waterings, but irrigation occurs before plants wilt [3, 4, 10, 15, 17].

Planting directly into large containers, such as hanging baskets, presents a greater challenge. If the entire mass of growing medium is thoroughly watered, it may take several days for it to dry. In this situation, it may be best to water only the area immediately surrounding each plant until the roots extend into the growing medium. Establishing plants in smaller (3- to 4-inch) containers and then transplanting them to the larger containers is another way to avoid overwatering [14].

As plants become established their water requirements increase. Keep the growing medium evenly moist for best results, as the amount of water available to the plant influences the finished product's size and quality [6]. A constantly wet growing medium produces large, lush plants that are strongly vegetative. When grown on the drier side, the plants will be smaller and more compact with tough leaves and more flowers. New Guinea impatiens will tolerate slight wilting without permanent damage, however, severe wilting or alternating between very wet and very dry growing medium may result in leaf burn and flower drop [6, 15].

Watering systems
New Guinea impatiens may be watered with any of the commonly used irrigation systems. Hand watering with a hose is the most common and most practical method to get the small plants established without over-

watering. Once established and spaced, drip systems provide good watering control and the ability to leach the growing medium when desired. Drip tubes are especially useful for hanging baskets and often result in improved uniformity and quality over hand watering (fig. 4.1). Drip systems are programmable to meet the multiple daily irrigations often needed for mature plants during the busy spring season [11].

Ebb and flood, trough and capillary mats are all bottom watering systems used for New Guinea impatiens irrigation, but they are not conducive to easy leaching. Therefore, the nutrient levels in the irrigation water is often lowered to avoid a soluble salts build-up in the growing medium. Capillary mats that are constantly moist often produce large, lush plants, not well acclimated for the consumer environment (fig. 4.2).

Nutrient requirements

New Guinea impatiens require the same essential mineral elements as most other plants. Leaf tissue analysis shows the mineral content is not much different than that of other floricultural crops (table 4.1). All six essential macronutrients (N, P, K, Ca, Mg, and S) and seven essential micronutrients (Fe, Mn, Zn, Cu, B, Mo, and Cl) must be available for the plant's use. Although it's possible for some of these elements to be absorbed by the foliage, they are usually taken up by the roots. The growing medium, water, and fertilizers are all nutrient sources in the root environment.

New Guinea impatiens are somewhat unique in their ability to extract their mineral requirements from less concentrated nutrient

Fig. 4.2. *New Guinea impatiens grown on capillary mat watering systems often produce large, lush plants that aren't well acclimated for the consumer environment.*

TABLE 4.1

Normal leaf tissue mineral analysis levels for New Guinea impatiens

	University of Minnesota [3]	Soil and Plant Laboratory [18]
Macronutrients	(percentage of dry weight)	
Nitrogen	2.5 to 4.5	3.4 to 4.6
Phosphorus	0.3 to 0.8	0.4 to 0.64
Potassium	1.9 to 2.7	1.2 to 2.4
Calcium	1.0 to 2.0	2.2 to 3.0
Magnesium	0.3 to 0.8	0.66 to 1.0
Micronutrients	(ppm of dry weight)	
Iron	150 to 300	75 to 300
Manganese	100 to 250	100 to 250
Zinc	40 to 85	60 to 86
Copper	5 to 10	8 to 14
Boron	50 to 60	40 to 80

solutions than are needed for optimum growth of other floricultural crops [3, 5, 15]. In fact, high nutrient levels or high soluble salts in the growing medium are detrimental to New Guinea impatiens growth [3, 6, 7, 8, 9, 15, 17]. This is especially true in the early stages, just before and immediately after transplanting a rooted cutting or seedling. A common recommendation is to apply no fertilizer for the first two to three weeks or until the roots reach the pot's side [3, 4, 7, 8, 9, 15].

Macronutrients

Macronutrients are usually supplied by adding slow release fertilizers to the growing medium and soluble fertilizers to irrigation water. Finely ground limestone or dolomite are added to the growing media to neutralize some of the acidity, especially in peat-moss-based mixes, but they are also sources of calcium (limestone) or calcium and magnesium (dolomite). Nitrogen, phosphorus, and potassium are most often provided as water soluble fertilizers. Formulations that have nearly equal percentages of nitrogen and potassium (K_2O), such as 20-10-20 or 15-16-17, are most frequently recommended [1, 2, 11, 16]. Lower phosphorus ratios (P_2O_5) are needed and are sufficiently supplied in these commonly used formulations. An alternative is to add super phosphate to the growing medium. Often a phosphorus application is unnecessary if phosphoric acid is being used to acidify irrigation water.

New Guinea impatiens are very efficient in their micronutrient uptake, especially iron and manganese, and are very sensitive to high micronutrient levels in the plant tissue that may severely impede growth [3]. Only moderate amounts of micronutrients should be provided, either in the growing medium or with the liquid fertilizer, but not both [13].

Fertility management

Fertility management details are very important for successful New Guinea impatiens production. Optimum nutrient and soluble salt levels are relatively lower and pH ranges more exacting than for other floricultural crops. Overfertilization is one of the most common cultural problems [17].

Fertility management begins with the growing medium. If needed, amend the medium with limestone or dolomite so the pH will be 5.8 to 6.5 [3, 4, 20]. The availability of micronutrients increases rapidly as the pH of the growing medium falls below 5.8, resulting in potential micronutrient toxicity [3]. Maintain soluble salts levels in the 1 to 1.5 EC (electrical conductivity) range (1:2 extract). University of Massachusetts research demonstrated that New Guinea impatiens growth was suppressed when the EC exceeded 1.5 mmhos/cm [9]. Growing media should be monitored for soluble salts and pH on a regular basis [7, 8, 15].

Soluble salts sensitivity

New Guinea impatiens are sensitive to high soluble salts levels in the growing medium, especially in the early growth stages [3, 6]. For this reason, newly transplanted plants perform best at lower fertilization levels. Little, if any, fertilizer should be applied the first two to three weeks after transplanting [3, 4, 7, 8, 19, 20]. Begin fertilization after the roots start to grow [2]. Start a liquid fertilizer program when the roots have reached the side of the pot [3, 4, 6, 15, 19, 20]. Constant liquid fertilizer (CLF) applications of 100 to 200 parts per million nitrogen using complete NPK fertilizers such as 20-10-20 have given excellent results (see Color Plate section, CP 4.1).

Leach with clear water when needed to avoid a soluble salts build-up. If fertilizer is not applied with each irrigation, make single applications of 300 to 350 ppm every other watering or on a weekly basis. As plants mature, CLF rates may be increased to 200 to 250 ppm as long as the growing medium's soluble salts level doesn't exceed an EC reading of 1.5 to 2.25 (1:2 extract). Avoid constant liquid fertilizer rates higher than 250 ppm N.

Micronutrients shouldn't be part of the liquid fertilizer solution if micronutrients were used as an amendment to the growing medium. Using controlled or slow-release fertilizers is usually not recommended because they may raise soluble salts to undesirable levels. If they are used, apply at very low rates and reduce the amount of liquid fertilizer.

Supply magnesium by adding dolomitic limestone to the growing medium or magnesium sulfate (Epsom salts) to the liquid fertilizer solution. Four ounces (113.4 g) of Epsom salts per 100 gallons (378.5 l) of water provide about 28 ppm magnesium, or apply 8 ounces (226.8 g) of Epsom salts per 100 gallons (378.5 l) of water as a separate drench every two weeks.

New Guinea impatiens propagated from seed should be fertilized in plug trays with 50 to 75 ppm N, using fertilizers such as 15-16-17 or 20-10-20. After transplanting, fertilize with 150 to 200 ppm N, constant liquid feed, using a complete NPK fertilizer [16].

Controlling soluble salts

New Guinea impatiens are extremely sensitive to high soluble salts levels in the growing medium. Soluble salts levels are measured as the electrical conductivity (EC) of the growing medium solution in mmhos/cm. Samples for measuring EC are prepared by extracting solutions from 1:2 (soil to water) or saturated paste preparations.

Whereas an EC of 3.0 mmhos/cm is considered a relatively high but acceptable level for many floricultural crops, levels above 1.5 (1:2 extract) suppressed the early growth stages of New Guinea impatiens in a University of Massachusetts test [9]. EC readings of 1.5 to 2.25 (saturated paste extract) are recommended for soilless media by the University of Minnesota [3] (table 4.2).

Soluble fertilizers are the most common source of soluble salts, but excessive EC levels can build for reasons other than high fertilizer rates [8]. Water quality, type of growing medium, amount of leaching, and frequency of fertilization all interact to contribute to soluble salts levels. It's not uncommon for irrigation water EC to be 1.0 or above before any soluble fertilizer is added.

Overfertilization

Overfertilization and/or high soluble salts levels result in poor growth of New Guinea impatiens. Young plants appear stunted and lack vigor.

TABLE 4.2

Recommended soil test readings for New Guinea impatiens grown in a soilless medium

Soilless medium	pH	SS	NO3	NH4	P	K	Ca
Spurway	6.2-6.5	60-80	75-100	0-5	5-10	30-40	80-120
Saturated media (paste)	6.0-6.5	1.5-2.25	75-125	0-10	5-10	75-125	100-200

Soilless medium	Mg	Na	Fe	Mn	Zn	B
Spurway	30-40	1-10	0.1-0.5	0.1-0.5	0.1-0.5	0.1-0.5
Saturated media (paste)	30-70	<10% total SS	0.3-3.0	0.02-3.0	0.3-3.0	0.05-0.50

Source: Minnesota Commercial Flower Growers Association Bulletin 41(3): 1-15 [3].

Roots don't develop, and plants wilt in moist growing medium. Often the leaf color will intensify to deep green or dark purplish green, depending on the cultivar [4, 17] (CP 4.2).

Shiny, dark green leaves, with a rippled or wavy leaf surface and cupping at the leaf margins are symptoms of high fertility levels in established New Guinea impatiens plants [3, 17] (CP 4.3). At this sign, check the soluble salts level, leach the growing medium with clear water, and reduce fertilizer rates. A general reduction in plant and root growth will result if overfertilization and/or high soluble salts persist and leaf tip and edge browning will become evident [6] (CP 4.4).

Underfertilization

Underfertilization results in a general growth reduction. Young plants are short and leaves are small and chlorotic; purplish-green leafed cultivars have reddish leaves and green leafed cultivars have a light green to yellowish appearance [17]. In more established plants, poor nutrition may result in leaf yellowing, leaf drop, and small flowers [15].

A weekly soluble salts test is suggested for New Guinea impatiens, especially in the beginning when it is uncertain how water quality, watering, leaching practices, and fertilizer rates will affect soluble salts levels. The methods are rather simple, and soluble salts meters are relatively inexpensive for those who wish to do their own testing. If a commercial testing laboratory is used, choose one that can report the results within a few days of sampling.

Why pH is important

The growing medium pH controls nutrient availability. A slightly acid growing medium provides optimum levels of most nutrients for New Guinea impatiens. Optimum pH ranges may differ slightly for soilless media and media containing mineral soils. Some recommend a 5.6 to 6.0 pH for soilless media and 5.8 to 6.5 for soil mixes [15], while others suggest a single range of 5.8 to 6.4 [3, 4] or 5.8 to 6.5 [20]. Regardless, the optimum range (5.8 to 6.5) is fairly well defined. Higher pH levels limit the availability of most micronutrients, while lower levels increase the availability of micronutrients to a point where micronutrient toxicity is possible [17].

New Guinea impatiens need only moderate micronutrient levels [15]. The growing medium pH shouldn't drop below 5.8 if iron or manganese levels are moderate to high. New Guinea impatiens take up unusually large amounts of iron and manganese at pH levels below 5.8 [3]. Excess micronutrients will cause distortion, stunting and cupping of the upper leaves, shoot tip dieback, necrosis of lower leaves or leaf margins and total plant collapse [3, 15]. If micronutrient toxicity is suspected, have the leaf tissue analyzed to confirm whether iron or manganese levels are excessive [3]. To correct micronutrient toxicity, leach the growing medium with clear water or a fertilizer solution with no micronutrients. Adjust the pH upward to the 6.0 to 6.5 range.

Water quality affects the growing medium pH. Alkaline water (i.e., water with a moderate to high bicarbonate level), neutralizes the growing medium's acidity and causes the pH to rise. Irrigation water with more than 200 ppm is often neutralized with acid to help maintain the growing medium pH below 6.5. On the other hand, irrigation waters low in alkalinaity (bicarbonates) often drive the pH below 5.8, causing excessive uptake and toxicity of micronutrients. Those who use water with low alkalinity often need to amend the growing medium with limestone and/or use soluble calcium fertilizers that raise and maintain a pH above 5.8.

References

[1]   Andrews, B. 1992. Ball Seed's New Guinea impatiens: cause for celebration. *Greenhouse Grower* July:112.
[2]   *The culture advisor—New Guinea impatiens culture.* 1991. West Chicago, Ill.: Ball Seed Co.
[3]   Erwin, J., M. Ascerno, F. Pfleger, and R. Heins. 1992. *New Guinea impatiens production.* Minn. Comm. Fl. Gr. Assoc. Bul. 41 (3):1-15.

[4]   ——. 1993. Getting to know New Guineas. *Greenhouse Grower*. Sept: 58, 60.

[5]   Fischer, P. Nahrstoffbedarf von impatiens New - Guinea - Hybriden. 1990. *Deutscher Gartenbau* 44 (18):1208, 1210-1213.

[6]   Grueber, G. 1992. Secrets to success with New Guinea impatiens. *Floriculture Indiana* 6 (1):4-6.

[7]   Judd, L.K., and D.A. Cox. 1991. *Soluble salts buildup as a cause of early growth suppression in New Guinea impatiens.* Mass. Fl. Gr. Assoc. Research Report No. 1.

[8]   ——. 1992. New Guinea impatiens—watch out for soluble salts. *Greenhouse Grower*. Feb: 68, 70-71.

[9]   ——. 1992. Growth of New Guinea impatiens inhibited by height growth—medium electrical conductivity. *HortSci.* 27 (11):1193-1194.

[10]   Koch, S. 1989. No patience required for Ecke's New Guineas. *Greenhouse Grower*. Dec:96.

[11]   Konjoian, P. 1990. New Guinea impatiens: optimism abounds. *PPGA News* XXI (12):2-3.

[12]   ——. 1994. When scheduling New Guinea impatiens, pay attention to the details. *PPGA News* XXV (1):4-5.

[13]   Mikkelsen, E.P. 1990. Rays of sunshine from Mikkelsens. *Greenhouse Grower*. Jan:118-119.

[14]   ——. 1989. Culture notes—New Guinea impatiens. *GrowerTalks*. Oct:16.

[15]   Cultural information for lasting impressions and sunshine New Guinea impatiens. 1993. Ashtabula, Ohio: Mikkelsens Inc.

[16]   *Spectra New Guinea impatiens.* 1991. West Chicago, Ill.: PanAmerican Seed Co.

[17]   *Cultural requirements for Paradise and Pure Beauty New Guinea impatiens.* 1992. Encinitas, Calif. Paul Ecke Ranch.

[18]   *Mineral analysis interpretation key for New Guinea impatiens.* 1988. Orange, Calif.: Soil and Plant Laboratory, Inc.

[19]   Watt, J.R. 1992. Mikkelsens' New Guinea impatiens: creating a lasting impression. *Greenhouse Grower*. Nov: 76.

[20]   ——. 1993. Mikkelsens' New Guinea impatiens: twice as nice. *Greenhouse Grower*. Dec:89.

CHAPTER 5

Light and Temperature

John Erwin

Cultural requirements for New Guinea impatiens are relatively easy and consistent across cultivars. Growers, however, often experience difficulties when New Guinea impatiens are placed in an environment that is either too cold or too hot. This chapter emphasizes how New Guinea impatiens environmental culture differs from that of other bedding plant crops.

New Guinea impatiens were originally collected by H.F. Winters and J.J. Higgins in 1970 [2]. The cultivars available today were developed from *Impatiens herzogii*, *I. schlecteri*, *I. linearifolia*, and *I. hawkeri*. All of these species are native to the Australian New Guinea subtropical highlands where average day temperatures are 77F to 86F (25C to 30C) and at night, 65F to 70F (18C to 21C) (Robert Quene, personal communication).

Light _____

Light essentially results in two biologically significant processes in plants: the use of light for chemical reduction or oxidizing power (photosynthesis), or as a trigger effect to release a large amount of stored energy (photo- or light perception). Photosynthesis is the use of light to capture energy for growth. Photo- or light perception is a process where an organism obtains information about the environment surrounding it.

Photoperiod
New Guinea impatiens are not photoperiodic—the length of the day or night period does not stimulate flowering [2, 4, 5]. However, flowering

increases as the total light that a plant is exposed during a 24-hour period increases, i.e., as the total daily carbohydrates produced as a result of photosynthesis increase [2, 4, 5, 6, 7]. Therefore, bright conditions and/or long days result in more flowering due to the greater amount of light that the plant receives over a day/night cycle.

Irradiance (light intensity)

New Guinea impatiens prefer bright light [2, 4, 5, 6, 7]. During the middle of the day, irradiance (light) levels of 3,000 to 4,500 foot-candles (32.3 to 48.4 klux) are recommended [2, 5, 6]. Irradiance levels lower than 3,000 f.c. can encourage stem elongation and reduce flowering [2, 5, 6, 7]. They should be shaded if irradiance levels exceed 5,000 f.c. (53.8 klux) regularly. Irradiance levels higher than 5,000 f.c. (53.8 klux) can slow growth and reduce leaf and/or flower expansion.

Plants grown outdoors should not be grown in direct sunlight for the entire day. Ideally, plants should receive bright light only. Keep in mind that light heats plants. High irradiance conditions may reduce flowering because plant temperatures get too warm.

Light quality

Light quality or color can have a dramatic impact on the appearance of a plant [3]. Light quality affects plant height, leaf color and size, and leaf orientation. Growers regularly alter the light color that crops are exposed to by turning lights on, spacing plants, or moving plants to greenhouses with different coverings. In addition, the light color that plants are exposed to on a bench changes as plants grow together.

Light color is perceived primarily by a pigment in the plant leaf called phytochrome that absorbs primarily red or far red light [3]. Perception of red and/or far red light by phytochrome leads to a number of physiological responses that change growth.

Leaves are preferential filters [3]. They absorb some light and let some light pass through. Green leaves absorb more red light than far red light (fig. 5.1). Therefore, plants growing under a canopy are exposed to more far red light than red light compared to plants grown in direct sunlight.

The ratio of red to far red light that a leaf is exposed to allows a plant to determine if it is being shaded by another plant or if a plant is near other plants. When a plant is exposed to more far red than red light, it uses its resources to grow above the canopy [3]. As a result, stem elongation increases while branching decreases and plant growth is concentrated on shoot development as opposed to root development. Plants will also capture as much light as possible by increasing leaf area and orienting leaves in a more upright position.

Difficulty in controlling New Guinea impatiens height is often relat-

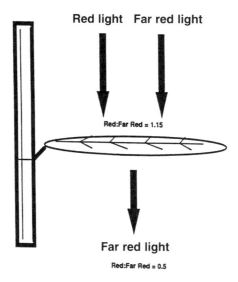

Fig. 5.1. *Ratio of red and far red light incident and red and far red light transmitted through a leaf.*

ed to excessive crowding of plants on a bench. It is critical that these impatiens be spaced adequately or that hanging baskets are not grown above a New Guinea impatiens crop. It's also important that lamps producing light high in far red light (incandescent lights) are not left on during the day and especially during the night. In fact, it's important not to turn on incandescent lights at all during the night.

It is often best to transplant cuttings delivered and/or propagated in a plug tray to a larger pot as soon as possible—cuttings can easily stretch in the flat due to crowding. Failure to transplant early will result in longer, lower internodes. If plants must be crowded due to space, you'll need to apply growth regulators or manipulate the difference between day and night temperature to reduce stem elongation.

Temperature

Development rate

The temperature a plant is exposed to affects its development rate, which is usually measured by determining the leaf unfolding rate per day [2]. In general, there is a certain temperature, called the base temperature, at which leaf unfolding is arrested (fig. 5.2). As the temperature increases above the base temperature, leaf unfolding rate increases proportionally until plant development reaches some maximum

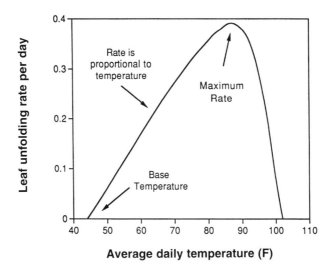

Fig. 5.2. *Effect of average daily temperature on a plant leaf unfolding rate. Data are not specific to New Guinea impatiens but represent a general plant temperature response curve.*

rate. This range of temperatures is called the linear range. As temperature increases further, the leaf unfolding rate decreases. As long as the day and night temperature are in the linear range, the leaf unfolding rate is a function of the average daily temperature used to grow the crop.

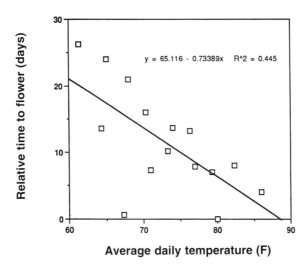

Fig. 5.3. *Average daily temperature effect on the relative time to flower of the cultivar Mimas. Relative time to flower was calculated by determining the average increase in time to flower relative to the most rapid flowering day/night treatment.*

New Guinea impatiens have a relatively narrow temperature range for optimal plant growth [2]. The base temperature range is between 50F and 55F (10C to 13C). Plant development rate increases as temperature increases from 60F to 80F (16C to 27C) (fig. 5.3 and also see Color Plate section, CP 5.1). The plant development rate is greatest when New Guinea impatiens plants are grown at constant 77F to 80F (25C to 27C) [2]. Increasing day or night temperature above 80F (27C) reduces the plant development rate (leaf unfolding) and plant quality.

Plants grown at a constant temperature of 63F (17C) require 10 to 14 days longer to first flower than plants grown at a constant temperature of 73F (23C) (fig. 5.3) [2]. It's important to realize that plant development slows dramatically when the temperature drops below 60F to 63F (16C to 17C). In particular, young plant growth is severely depressed when night temperatures drop below 63F (17C). However, night temperatures can drop to 60F (16C) on large, established plants without significant detrimental effects on plant growth [6, 7].

It's important to remember that plants grown in direct sunlight can be 4F to 8F (2.2C to 4.4C) warmer than the air temperature. For example, if plants are grown in direct sunlight in a 75F (24C) greenhouse, the plant temperature may be over 80F (27C) and plant development rate may be slowed.

Development of new, more heat tolerant New Guinea impatiens may increase the maximum temperature at which growth rate is slowed by warm temperatures. There appears to be great performance variation in the landscape environment. Both Pennsylvania State University and Disney World have conducted extensive cultivar trials that identify a variety of New Guinea impatiens with superior landscape performance (T. Smith, personal communication). This chapter's information was primarily derived from experiments on the cultivar Mimas [2]. Superior landscape performance of new cultivars is probably due to better heat and/or water stress tolerance. Mark Strefeler and Robert Queñe at the University of Minnesota are currently breeding New Guinea impatiens for heat and cold and water stress tolerance.

Plant morphology

Plant morphology refers to a plant's appearance such as its height, internode length and caliber, leaf size and color, and branch number.

New Guinea impatiens stem elongation is affected by the average daily temperature (ADT) plants are grown under and the difference between the day and night temperature (fig. 5.4) [2]. Stem elongation increases as temperature increases to approximately 80F (27C) on the cultivar Mimas (fig. 5.4). Increasing temperature above 80F (27C) reduces stem elongation. For example, Mimas' internode length (the stem segment between two leaves) increased from 1.1 to 3.3 cm (0.43

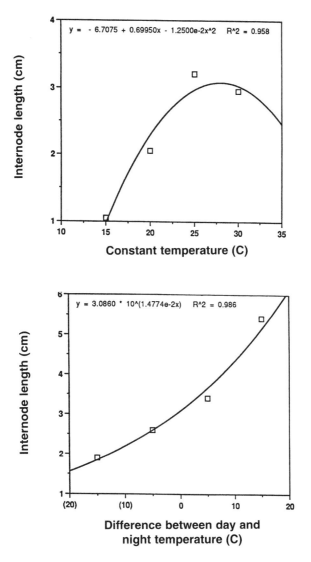

Fig. 5.4. *Effect of constant temperature treatments and the difference between day and night temperature (day temperature - night temperature) on Mimas New Guinea impatiens internode length. Temperatures of 15, 20, 25 and 30C are similar to 59, 68, 77 and 86F.*

to 1.3 inches) as temperature increased from 59F to 77F (15C to 25C) then decreased to 3.0 cm (1.18 inch) as temperature was further increased from 77F to 86F (25C to 30C) (fig. 5.4) [2].

Stem elongation also increases as DIF increases (fig. 5.4) [2]. DIF refers to the difference between the day and night temperature (DIF = day temperature - night temperature) [1]. For example, Mimas' inter-

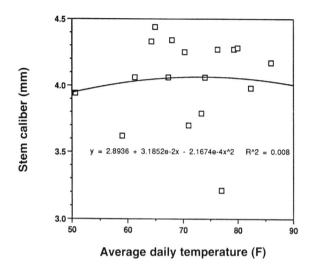

Fig. 5.5. *Effect of average daily temperature on the stem caliber of Mimas New Guinea impatiens.*

node length increased from 1.9 to 5.6 cm (.75 to 2.2 inches) as DIF increased from -27F to +27F (fig. 5.4) [2].

Stem elongation can be significantly reduced by growing the crop with an equal day and night temperature (0 DIF) or a cooler day than night temperature (negative DIF) [1]. For instance, internode length was 3.8 cm (1.5 inch) on Mimas plants grown with a 77F (25C) day and 59F (15C) night temperature (+18F DIF) while Mimas plants grown at constant 68F (20C) (0F DIF) had internode lengths of 2.0 cm [2]. In other words, stem elongation was reduced 47% by growing plants in a 0F DIF environment versus a +18F DIF environment [2].

The response of New Guinea impatiens stem elongation to DIF is affected by other environmental factors. DIF's effect on stem elongation increases as daylength decreases, irradiance increases, and plant spacing increases [1].

An alternative to growing a New Guinea impatiens crop with either a 0 or negative DIF environment is to drop temperatures during the first three hours of the morning. This is almost as effective in controlling stem elongation as maintaining cool temperatures all day [1]. The degree of elongation reduction is enhanced as temperature drop increases [do not drop below 58F and 55F (14C and 13C) on young and old plants, respectively] and the earlier in the day the temperature drop occurs [1].

Stem caliber is unaffected by temperature (fig. 5.5) [2]. However, stem dry weight is affected by temperature. Temperature effects on stem dry weight for either finishing a New Guinea impatiens crop or

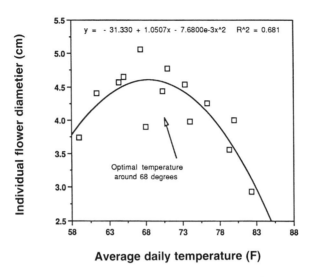

Fig. 5.6. *Effect of average daily temperature on Mimas New Guinea impatiens flower diameter.*

growing stock plants is discussed in the following sections on **carbon partitioning** and **practical implications**.

Flower size is greatest when day and night temperatures are 68F to 72F (20C to 22C) (CP 5.2) [2]. If either day or night temperature increases or decreases from 68F to 72F (20C to 22C), flower size is reduced [2]. For example, flower diameter decreased from approximately 4.5 to 2.6 cm (1.77 to 1.02 inches) as temperature increased from 68F to 82F (20C to 28C) (fig. 5.6). Mimas plants grown at temperatures above 82F (28C) average daily temperature failed and/or aborted flowers [2].

In contrast to flower size, leaf number per node and individual leaf area are primarily influenced by the average daily temperature that plants are grown under. Mimas leaf number per node increased from 4 to 7.5 as average daily temperature increased from 50F to 75F (10C to 24C) (fig. 5.7) [2]. Increasing the average daily temperature from 75F to 86F (24C to 30C) slightly decreased leaf number per node. Similarly, leaf area increases as average daily plant growth temperature increases to 75F (24C), then decreases as average daily temperature increases above 75F (24C) (fig. 5.7) [2].

Carbon partitioning

Total shoot dry weight (stem + leaves + flowers) is highest (7.1 g/0.25 oz.) when plants are grown with day/night temperatures of 77F (25C)/59F (15C) (table 5.1). Shoot dry weight decreased to 6.3 g (0.22

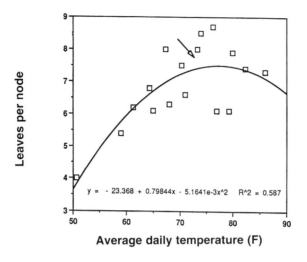

$y = -23.368 + 0.79844x - 5.1641e\text{-}3x^2 \quad R^2 = 0.587$

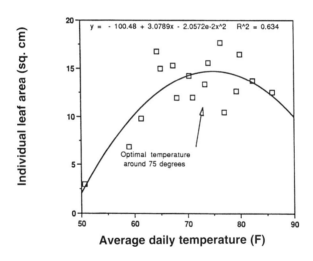

$y = -100.48 + 3.0789x - 2.0572e\text{-}2x^2 \quad R^2 = 0.634$

Optimal temperature around 75 degrees

Fig. 5.7. *Effect of average daily temperature on number of leaves per node and individual leaf area of Mimas New Guinea impatiens.*

oz.) when plants were grown with a 68F (20C) day and 59F (15C) night temperature (table 5.1) [2].

Stem dry weight is affected primarily by day temperature (fig. 5.8). Stem dry weight is greatest when plants are grown with warm day temperatures, i.e., 77F to 86F (25C to 30C) (table 5.1). For instance, stem dry weight increased from 0.1 g to 1.4 g (0.04 oz.) per shoot as day

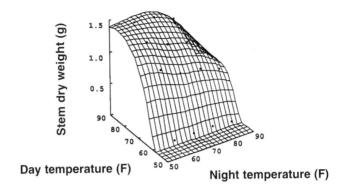

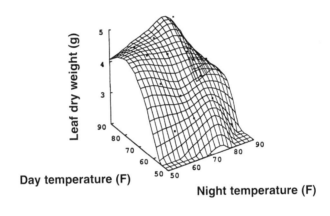

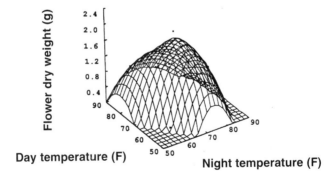

Fig. 5.8. *Three dimensional surface plots showing the effect of day and night temperature on stem, leaf, and flower dry weight (g) of Mimas New Guinea impatiens. Data was collected 51 days after temperature treatments were initiated.*

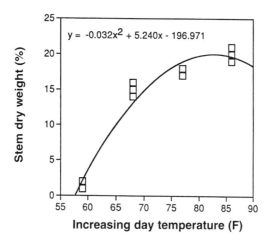

$$y = -0.032x^2 + 5.240x - 196.971$$

Fig. 5.9. *Increasing day temperature effect on the percent of total shoot dry weight that was partitioned to Mimas New Guinea impatiens stems.*

temperature increased from 59F to 86F (15C to 30C) (table 5.1). Carbon partitioning to the stem also increases as day temperature increases. The percent of Mimas total shoot dry weight that is in the stem increased from 1% to 21% as the daily plant growth temperature increased from 59F to 86F (15C to 30C) (fig. 5.9).

Leaf dry weight per shoot was also affected primarily by day temperature (fig. 5.8). Mimas leaf dry weight increased from 2.7 g to 4.4 g (.09 to .15 oz.) per shoot as day temperature increased from 59F to 86F (15C to 30C), and the night temperature was held at 59F (15C) (fig. 5.8 and table 5.1). Carbon partitioning to the leaves was the lowest at a constant temperature of 68F (28C) and greatest when carbon partitioning to flowers was least (table 5.1).

Carbon partitioning to flowers or the percent of total shoot dry weight that was dedicated to flowers was highest when plants were grown at a constant 68F (20C) (fig. 5.8). If either day or night temperatures varied from 68F (20C), flower dry weight per shoot decreased.

Practical implications

Dry weight is a determinant of plant quality. Adequate cutting weight is critical for plant propagators since high cutting weight is associated with increased rooting and cutting vigor. In addition to cutting dry weight, it's important to have adequate internode length on cuttings for ease in harvesting and to hold the foliage above the rooting medium. A positive DIF stock plant environment promotes greater cutting dry weight and internode elongation. Day temperatures of 77F (25C) and night temperatures of 66F (19C) promote high cutting dry weight, high

Day and night temperature effects on leaf, stem, flower and total shoot dry weight of Mimas New Guinea impatiens [a]

Night temperature	Day temperature			
	59/15 (F/C)	68/20 (F/C)	77/25 (F/C)	86/30 (F/C)
(F/C)	**Total shoot dry weight (g)**			
59/15	2.83	6.27	7.08	6.73
68/20	4.55	6.26	6.73	6.78
77/25	4.67	5.87	6.30	6.84
86/30	2.33	4.77	4.71	4.24
(F/C)	**Stem dry weight (g)**			
59/15	0.06 (2%)	1.02 (16%)	1.28 (18%)	1.43 (21%)
68/20	0.07 (1%)	0.86 (14%)	1.14 (17%)	1.42 (21%)
77/25	0.07 (1%)	0.83 (14%)	1.08 (17%)	1.30 (19%)
86/30	0.04 (2%)	0.72 (15%)	0.82 (17%)	0.83 (20%)
(F/C)	**Leaf dry weight (g)**			
59/15	2.69 (95%)	3.87 (62%)	4.46 (63%)	4.41 (66%)
68/20	2.88 (63%)	3.28 (52%)	4.29 (64%)	4.49 (66%)
77/25	3.30 (71%)	3.71 (63%)	4.16 (66%)	4.95 (72%)
86/30	2.26 (97%)	3.67 (77%)	3.71 (79%)	3.37 (79%)
(F/C)	**Flower dry weight (g)**			
59/15	0.08 (3%)	1.38 (22%)	1.34 (19%)	0.87 (13%)
68/20	1.60 (35%)	2.12 (34%)	1.29 (19%)	0.87 (15%)
77/25	1.30 (28%)	1.33 (23%)	1.05 (17%)	0.59 (9%)
86/30	0.03 (1%)	0.38 (8%)	0.18 (4%)	0.04 (1%)

[a] Data on the percent of total shoot dry weight are presented in parentheses. Plants were grown under a nine-hour photoperiod. Data were collected 51 days after temperature treatments were initiated.

stem dry weight, and adequate internode length. In addition, leaf unfolding rate would be higher and leaf and stem growth would be promoted at the expense of flowering.

In contrast to a propagator, a grower who finishes New Guinea impatiens for market desires a high percentage of the total plant dry weight as flowers. Based on this, the optimal temperature to finish New Guinea impatiens is constant 68F to 72F (20C to 22C). At this temperature, stem elongation is reduced compared to a positive DIF environment, flower size is maximized, and a greater proportion of the total shoot dry weight is in flowers (34% on Mimas) (figs. 5.8 and CP 5.3).

Enviromental interaction

Use of growth retardants

New Guinea impatiens usually don't need any growth retardant applications. This is fortunate since Cycocel, B-Nine, and A-Rest have relatively little effect on New Guinea impatiens stem elongation. Bonzi, however, has been shown to be effective [2].

Controlling stem elongation with temperature is possible to some degree. Use of DIF and/or a cool morning drop in temperature can reduce stem elongation significantly.

Stem elongation is most difficult to control when plants are crowded and/or hanging baskets are grown above a crop. As mentioned before, crowding plants changes the light quality that lower internodes are exposed to and results in greater stem elongation [3]. Excessive crowding will stimulate stem elongation. However, this can be overcome by using either DIF or growth retardant applications [1].

The best methods to control height on a New Guinea impatiens crop are to:

1. space plants adequately so as to not alter light quality,
2. grow plants at adequate irradiance levels,
3. maintain a zero or low positive DIF temperature environment,
4. minimize the use of high ammonium fertilizers.

Insect pests

The most common pests are the two-spotted mite, cyclamen mite, aphids, fungus gnats, and western flower thrips. Western flower thrips have become a severe problem for production throughout the United States. Although thrips can damage the plant directly, the greatest danger is the thrips' ability to transmit tomato spotted wilt virus (TSWV). A thrips life cycle, as with all insects, is also dependent on the average daily temperature. Therefore, if a crop is early, an effective thrips control measure is to reduce the average daily plant growth temperature. This decreases the thrips reproduction rate and activity in conjunction with either bio- or chemical control measures. Don't reduce the average daily temperature below 65F to 67F (18C to 19C), or there will be a reduction in flowering.

References

[1]   Erwin, J.E., R.D. Heins, W. Carlson, and S. Newport. 1992. Environmental and mechanical manipulation of stem elongation. *PGRSA Quart.* 20:1-7.
[2]   Erwin, J.E., M. Ascerno, F. Pfleger, and R.D. Heins. 1992. *New Guinea impatiens production.* Minn. Comm. Flow. Grow. Bull. 41(3):1-15.
[3]   Erwin, J.E. 1993. *Light quality: A brief overview.* Minn. Comm. Flow. Grow. Bull. 42(1):1-5.
[4]   Grueber, G. 1992. Secrets to success with New Guinea impatiens. *Floriculture Indiana* 6(1):4-6.
[5]   Kasperski, M., and W. Carlson. 1989. *New Guinea impatiens production.* Mich. State Univ. Ext. Bull. E-2179.

[6]   *Cultural information for Mikkel Sunshine New Guinea impatiens.* 1989. Ashtabula, Ohio: Mikkelsens, Inc.

[7]   *New Guinea impatiens: Cultural information.* 1989. Encinitas, Calif.: Paul Ecke Ranch.

CHAPTER 6

Certified Stock

Michael J. Klopmeyer

Successful production, finishing, and sales of New Guinea impatiens can be severely impacted by plant disease. With the increased demand for New Guinea impatiens in the home garden, propagators and finishers need to focus on bringing a top quality, clean plant to market. As this crop's popularity has grown over the past 10 to 15 years, so have new and potentially devastating plant diseases. For example, the appearance in North American greenhouses in the late 1980s of tomato spotted wilt virus (TSWV) and impatiens necrotic spot virus (INSV) as well as their vector, the western flower thrips, significantly impacted grower's success with New Guinea impatiens. One way for growers to combat this problem is to adopt clean plant production practices including the purchase of disease-free, certified cuttings.

Major pests affecting New Guinea impatiens include fungal, bacterial, and viral pathogens and various insects. Their control methods are covered elsewhere in this book. This chapter will describe the general methods employed by the major breeder/propagators to eliminate these pathogens and provide clean, certified plants to the industry.

What is certified stock?_____

Certified stock can best be described as plants that have been thoroughly tested and retested under controlled conditions for the presence of plant pathogens including fungi, bacteria, and viruses. If careful testing doesn't reveal the presence of plant pathogens, the stock can be certified disease-free. But this stock is still susceptible to diseases.

Careful build-up and production of certified stock under disease-free and insect-free conditions will adequately guarantee the continuation of a "certified" stock base.

A long history of certification programs for vegetatively propagated crops exists in the floriculture industry [17]. Due to serious and often devastating disease outbreaks in crops such as chrysanthemums, carnations and geraniums, major specialist propagators need to provide clean, certified plants to the industry to remain competitive. Fortunately, many of these same concepts can be applied toward producing certified New Guinea impatiens stock.

Pathogen review

As described in Chapters 12 and 13, the major pathogens of New Guinea impatiens are: the tospoviruses (INSV and TSWV) and other miscellaneous viruses; root and stem rot fungi such as Rhizoctonia, Pythium; leaf spot fungi such as Botrytis and Myrothecium and leaf spot bacteria such as *Pseudomonas syringae*. Different methods are available to eliminate specific pathogens from New Guinea impatiens in a certification program.

Eliminating pathogens ————————

Little information has been published in either scientific or trade journals about eliminating pathogens from New Guinea impatiens, but the basic concepts developed for pathogen elimination from geraniums, for example, can be applied. An understanding of each pathogen's basic biology and the type of diseases they produce is necessary.

Fungal pathogens such as Rhizoctonia and Pythium are typically encountered in greenhouses where poor sanitation practices are employed. Infection sources of these fungi usually are contaminated media, water, or greenhouse benches. In a certification program, problems associated with these fungi can be reduced by utilizing steam-pasteurized potting media as well as sterilized pots, benches, and greenhouse structures.

Eliminating fungi and bacteria

Fungi can be eliminated from plants by using a simple laboratory technique called culture indexing. In the 1940s, culture indexing was developed to free chrysanthemums of the fungal wilt pathogen, Verticillium [6, 7, 17]. This method was later expanded to eradicate systemic carnation pathogens [19] and bacterial blight (*Xanthomonas campestris* pv. *pelargonii*) from geraniums [15, 20].

Culture indexing is a simple yet very effective method for selecting New Guinea impatiens that are free of systemic pathogens. Steps in culture indexing include:

1. Establishing mother plants in an incubation greenhouse at temperatures optimal for disease development 77F to 86F (25C to 30C) day, 68F to 77F (20C to 25C) night.
2. Remove top cuttings (3 to 4 cm long) (1.17 to 1.56 inches) from this mother plant; number them individually and take them to the laboratory for testing (without storage).
3. Excising the bottom 1 to 2 cm (0.39 to 0.78 inch) portion of the cutting with a sterile knife. The surface is sterilized with a 10% bleach solution for approximately 10 minutes.
4. Aseptically slicing the stem section into thin (2 mm) (0.078 inch) sections that are placed in a test tube containing sterile nutrient broth and incubated at room temperature, 73F to 77F (23C to 25C), for 10 to 14 days.
5. After incubating, if the nutrient solution appears cloudy due to bacterial or fungal contamination from the plant's vascular system, the original numbered cutting tested is discarded. Only those cuttings that yield no growth of any microorganism in the nutrient broth tube are retained. The original mother plant is also destroyed.
6. Planting all cuttings that culture index free of pathogens in an incubation block (at temperatures optimal for disease development) and retesting after three to four months. If cuttings from these mother plants test clean, they are kept while the original mother plant is destroyed. This process is repeated one more time for a total of at least three times. One complete year of testing (three to four culture indexings) should be done to assure freedom from systemic bacterial and fungal pathogens.

Key points to remember about culture indexing are:

- All bacterial and fungal systemic pathogens and nonpathogens are detected.
- Theoretically, one bacterial cell or fungal spore can be detected.
- The identity of the organism(s) in the broth tube isn't required. Zero tolerance for all systemic organisms is the rule.

Eliminating systemic fungal and bacterial pathogens from New Guinea impatiens can also be exploited via tissue culture techniques. New Guinea impatiens can be readily established in tissue culture [18]. Excised shoot tips or meristem tips (2 to 4 mm long), after surface sterilization in a 10% bleach solution, can be established on a simple agar-based tissue culture medium [16] consisting of mineral salts and plant hormones. Establishment of excised plants on this medium doesn't assure that these plants are clean. Many fungi and bacteria are capable of surviving in laboratory-raised tissue culture plants without showing visible plant symptoms or contamination. Selection and maintenance of clean plants can be attained by using the culture indexing process described earlier. Culture indexing of in-vitro-maintained New Guinea impatiens is a relatively simple method for selecting explants free of systemic and epiphytic bacteria and fungi.

An additional advantage of tissue culture maintenance of certified New Guinea impatiens is the ability to maintain this stock in a protected environment (i.e., laboratory growth chamber) rather than in the greenhouse. It is highly unlikely that pathogens, insects, and other pests can attack a plant maintained in the laboratory.

Eliminating viruses

Viruses can be eliminated from infected plants in a number of ways, including:
1. exploiting erratic virus distribution within plants,
2. chemotherapy,
3. heat therapy [9], and
4. meristem tip culture [10].

Many of these techniques have been used for vegetatively propagated crops such as potatoes, chrysanthemums, carnations and geraniums.

Major viral pathogens of New Guinea impatiens include INSV, TSWV, tobacco mosaic virus (TMV), cucumber mosaic virus (CMV) and other miscellaneous viruses. Eliminating these viruses from stock plants is best accomplished by exploiting the virus strain's biology within the plant. For example, some viruses may be evenly distributed throughout the plant while other viruses can only be found in specific plant parts.

Viruses that are unevenly distributed in the plant, such as INSV and TSWV [12], can usually be eliminated by meristem tip culture. Most viruses are incapable of advancing into the plant's youngest growing portion, the meristem tip. This small plant part, approximately 1 to 2 mm (.039 to .078 inches) long, consists of the apical dome and one to two young leaves called leaf primordia. The vascular system (water and food conducting vessels called xylem and phloem) has not developed in this region, making it difficult for the virus to move into this area.

Viruses that are evenly distributed such as TMV are also very stable and easily spread. Utilizing heat therapy (36C to 38C) or chemotherapy (ribavirin) can reduce the virus concentration (titer) by inhibiting viral replication [8]. Since New Guinea impatiens are quite amenable to routine tissue culture work, the combination of virus titer reduction (by heat or chemotherapy), along with meristem tip culture, is very effective in eliminating major viruses from New Guinea impatiens.

After four to six weeks in culture, the tiny meristem tips develop into a small rooted plant approximately 3 to 4 cm (1.17 to 1.56 inches) high.

This plant is then taken to an insect-free greenhouse and placed under mist for five to six days to harden off. Successful virus elimination from these plants needs to be verified by virus indexing.

Virus indexing

Virus indexing or testing is the most important part of the certification process. Up to this point, a significant amount of time and money has been invested in the elimination of fungal, bacterial, and viral pathogens from these New Guinea impatiens stock plants. Since the production-limiting diseases of New Guinea impatiens are primarily the viruses, sensitive virus indexing techniques are required to assure healthy plants.

There are a number of virus indexing techniques that can be utilized in a certification program. These are:

1. ELISA (enzyme-linked immunosorbent assay) or other antibody tests (i.e., immunoblot, immunofluorescence and immunosorbent electron microscopy [13]),
2. bio-indicator plant inoculations,
3. RNA analysis [22], and
4. viral inclusions [4].

Each indexing technique has strengths and weaknesses. The best technique is one that is sensitive, not dependent on plant sampling location and low cost. Unfortunately, there is no one technique that fits all of these criteria. The major weakness that all techniques have is the

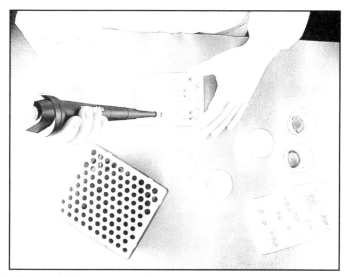

Fig. 6.1. *Enzyme-linked immunsorbent assay (ELISA) used for the detection of plant pathogenic viruses.*

sampling method. Even if the testing method used is very sensitive, it cannot be effective if the wrong plant parts are sampled or the test is done at the wrong time of the year. These problems have been documented for ornamental plants infected with either, TSWV or INSV.

For example, during periods of higher temperatures, TSWV concentration may be below the level of detection due to a decrease in viral replication [3]. Plants that are known to be infected with TSWV or INSV vary in their ability to be detected at different times of the year by ELISA [21]. Also, in some instances, INSV can be more readily detected in the roots of infected plants than in above-ground parts [3].

The two techniques most commonly used in certification programs are ELISA and bio-indicator plant inoculations. The ELISA technique is a low-cost, sensitive technique that allows for relatively quick testing of a large number of plant samples. Currently in the United States, there are commercially available ELISA kits that target the major virus pathogens of New Guinea impatiens (Agdia, Inc., Elkhart, Ind.). These tests are in a 96-well microplate format using a double antibody sandwich (fig. 6.1). They utilize a combination of monoclonal and/or polyclonal antibodies for maximum sensitivity.

For example, the microplate ELISA test for INSV uses a polyclonal antibody as the capture antibody and a cocktail of several monoclonal antibodies as the enzyme-conjugate (C. Sutula, personal communication). ELISA is also sensitive enough to detect TSWV in individual

Fig. 6.2. *Symptoms of impatiens necrotic spot virus (INSV) seven to 10 days after mechanical inoculation onto the bioindicator tobacco plant species,* Nicotiana benthamiana.

TABLE 6.1

Symptom expression of the major viral pathogens of New Guinea impatiens on various bio-indicator plant hosts

Virus	Symptoms on New Guinea impatiens	Nb [1]	Ng	Cq	Gg
Impatiens necrotic spot virus (INSV)	necrotic target spots, blackened stems, stunting, deformed leaves	necrotic local lesions, systemic mosaic	necrotic ringspots, systemic necrotic pattern	necrotic angular local lesions	necrotic local lesions with white centers on inoculated leaves
Tomato spotted wilt virus (TSWV)	necrotic target spots, blackened stems, stunting, deformed leaves	necrotic local lesions, systemic mosaic	necrotic ringspots, systemic necrotic pattern	necrotic angular local lesions	necrotic local lesions with white centers on inoculated leaves
Tobacco mosaic virus (TMV)	plant stunting, mosaic on leaves	systemic mosaic	necrotic local lesions	necrotic local lesions	unknown
Tobacco ringspot virus [2] (TbRSV)	unknown	systemic whitish mosaic	necrotic local lesions	chlorotic local lesions, systemic apical necrosis	unknown
Tomato ringspot virus [2] (TmRSV)	unknown	systemic mosaic	necrotic local lesions	chlorotic local lesions, systemic apical necrosis	unknown
Cucumber mosaic virus [2] (CMV)	unknown	systemic mosaic	systemic mosaic	chlorotic or necrotic local lesions	unknown
Carlavirus [3]	asymptomatic	systemic mosaic	unknown	chlorotic local lesions, systemic mottle	unknown

[1] Nb=*Nicotiana benthamiana*; Ng=*N. glutinosa*; Cq=Lambsquarters (*Chenopodium quinoa*); Gg=*Gomphrena globosa*
[2] Detected by ELISA in a mixed infection with INSV.
[3] Isolated from double impatiens.

thrips [5]. ELISA kits require some specialized laboratory equipment and expertise for consistent results.

Another sensitive virus detection technique is using indicator plants, which are plant species that are susceptible to many different plant pathogenic viruses. This virus detection method is more laborious and costly than ELISA, but it provides a means of detecting unknown viruses where no ELISA kit is available or viruses that are at low concentrations. Reliable indicator plant species for viruses infecting New Guinea impatiens include various tobacco species [14], lambsquarters (M. Tiffany, personal communication), gomphrena [1], and petunia [2].

The method consists of removing 0.5 to 1.0 g of symptomatic or non-symptomatic leaves, stems, or roots of New Guinea impatiens and macerating them in a 5 to 10 ml (0.17 to 0.34 fluid ounce) buffered solution containing anti-reducing agents [14]. This ground-up extract is then gently rubbed over the indicator plant's leaf surface that has previously been sprinkled with an abrasive such as carborundum or celite. The abrasive creates small wounds in the cell wall, allowing for virus penetration and subsequent cell wall healing.

After 20 to 30 minutes, the inoculated leaves are gently rinsed with sterile water and the inoculated indicator plants incubated in a greenhouse to await symptom expression. If a virus or viruses are present in the New Guinea impatiens test plant, symptoms may appear on the indicator plant seven to 21 days after inoculation (fig. 6.2).

Different viruses may produce different symptoms on the indicator plants ranging from distinct, localized necrotic or chlorotic lesions on inoculated leaves to systemic mosaic symptoms on noninoculated leaves. Indicator plant symptoms of the most important viruses infecting New Guinea impatiens are outlined in table 6.1. If symptoms appear on the indicator plants, repeat virus elimination procedures to achieve virus-free plants. As with all virus indexing methods, repeated testing of individual plants at different times of the year are necessary for accurate results.

Clean plant production _____

The development, maintenance, and production of certified stock requires strict adherence to four fundamental principles of clean plant production.

Annual renewal. After completing each production year, all old stock should be destroyed, the greenhouses disinfected, and the stock base renewed with clean plants.

Unidirectional flow. During annual renewal of the stock base, the new stock should always come from a cleaner source. Never use cuttings from old stock to re-establish a new stock base.

Repeated testing. Repeat indexing of certified stock over at least a one year time period. This allows maximum opportunity to detect plant pathogens under different environmental conditions.

Clonal selection. After intensive indexing procedures, including tissue culture maintenance, the certified stock base should be flower trialed under controlled conditions. This allows for selection of superior clones that flower earlier and more often on a plant with an excellent habit. Since all New Guinea impatiens are protected by a plant patent, clonal selection criteria should also closely approximate the variety description outlined in the patent application.

With the continued threat of major diseases and pests such as INSV/TSWV and thrips in most U.S. greenhouses, a grower's success in producing a disease-free New Guinea impatiens crop is difficult. Thus, the requirement for clean, certified stock is more important than ever before. Accurate and dependable certification techniques along with clean plant production practices will allow New Guinea impatiens breeders, producers, and finishers to expand markets and opportunities with this exciting crop.

References

[1]   Allen, T.C., J.P. McMorran, and E.A. Locatelli. 1983. Isolation of tomato spotted wilt virus from hydrangea and four weed species. *Plant Disease* 67:429-431.

[2]   Allen, W.R., and J.A. Matteoni. 1991. Petunia as an indicator plant for use by growers to monitor for thrips carrying the tomato spotted wilt virus in greenhouses. *Plant Disease* 75:78-82.

[3]   Allen, W.R., J.A. Matteoni, and A.B.Broadbent. 1991. Factors relating to epidemiology and symptomatology in florist's chrysanthemum infected with the tomato spotted wilt virus. In *Proceedings*, USDA workshop. USDA-ARS. pp. 28-45.

[4]   Brown, L.G., G.W. Simone, and R.G. Christie. 1991. Diagnostic strategy development for tomato spotted wilt virus. In *Proceedings*, USDA work shop. USDA-ARS. pp. 94-100.

[5]   Cho, J.J., R.F.L. Mau, R.T. Hamasaki, and D. Gonsalves. 1988. Detection of tomato spotted wilt virus in individual thrips by enzyme-linked immunosorbent assay. *Phytopathology* 78:1348-1352.

[6]   Dimock, A.W. 1943. A method of establishing Verticillum-free clones of perennial plants. *Phytopathology.* 33:3.

[7]   ———. 1962. Obtaining pathogen-free stock by cultured cuttings techniques. *Phytopathology.* 52:1230-1241.

[8]   Griffiths, H.M., and S.A. Slack. 1988. Potato virus elimination by heat and ribavirin. *Phytopathology.* 78:838 (Abstr.).

[9]   Grondeau, C., and R. Samson. 1994. A review of thermotherapy to free plant materials from pathogens, especially seeds from bacteria. *Critical Reviews in Plant Sciences.* 13:57-75.

[10] Hollings, M. 1965. Disease control through virus-free stock. *Ann. Rev. Phytopathol.* 3:367-396.

[11] Horst, R.K., and M.J. Klopmeyer. 1993. Controlling viral diseases. In *Geraniums IV*, Ed. John White. Batavia, Ill.: Ball Publishing.

[12] Hsu, H.T., and R.H. Lawson. 1989. Detection of tomato spotted wilt virus in Impatiens using biotinylated mouse monoclonal antibodies. *Phytopathology.* 79:1197.

[13] ———. 1991. Detection of tomato spotted wilt virus by enzyme-linked immunosorbent assay, dot-blot immunoassay and direct tissue blotting. In *Proceedings,* USDA workshop. USDA-ARS.

[14] Law, M.D., and J.W. Moyer. 1990. A tomato spotted wilt-like virus with a serologically distinct N protein. *J. General Virology.* 71:933-938.

[15] Munnecke, D.E. 1956. Development and production of pathogen-free geranium propagative material. *Plant Disease Reptr. Suppl.* 238:93-95

[16] Marashige, T., and F. Skoog. 1962. A revised medium for rapid growth and bioassays with tobacco tissue cultures. *Physiol. Plant.* 15:743-749.

[17] Raju, B.C., and C.J. Olson. 1985. Indexing systems for producing clean stock for disease control in commercial floriculture. *Plant Disease.* 69:189-192.

[18] Stephens, L.C., S.L. Krell, and J.L. Weigle. 1985. In vitro propagation of Java, New Guinea, and Java and New Guinea Impatiens. *HortSci.* 20:362-363.

[19] Tammen, J., R.R. Baker, and W.D. Holley. 1956. Control of carnation diseases through the cultured cutting technique. *Plant Disease Reptr. Suppl.* 283:72-76.

[20] Tammen, J.F. 1960. *Disease-free geraniums from cultured cuttings.* Pennsylvania Flower Growers Bulletin.

[21] Vali, R.J., and F.E. Gildow. 1992. Symptomology, cytopathology and distribution of tomato spotted wilt virus in infected greenhouse ornamentals. *Phytopathology* 82: 248 (Abstr.).

[22] Valverde, R.A., S.T. Nameth, and R.L. Jordan. 1990. Analysis of double stranded RNA for plant virus diagnosis. *Plant Disease* 74: 255-258.

CHAPTER 7

Stock Plant Production

Jack E. Williams and Pamela Ruis

New Guinea impatiens have come from being considered a minor flowering crop in the 1980s to being one of the more important greenhouse crops of the 1990s. Part of this change is due to the outstanding flower size, color, and growth habit bred into today's cultivars. This success is also due to the increased awareness of plant health that has influenced the stock buildup programs for plants developed through breeding programs. The commitment to establishing and maintaining clean stock plants has extended into the distribution system as well.

New and innovative programs of insect and disease prevention have been developed and implemented by specialty propagators responsible for the production of young cuttings. The effort put forth by these producers is reminiscent of clean stock programs first used by carnation and geranium growers in the 1960s. The benefits to growers and consumers alike have justified investments made to produce top quality New Guinea impatiens stock plants.

A New Guinea impatiens stock plant program's goal is to produce healthy mother plants yielding vegetative cuttings free of insects and diseases.

Start clean and stay clean _____

Obtain all mother plants from breeders after cultivars have been indexed and confirmed free of plant diseases. Stock plants may be multiplied from these "clean" mother plants. Index all plants periodically to assure they are free of plant pathogens including virus diseases.

Fig. 7.1. *Stock range with exclusion screening, Paul Ecke Ranch.*

The pathogens of greatest concern are tomato spotted wilt virus (TSWV) and impatiens necrotic spot virus (INSV) [1]. Western flower thrips (WFT), the primary vector for TSWV, is difficult to control. Thrips have transmitted TSWV to New Guinea impatiens plants in as little as 15 to 30 minutes of feeding [2]. Thrips populations are difficult to control because of their many hosts and insecticide resistance [3]. Stock producers begin production in late summer/early fall, during weather conditions that are conducive to thrips activity both inside greenhouses and outdoors. This extremely small, but damaging, insect may enter the greenhouse during ventilation. Most chemicals have proven only mildly successful in controlling western flower thrips. None are able to prevent them from attacking the crop.

Screening

Exclusion screening is the most effective method of minimizing insect pressure on stock plants (See Chapter 15). Screening that will exclude the narrow bodied thrips must be chosen (fig. 7.1). New screening materials are more durable and allow for greater air flow. These improved screening materials make it possible and practical for growers to use exclusion, even in areas with climatic conditions requiring rigorous ventilation.

Isolation

Stock plant producers should make every effort to grow New Guinea impatiens stock within an insect-free environment. However, this alone is not enough to prevent the occurrence of WFT or TSWV/INSV. Thrips may still enter the greenhouse on plant material, on clothing of employees or visitors, on equipment and supplies moved into the greenhouse or anytime the greenhouse is open to an external environment. For these reasons, it is important to isolate stock plant growing areas. No other plant material should be brought into this area unless it has been thoroughly checked and verified free of insects and diseases.

Special employees should be assigned to work in this area, and any unnecessary movement of people in or out of the greenhouse should be avoided. If it is impossible to maintain separate employees, be sure that this is the first greenhouse and crop they come into contact with daily. Working around other plants, including home gardens, prior to entering the stock area allows opportunity to "pick up" WFT or other potentially damaging insects or diseases and move them into the greenhouse. It is equally important for employees to wear clean clothing to work. Supplies used for packing or other crop activities may also be an introduction point for insect and disease pests. Be sure to inspect these items for potential problems as well.

Before stock plant cuttings arrive at the greenhouse, growing areas should be prepared to minimize potential problems. Some steps to follow in a good sanitation program are as follows:

1. Remove any plants, debris, weeds, or other potential insect/disease hosts from the greenhouse area to minimize carry-over of problems from one crop to another.
2. Clean around the greenhouse area to reduce pest pressure from the surrounding environment. Keep weeds and grasses mowed or use pavement to prevent their growth in the immediate area.
3. Thoroughly disinfect the production area before moving any stock plants into the greenhouse. Wash down the roof, walls, benches and other inside structures with disinfectant solutions such as chlorine solutions, Physan, or Green-Shield.
4. Ventilate and rinse greenhouses with clear water to remove any potentially damaging residues.
5. Keep greenhouses closed up for at least two weeks before plants are moved in. During late summer/early fall, elevated temperatures in a closed greenhouse will accelerate the speed of insects completing their life cycle. If the greenhouse has been closed down during periods of cold weather, be sure to heat for at least two weeks prior to starting the crop. Some stages of the pest's life cycle may survive in the cold and will become active again once the greenhouse temperatures rise. Also do some form of fumigation (using smoke formulated insecticides or other similar chemicals) to control surviving adults. When plants are ready to be moved in, pests should be gone.

6. Once crops are in the greenhouse, keep the area free of weeds, plant debris, or other potential hosts for the various insects and diseases that can attack the crop.

Containers

Stock plants may be grown in a variety of containers, including pots, bags, raised beds, or rock wool slabs. Decisions regarding the container type and size should be based on the length of time the crop will be managed. Long-term stock production (five months or more) usually benefits from larger container sizes and more liberal spacing, while short-term stock production (less than five months) does well in smaller pots and less space. In either case, containers and media must provide plants with adequate water holding capacity to support normal growth. This capacity is directly influenced by soil volume, container size, and the growing media used. Individual containers are desirable for insect and disease management, so that infested plants can be easily removed from the greenhouse. In long-term stock programs, more permanent installations, such as raised beds, rock wool slabs, etc., may provide superior conditions for water reserves and root development that enhances the overall quantity and quality of cuttings produced. This method is less flexible in terms of space utilization and pest management.

Media

Use a growing medium that encourages strong, healthy root systems to support the growth demands of the stock. The growing medium must provide adequate water holding capacity and aeration as irrigation

TABLE 7.1

Suggested stock plant spacing and container size

Crop cycle	Container size	Suggested spacing	Tight spacing
less than 4 months	5.5 to 6 inches	0.6 to 0.9 sq.ft./pot	0.5 sq.ft./pot
	(14 to 15 cm)	(557 to 836 cm²/pot)	(464 to 697 cm²/pot)
4 to 6 months	6.5 to 7 inches	0.6 to 1 sq.ft./pot	0.5 to 0.75 sq.ft./pot
	(16.5 to 17.8 cm)	(557 to 929 cm²/pot)	(464 to 697 cm²/pot)
6 to 8 months	7 to 8 inches	1 to 1.4 sq.ft./pot	0.75 sq.ft./pot
	(17.7 to 20.3 cm)	(929 to 1,300 cm²/pot)	(697 cm²/pot)

management is paramount for successful stock production. A medium's physical properties should provide about 50% moisture retention and 20% free porosity for suitable available water levels and gas exchange. An appropriate medium may be composed of about 50% coarse peat moss with aggregate components such as bark, perlite, or scoria added. Use mixes with components that will maintain media structure for the length of stock production time.

The growing medium's chemical properties are equally important for supporting optimum growth. It is very important to manage the soluble salts (electrical conductivity measured as mmhos/cm) of the medium. Most New Guinea impatiens cultivars are very sensitive to elevated salts levels (2.0 mmhos/cm or higher). Monitor salts closely to avoid damage to the stock block or young cuttings. Nutrient additions should be based on crop needs considering the water source used and other factors that influence your irrigation and fertilization programs.

Spacing

Stock plant spacing depends upon length of time in production and containers used (table 7.1). Allow space around each stock plant for adequate light and air circulation. Full access to a stock plant during harvesting and trimming makes it easier to remove cuttings. However, the production per square foot/meter may be increased by reducing the amount of space provided per plant. Stock plants grown in tight spacing have a higher disease pressure resulting from the lack of air circulation around the crop and lack symmetrical growth on individual plants. This is particularly true in areas with low light and low ventilation, such as in a northern greenhouse during the winter. Plant symmetry is only important if the grower sells stock plants after the production season. Considerable trimming, respacing, and time is necessary to make salable blooming plants out of tightly grown stock plants.

Fertilization and irrigation —————————

New Guinea impatiens are grown with relatively light (less than 200 ppm), constant liquid feed. New Guinea impatiens stock plants benefit from constant fertilization, but care must be given to provide thorough watering and leaching of excess salts. Salts can be flushed from the medium by using a drip or tube irrigation system that waters from the top of the medium. If irrigating by capillary uptake, or methods that do not provide for physical removal of salts, use lower fertilizer concentrations. No matter what irrigation system is used, periodic leaching by overhead irrigation will minimize salts accumulation in the media.

Fertilization program

- During the initial two to three weeks of growth, it's important to apply little if any fertilizer to the crop. This will encourage rapid root growth and development during establishment.
- After about three weeks regular fertilization may begin. Use a complete and balanced fertilizer mix on a constant liquid feed (CLF) solution at 125 to 150 ppm nitrogen.
- Select fertilizer mixes, or mix your own, based on compatibility with your water source and media. Use fertilizers that do not contain elevated levels of minor elements. New Guinea impatiens are sensitive to minor elements and should not have them supplied on a constant basis.
- Use of constant release fertilizers (CRF) or slow release fertilizers (SRF) is not recommended for New Guinea impatiens stock.
- Maintain a media pH between 5.5 and 7.0.
- Maintain a media soluble salts (EC) level below 2.0 mmhos/cm using a saturated paste extract, or 1.2 mmhos/cm for a 1:2 soil-media extract.
- Monitor the crop through regular soil and tissue analysis to determine trends towards nutritional imbalances or problems.

Environment

The greenhouse environment is critical in keeping stock plants vegetative. Budded cuttings are considered less desirable. Good quality cuttings may be produced using environmental controls. Some producers treat stock plants with chemicals like Florel, which is now labeled for New Guinea impatiens. To minimize budding without chemical intervention, control the temperature, humidity, and light intensity under which stock plants are grown.

Temperature

New Guinea impatiens require relatively warm growing conditions. This is true of both the blooming crop and the stock plants. University of Minnesota research indicates that New Guinea impatiens leaf production and development are optimum at 68F to 72F (20C to 21C) [4]. These are ideal night temperatures for establishing and growing stock plants. Day temperatures may be warmer depending upon weather conditions, but should not exceed 85F (29C). Flower development in New Guinea impatiens is encouraged by cooler temperatures. University of Minnesota research shows budding is stimulated at 65F (18C).

Humidity

A constant relative humidity of 60% encourages soft growth and leaf expansion. Depending upon temperatures, hosing down greenhouse walkways during the day can help create additional humidity. Avoid humidity above 60% as it is favorable for diseases such as Botrytis. Preventing this disease is important to keep stock plants healthy and minimize problems with young cuttings.

Light intensity

New Guinea impatiens flower development is encouraged by higher light intensities (4,000 footcandles/43.1 klux). To keep stock plants vegetative, the grower may need to use shading to reduce light intensities. In the fall and winter, light intensities in North America are reduced naturally. It is still important, however, to maintain light levels of about 3,000 f.c. (32.3 klux) maximum.

Insect exclusion screening is likely to elevate temperature and humidity in the greenhouse. Gutter to gutter screening also affects light levels available for crop growth. These conditions can help keep stock plants vegetative.

Stock plant management —————————

Once New Guinea impatiens stock plants are established and actively growing, growers must manage the crop through pinching, trimming, and careful maintenance (fig. 7.2). Without constant "working," the

Fig. 7.2. *Workers trimming stock plants.*

Fig. 7.3. *Cuttings that have stretched and developed a palm-tree-like whorl of foliage and buds are undesirable for stock use. Rogue if possible.*

stock plants will begin to bud and flower. Pinching develops the stock plants' structure creating a framework from which branching and cuttings will develop. Trimming also influences timing and size of cuttings.

Pinching

Although modern New Guinea impatiens cultivars rarely require pinching to develop good branching, it is necessary to pinch stock plants. The initial pinch removes flower buds and redirects the plants' growth habit. The pinch may be either hard or soft. A soft pinch, defined as the removal of less than one-half inch (1.27 cm) of the growing tip, is usually desired. Strongly budded cuttings may stretch and develop a whorl of foliage and buds resembling a palm tree (fig. 7.3). The stock grower should hard pinch these cuttings to force more vegetative growth out of the lower stem area, or better yet, rogue this plant from the stock block.

Trimming

A regular program of trimming (soft pinching secondary shoots) is necessary to stimulate increased numbers of shoots to time cuttings for harvest dates and to manage the size of developing cuttings. Stock plant producers require an extended harvest period, and trimming spreads out the availability of young cuttings. Trimming also helps prevent budding of shoots by limiting the age of any one shoot and by forcing new growth on the stock plants at all times. Trimming is a valuable tool to control the number of cuttings available during a given week.

Most New Guinea impatiens cultivars require four to five weeks from pinching to usable cuttings. Producers should plan the number of shoots to trim four to five weeks prior to harvest based on the weekly quantity of cuttings required. The small size of shoots makes it best to use knives for trimming and harvesting cuttings.

Thinning

Periodic thinning helps expose new cuttings to available light. Regularly trimmed or harvested plants won't need this additional step. On over-grown stock, young growth below the canopy becomes weak and spindly due to lack of light and air, rendering these cuttings undesirable. Thinning also increases air and light availability to young cuttings, which enhances insect and disease management. Thinning should only be done as needed so as not to limit photosynthetic potential through excessive foliage removal. Experiment with a small number of plants before thinning on a large scale. Some cultivars respond poorly to thinning, resulting in dieback or stunted growth. The secret to a reliably high cutting yield lies in the early stock development phase.

- Trim stock plants weekly to rapidly increase branching in preparation for the peak demand. Shoots can be trimmed before reaching standard cutting length.
- Keep early season harvest volumes low. Avoid overcutting or knuckle-cutting a main stem as this reduces cutting availability later in the season.

Cutting characteristics ⸻⸻⸻⸻

The job of stock plant growers is to produce vegetative cuttings that have the potential to grow into superior blooming crops. Cutting size includes total shoot length, size, and number of leaves, potential flower buds present, and basal stem length. Most growers propagate New Guinea impatiens under fairly tight spacing, so large, leafy cuttings have more problems under mist than smaller cuttings. The incidence of budding is significantly higher with older, larger cuttings, which may be undesirable to the blooming plant grower. As seen in fig. 7.4, the characteristics desirable for New Guinea impatiens cuttings are:

Total length: 3/4 to 1½ inches (1.9 to 3.8 cm) from stem base to shoot tip.
Number of leaves: No more than two expanded leaves and three to four immature leaves evident.
Basal stem length: 3/16 to 1/2 inch (0.4 to 1 cm).

Fig. 7.4. Quality New Guinea impatiens cuttings.

Stock plant production _____

New Guinea impatiens stock can be predictably managed and scheduled much like geranium or poinsettia stock plants (table 7.2). By
keeping an interval of four to five weeks between pinch and cutting
harvest, stock plants provide cutting quantities based on the number
of nodes left on each shoot after trimming or cutting removal. Not all
cultivars respond alike, leaving it up to growers to observe and learn
from the characteristics unique to each cultivar produced. Cultivars
that produce fewer cuttings due to less plant vigor or slow return time
from pinch usually benefit from double planting in a container.
Another option is to produce additional stock plants of these low yield
cultivars to maintain reasonable cutting supplies through the season.
The differences in response characteristics of cultivars extend beyond
stock production. Varying responses have been noted to chemical
growth regulators, fertilization levels, pesticides, and insects or diseases. It is important for growers to learn about the plants they produce and to take into account their individuality.

Insect and disease management _____

Insect and disease management is paramount with New Guinea impatiens stock plants. This crop's grower is charged with preventing poten-

TABLE 7.2

Stock production program

Week 1	Propagate unrooted cuttings in rooting medium.
Week 4	Transplant rooted cuttings to final container.
Week 6	Pinch main terminal of each cutting to increase branching.
Week 8	Begin trimming of side shoots for increased production and timing. Soft pinch shoots to allow maximum node count for buildup of future cuttings.
Week 9	Continue trimming as described in week 8.
Week 10	Continue trimming as described above.
Week 11	Continue trimming as described above.
Week 12	Begin cutting harvest on shoots returning from week 8 trim.

tially devastating crop problems from occurring while battling some of the toughest insects known today.

Insects

The western flower thrips (WFT) has proven to be an extremely difficult pest to control in a wide range of crops. The ability to transmit plant virus has forced stock plant growers to take unusual steps to prevent this insect from entering the greenhouse. Other pests, such as aphids, spider mites, and beet armyworm, may become active on the crop as well. With the exception of aphids, these pests do not pose a serious risk to crops as they are not associated with the transmission of virus diseases. Pest exclusion programs have emerged as the most effective method of keeping stock plants "clean" to date. The exclusion programs and IPM practices discussed in Chapters 15 and 16 provide excellent guidelines for pest control. Stock plant production differs from blooming plant culture, and therefore involves issues unique to this phase of crop production management.

- Initial pest pressure is greater with stock than with blooming plants. Stock plants are generally started in late summer when greenhouse ventilation needs increase the opportunity for pests to enter the greenhouse and become established.
- Monitor plants closely and respond to any evidence of pest presence or disease activity. Use sticky cards (blue or yellow) to help identify insects that enter the greenhouse. Place cards randomly through out the crop and use extra cards near vents, doors, or other greenhouse openings through which pests might enter.
- Train all employees to recognize signs of insect pests or their damage. Greenhouse workers see more of the plants than anyone else, and they may be your greatest assets in a good scouting program.

- Consider a schedule of regular virus indexing on stock plants to reconfirm their healthy status before cuttings are harvested for propagation. As cold weather develops and pest pressures are reduced, the need for extensive indexing will also be reduced. However, it is advisable to form a schedule of testing to monitor crop health.
- Use good pesticide application technology, and base chemical choices on the pest being treated. Understand the insect's biology and increase treatment effectiveness by targeting the application to the insect's current stage of development. Even in a screened growing environment there is no guarantee that insects will not find their way into the greenhouse!

Diseases

Disease control, like insect control, should be focused on prevention. Control of WFT has already been emphasized as the key issue for preventing TSWV, a disease for which there is no cure! Beyond this disease, New Guinea impatiens are relatively free of problems. Other diseases of New Guinea impatiens are reviewed in Chapter 13. The stock plants and blooming crops may be attacked by Botrytis or Rhizoctonia. It is also possible that Pythium may become established, particularly if improper crop moisture levels are maintained or if root systems are damaged due to soluble salts buildup. With a little effort, these situations may be easily prevented.

TSWV/INSV. Virus disease has been the most significant problem associated with New Guinea impatiens. Stock plants infected with TSWV or INSV serve as a source of infected cuttings. If growers receive infected cuttings from propagators, the expression of symptoms may come late in the crop and without warning. The results can be devastating if this same grower has WFT present, as the disease may be easily spread to other ornamental crops. Stock plant growers should take a lead role of responsibility and develop a program of regular virus index testing to help track and understand the status of their mother plants and the resulting cuttings.

Botrytis. Stock plants are especially susceptible to attack by Botrytis for a number of reasons. As stock plants grow and increase in size, the amount of air circulation in the lower plant structure is greatly reduced. After pinching, trimming, or harvesting cuttings, plan time for employees to clean up any plant debris that may have fallen on the benches and floors. During cutting or trimming, avoid leaving debris on the stock as it may become a source of dead tissue on which Botrytis can develop. The resulting spores are capable of infecting adjoining stock plants and their cuttings. Regular fungicide applications to the foliage may be effective in reducing the threat of Botrytis. Weekly treatments are best made directly following cutting harvest to provide a protective residue on young shoots. Studies conducted on the incidence of Botrytis in stock plant geraniums show that "in air" conidia counts peak during the time immediately after harvest [5]. At this time, the abundance of open wounds on the stock plants make them susceptible to infection by the fungus. As frequency of cutting and density of plant material increase with age, this disease becomes more difficult to control. Similar conclusions may be drawn for New Guinea impatiens stock plants.

Rhizoctonia. This fungus generally attacks the stem near the soil line causing a brown to reddish-brown rot. The disease is capable of moving up the stem or down into the root system. Warm temperatures and conditions that cause stress on the plant (improper irrigation practices, high soluble salts, etc.) favor this disease. Prevent Rhizoctonia with periodic fungicide drench applications using chemicals known to control this disease, such as Banrot, Chipco 26019, Terraclor, Cleary's 3336, and Fungo Flo.

Pythium. This organism is generally responsible for root rot and belongs to the family of water mold fungi. Pythium is a common disease of a wide range of crops and is best controlled through selecting an appropriate, sterile growing medium and good irrigation practices. Damage is most likely to occur whenever the soil is kept excessively wet or whenever damage results from excess fertilization or lack of leaching the soluble salts. The problem is also frequently associated with the presence of fungus gnat larvae that may feed on the young, tender root systems of the crop. Stock plants attacked by this disease are likely to show symptoms of frequent wilting, yellow foliage, and eventual drop, and, of course, a root system that develops brown rot. Prevent Pythium through good fertilization and irrigation practices and the use of periodic fungicide drench applications using chemicals known to control this disease such as Banrot, Chipco, Aliette, Subdue, and Truban.

Other production issues _____

Several issues regarding the use of growth altering chemicals and hormones require review when discussing New Guinea impatiens stock production. There are different schools of thought regarding the application of any such agents. Growers need to educate themselves about the use of these materials and decide for themselves whether using them is appropriate under their unique conditions.

CO_2 injection

It is not uncommon for carbon dioxide (CO_2) injection to be used with other stock production programs such as geraniums. Environmental conditions at the time of year New Guinea impatiens stock is grown may favor the use of this gas on the crop. Winter production's typically poor air exchange means ambient levels of CO_2 are rapidly depleted in the greenhouse. Growers using CO_2 at 800 to 2,000+ ppm have noticed accelerated growth on New Guinea impatiens crops. This effect might be beneficial to stock plants during peak cutting production, however, some equally undesirable reactions to this gas have been observed. The most obvious reaction to CO_2 is the size of leaves. Both the leaf length and width is increased to more than double the normal size when CO_2 is supplied on a regular basis. This characteristic would be undesirable on cuttings where propagation density is high. The other undesirable reaction to CO_2 is rapid flower bud development, and this response is contrary to what stock growers are trying to achieve. If CO_2 injection is used with New Guinea impatiens stock plants, the grower would also have to use plant hormones such as Florel.

Florel

The use of Florel is controversial on New Guinea impatiens stock plants. This particular plant hormone is effective in preventing flower bud formation and in stimulating lateral branching of treated crops [6]. This secondary effect is not nearly as important with today's cultivars, which have strong, natural branching characteristics. The newer cultivars do exhibit earlier flowering, which under some conditions may warrant the use of this material. Florel's ability to inhibit leaf blade expansion, resulting in smaller leaves (beneficial for propagation) may be useful.

It is important to remember that not all New Guinea impatiens cultivars react in a similar manner. Differences in branching, vigor, rate of development, and flowering time exist between cultivars of every series of plants. Florel may offer producers a selective tool in adjusting the growth characteristics of specific cultivars, resulting in more uniform cultural practices.

This is still a matter of experimentation with no set recommendations for usage; however, some success has been achieved by using 500 ppm at two to four week intervals. Growers should evaluate and trial this material before using it on the crop. Growers who receive cuttings from stock producers using Florel have concerns about the long term effects on their blooming plants. There are real issues that need to be resolved before the application of Florel can be suggested as a normal crop procedure.

References ─────────────────────────────

[1]   Moyer, James W., and Margaret E. Daub. 1994. Tomato spotted wilt virus/impatiens necrotic spot virus: Where we've been and where we're going. In *Proceedings*, 10th Conference on Insect and Disease Management on Ornamentals. In press.

[2]   Sakimura, K. 1962a. *Frankliniella occidentalis* (Thysanoptera; Thripidae), a vector of the tomato spotted wilt virus with special reference to the color forms. *Am. Entomol. Soc. Am* 55: 387-389.
───. 1962b. Present status of thrips borne viruses. In *Biological transmission of disease agents*. New York: Academic Press.

[3]   Robb, Karen L. 1990. Western flower thrips: their biology and control. In *Proceedings*, 6th Conference on Insect and Disease Management on Ornamentals.

[4]   Erwin, John, and Royal D. Heins. 1993. *Temperature effects on bedding plant growth*. Minn. Comm. Fl. Gr. Assn. Bull. 42, (3).

[5]   Hausbeck, Mary K., and Stanley P. Pennypacker. 1991. Factors influencing concentration of airborne conidia of *Botrytis cinerea* among geranium stock plants and cuttings. In *Proceedings*, 7th Conference on Insect and Disease Management on Ornamentals.

[6]   Konjoian, Peter S. 1993. Research update on the effects of Florel on flori-cultural crops. Presentation at International Floriculture Industry Short Course.

CHAPTER 8

Rooting

Edward P. Mikkelsen

The rooting of New Guinea impatiens is relatively easy compared to some other ornamental crops. Ignorance of sanitary propagation procedures, lack of attention to detail, and the failure to recognize the importance of clean cuttings can lead to problems. As with many crops, moisture (mist), temperature (bottom heat), light, and disease control play critical roles in the successful rooting of New Guinea impatiens. The added element of thrips control and subsequently preventing tomato spotted wilt virus (TSWV) from entering the crop requires strict pest exclusion procedures and properly designed facilities. Disease prevention is no better than the weakest link in the process. New Guinea impatiens can be rooted at relatively high densities often taking little space in the greenhouse. Remember the value per square foot (or square meter) and you will stop by more often to see how things are going.

Sanitation

Sanitation is as important in the propagation of New Guinea impatiens as with any other species. Benches, reusable trays, etc., should be sanitized between crops. Media should be pest-free and, if containing soil, pasteurized. With careful handling peat-based soilless media should not need pasteurization if all the additional components (for example, vermiculite, perlite, or styrofoam beads) are clean. Media that comes in contact with the ground or floor should not be used. Rhizoctonia infection is one of the worst diseases that can ruin New Guinea impatiens propagation and is easiest to control by proper sanitation. With the tight spacing that many growers use (about 50 cuttings per square foot or 538 cuttings per square meter), a Rhizoctonia infection can destroy hundreds of cuttings within a few days. Unless continual disease prob-

Fig. 8.1. *Unrooted New Guinea impatiens cutting of correct size.*

lems occur, a fungicidal drench before or after sticking the cuttings should not be necessary.

Cutting specifications

Successful propagation of New Guinea impatiens can be achieved with a range of cutting sizes. A good size includes the growing point, a pair of expanding leaves, and a pair of mature leaves (fig. 8.1). The length should be one-half to three-quarter inch (1.3 to 1.9 cm). The basal stem length, (stem below the first node) should be three-sixteenth to one-half inch (0.5 to 1.3 cm). Smaller cuttings take longer to root, and larger cuttings take more time on the stock plant to produce. If large cuttings are used in high density propagation, overlapping leaves can promote Botrytis infection. The use of root-inducing hormones should not be necessary. Cuttings should not have flower buds unless the finished crop is sold in market packs. Budded cuttings not only take longer to root, they also don't grow as rapidly and branch as well. Flower buds in the lateral axis replace the lateral vegetative bud. Rather than having good basal branching, flowers appear too early and underneath the foliage. They also take more time to fill out in larger pots after transplanting (see Chapter 7, Cutting characteristics).

Media

Propagation of New Guinea impatiens can be done in a number of diverse media. A typical peat-based soilless medium amended with perlite, vermiculite, rockwool granules, composted bark, and/or Styrofoam beads works well. The pH should be between 5.5 and 6.5. It's not necessary that the medium have an initial nutrient charge. Completely synthetic media, such as Oasis wedge strip or Grodan

Fig. 8.2. *Cutting after 10 days in propagation.*

Fig. 8.3. *Rooted cuttings after 24 days, ready for transplanting.*

rockwool cubes, can also be used. With any of these media, it is important that they aren't saturated with water. A water-soaked medium has reduced oxygen available to the stem where roots are formed, delaying root initiation and elongation. A water-soaked medium is also conducive to water mold infections.

Environment

A minimum temperature of 68F (20C) should be maintained in the propagation area. If at all possible, primary heat should be below the bench. Heating of the medium in this manner hasten rooting time by at least a week. Cuttings are propagated on misted open benches, or if mist isn't available, covered with plastic tents. Typical misting schedules begin with a frequency of every 15 minutes on sunny days and every two hours on heavily overcast days. Misting through the night is normally not required. As cuttings begin to callus, misting frequency is reduced to every half hour during sunny days and twice on heavily overcast days. Once roots are approximately one-quarter inch (0.6 cm) in length, then misting may only be required several times on hot or bright days. Misting should be discontinued as soon as possible, and the rooted cuttings placed on a feed program of 200-50-200 ppm N-P-K.

A typical propagation cycle is as follows:

5 to 7 days	Callus forms at the cutting's base.
10 to 12 days	Roots visible (fig. 8.2)
3 to 4 weeks	Cuttings well-rooted and transplantable (fig. 8.3).

Depending on the cutting size, tray size, temperatures, and medium, the time required to root cuttings varies by cultivar. The difference between varieties can be over three days.

If tents are used instead of mist, several precautions need to be taken, especially on sunny days. Tent sides may need to be lifted to vent excess heat. During these times carefully mist the cuttings using a hose with a fine mist nozzle that will not blow the cuttings out of the medium. Even on cloudy days the cuttings may need to be misted.

The light level in the propagation area should be below 2,000 f.c. (21.5 klux). During the winter in northern latitudes, shade may not be necessary. On extremely bright days, mist more frequently to reduce water stress. In the summer, shade on the roofs as well as over the plants may be needed. After rooting has begun, the interior shade can be removed.

Sometimes it's necessary to keep the rooted cuttings in the propagation area after they have rooted and are transplantable. Avoid delaying transplanting if at all possible. Several techniques can be used to prevent undesirable internodal stretching of the cuttings if held in the pack longer than necessary. First, withhold water although plants should not be water-stressed so much that they wilt. After the medium has been dried and the plants need water, water lightly. Second, if possible, remove any shade. Third, New Guinea impatiens respond to a negative DIF; therefore, a cool shock in the morning at sunrise will help reduce stretch. Fourth, generally lower both the day and night temperatures, but be sure that the foliage is dry before evening to reduce the chances of Botrytis infection. Finally, a light spray of Bonzi at 5 ppm may be used. Be extremely careful when using Bonzi that none of it gets into the soil. Other classes of chemical growth regulators are not effective.

Diseases

Aside from Rhizoctonia, cuttings may also succumb to other diseases during propagation, such as Pythium. Botrytis may also affect the above ground portions of cuttings. Good sanitation, healthy cuttings, and proper watering practices are important aspects in preventing these diseases. A preventive fungicidal spray program on the stock is also essential. The use of drip irrigation for stock is recommended to keep the foliage dry. Finally, if necessary, fungicides may be used on the cuttings. To help control soilborne pathogens, the cuttings can be drenched after sticking. If diseases infect the above-ground portion of the cuttings before they are sufficiently rooted to be sprayed, drench the cuttings lightly to cover the foliage but not to saturate the medium. There are several fungicides that are registered to use for these diseases. Terrachlor is not recommended since it can slow down the rooting process and cause stunting.

If the stock is in good condition, the rooting environment well maintained, and all other precautions taken, losses should be below 3%. Even a loss rate below 1% is achievable.

Other propagation systems

New Guinea impatiens cuttings can be stuck directly into 4- and 6-inch (10 cm and 15 cm) pots. Typically a larger cutting is used. One cutting is stuck in the 4-inch pot and two or three are stuck in the 6-inch pot. The environment, mist, and other considerations listed above apply to this method as well. More space is required in a direct stick program than with a transplant program, but there is a reduction of labor and no transplant shock. The plants remain more compact and better branched since there is increased space available for each cutting.

Flowering plants of New Guinea impatiens can be produced in market packs, such as the popular 1204 and 1801 configurations. In order to produce flowering plants in such small containers for the consumer, use cuttings with small flower buds rather than cuttings with large buds or open flowers. The latter tend to have few, if any, vegetative nodes and do not produce sizeable plants very rapidly when transplanted into the garden. Cuttings with flower buds may take three to five days longer to root and six to nine weeks to obtain plants with some open flowers. A growth regulator is used to keep the plants from stretching. Cultivar selection is also important. Choose cultivars that flower early and tend not to stretch.

Economic considerations

A thorough analysis of production costs of New Guinea impatiens is given in Chapter 18. The following range of factors may assist in propagation cost analysis. Good stock plants can produce 10 cuttings per square foot per week (108 cuttings/m^2/week). The cutting season may last 10 to 12 weeks so that the total cuttings harvested might be 100 to 120 per square foot (1,080 to 1,292/m^2) of stock. The stock may have been growing for six to eight months. The cutting cost is the overhead cost for one square foot (or square meter) of bench space for half of a year plus the cost of the stock plus the cost of labor and materials to maintain the stock divided by 100 to 120 (number of cuttings).

Cutting harvest rates may be anywhere from 750 to 1,200 an hour and sticking rates from 1,500 to 2,000 per hour. Material costs include packs, medium, fertilizer, water, and pesticides. Additional labor costs include cost to fill and set out packs, water and apply pesticides, and rogue diseased plants. Bench space cost for the cuttings depends on spacing and time to root. Typical figures would be four weeks to root and 50 cuttings per square foot (538/m^2). Therefore, the bench space cost would be the cost of 1 square foot per week times 0.08 square foot-weeks per cutting (4 weeks divided by 50 cuttings per square foot) or one square meter per week times 0.007 square meter-weeks per cutting (4 weeks divided by 538 cuttings/m^2). Additional labor is needed to maintain the cuttings after sticking until transplanting. Finally, the royalty charge of protected varieties needs to be added. These are likely cost ranges—growers have to determine costs for their own particular situation.

CHAPTER 9

Finishing

▬▬▬▬ Northeast ▬▬▬▬

Peter S. Konjoian

In the Northeast most New Guinea impatiens crops are scheduled to bloom between early May and early June. A few are scheduled for April and a few are scheduled for summer sales. In the past decade the demand for New Guinea impatiens has grown to the point where they are my second most popular flowering potted crop in the spring and third most popular crop annually. In my 55,000 square-foot (5,108 m²) range, we are handling about 15,000 geranium seedlings, 10,000 poinsettia cuttings, and 9,000 cuttings of New Guinea impatiens. The demand for New Guinea impatiens has been rising steadily, causing a shift in production away from geraniums (see Color Plate section, CP 9.1).

Container sizes and cultivar mix

The backbone of most growers' New Guinea impatiens crops is the 4- or 4¹/₂-inch (10.1 or 11.4 cm) pot. After several years of producing 4¹/₂-inch (11.4 cm) New Guinea impatiens, I have shifted to a 5-inch (12.7 cm) pot in order to provide my customers with a larger root ball. This was done to ease the shock of moving the plant from the greenhouse to the garden setting. Larger sizes of New Guinea impatiens start at 6-inch (15.2 cm) pots containing one to three cuttings per pot all the way up to 12 inch (30.5 cm), 14 inch (35.6 cm), and even larger tubs and patio planters with numerous cuttings per pot. As the size increases so do the combinations of colors that can be used. New Guinea impatiens are also popular in mixed containers and hanging baskets.

Smaller sizes are also produced, particularly for the wholesale and mass market outlets. Three- to 4-inch (7.6 to 10.2 cm) pot sizes are common. I produce a jumbo six-pack unit; three six-packs fit in a stan-

Fig. 9.1. *Moss baskets of New Guinea impatiens can be quite stunning in the landscape.*

dard 1020 flat. The cell size is comparable to a 3- to 3½-inch (7.6 to 8.9 cm) pot, and each pack has a handle for easier merchandising.

The most common hanging basket sizes include both 8- and 10-inch (20.3 and 25.4 cm) plastic containers and 12-inch (30.5 cm) moss baskets. The plastic containers are less expensive and a bit easier to produce; however, the moss baskets are the real eye-catchers (fig. 9.1). Most growers put three cuttings in an 8-inch (20.3 cm) hanger and either three or four in a 10-inch (25.4 cm). I use one cutting in my 8-inch (20.3 cm) hangers so that my customers have a better chance of

Fig. 9.2. *Eight-inch (20.3 cm) baskets showing one cutting per pot and drip irrigation tubes.*

Fig. 9.3. *Ten-inch (25.4 cm) basket showing four cuttings per pot.*

maintaining the basket throughout the summer (fig. 9.2). How well the limited volume of growing medium in an 8-inch (20.3 cm) hanger can support the water demands of three New Guinea impatiens plants during July is questionable. Four cuttings per 10-inch (25.4 cm) hanger work well for my production (fig. 9.3).

A well-grown moss basket of New Guinea impatiens is about as stunning as any hanging basket I produce. Fifteen cuttings per basket are used, 11 around the outside of the container in two circles and four in the top of the basket (fig. 9.4). It is considerably more expensive to produce with the added cost of the wire frame, sphagnum moss, and

Fig. 9.4. *Twelve-inch (30.5 cm) moss basket with cuttings planted through the outside of the container.*

labor needed to line the basket, added growing medium, and extra cuttings. However, the retail price can be quite a bit higher than that of a 10-inch (25.4 cm). The retail price range for our moss baskets is $50 to $55 (CP 9.2), while that for our 10-inch (25.4 cm) hangers is $25 to $30.

There has been a tremendous amount of breeding work done on this crop resulting in over 100 cultivars for growers to choose from. My family has gravitated toward the bronze leaf cultivars. We tried the variegated cultivars but felt that the yellow and green variegation detracted from the flowers. Newer introductions have larger flowers with more vivid colors, compact plant habits, and the tendency to branch freely without needing to be pinched. As cultivar series are expanded, it is becoming easier to grow different colors with the same plant habit in the same basket.

Scheduling

Scheduling New Guinea impatiens is quite similar to scheduling geraniums. Potted crops require anywhere from 10 to 14 weeks, depending on the size and desired quality. Hanging baskets may require a bit more time to mature because they must attain a larger size prior to sales. Spring production schedules are presented in table 9.1.

▰▰▰▰▰▰ TABLE 9.1 ▰▰▰▰▰▰

Spring production schedule

| | Sales period | | | | Cuttings/ container |
| | April | May | June | July | |
		Plant date			
5-inch pots (12.7 cm)	Jan. 24	Feb. 7	Feb. 28	April 4	1
6-, 8-inch pots (15.2, 20.3 cm)	—	Jan. 24	—	—	3, 4
8-inch hanging basket (20.3 cm)	—	Jan. 24	—	April 4	1
10-inch hanging basket (25.4 cm)	—	Jan. 24	Feb. 28	—	4
12-inch moss basket (30.5 cm)	—	Jan. 24	—	—	15

Fig. 9.5. *Soil medium mixing and steam pasteurization.*

My general crop scheduling rule is that in order to adjust the flowering date by one week in either direction, change the planting date by two weeks in the same direction. For example, if you want to delay a crop by one week, you need to plant the crop two weeks later. Conversely, to flower one week earlier, plant two weeks earlier. This rule accounts for the improving growing conditions that exist as the season progresses from winter to spring, such as higher light intensities, longer days, and warmer temperatures. In essence, one spring day equals two winter days in terms of crop development.

Growing medium

Most New Guinea impatiens crops are grown in soilless media. It used to be that a well-drained, well-aerated mix was ideal. However, as ground water contamination and excess leaching concerns become the rule instead of the exception, we must change our thinking slightly. Instead of the optimally drained mixes currently in use, we need to back off and look at adequately drained mixes with more water holding capacity. At the same time, we can't afford to diminish the mix's aeration properties.

I mix my own growing medium and have seen it change over the years from a fairly heavy mix to one that is almost soilless. My current mix is a blend of 15% topsoil, 60% sphagnum peat moss, and 25% rock wool. I like having the topsoil present as a buffer and decided to use rock wool to replace my perlite fraction several years ago. The perlite had been used to provide optimal drainage. Rock wool has been shown to improve water holding capacity and, at the same time, maintain aeration.

My reasons for changing to this mix included concern over excess leaching and providing my customers with a mix that would hold more water and be easier to maintain during the summer. After using this mix for three seasons, I find that I am irrigating less often and with lower volumes of water. A word of caution if you ever work with rock wool. It is essential that you lighten up on your watering practices or else you will run into trouble. You will not be successful with this "next generation" growing mix if you are a heavy-handed waterer.

Dolomitic limestone is added to adjust the pH into the 5.8 to 6.2 range and the mix is steam-pasteurized using aerated steam at 180F (82C) (fig. 9.5). Containers are filled by hand, moved to the greenhouse, dibbled, and planted.

Drip irrigation

New Guinea impatiens benefit from drip irrigation in the same way that geraniums and other potted crops do. Water and fertilizer are delivered in uniform amounts and in a timely manner when automated with time clocks. Foliar diseases such as Botrytis are prevented from becoming established in a crop because the foliage never gets wet. Root disease outbreaks are also minimized as a more constant soil moisture content can be maintained with fewer fluctuations. Of course, the most important reason to use automatic watering is the labor savings. Once New Guinea impatiens approach maturity they are among the thirstiest crops I have dealt with. They don't tolerate repeated wilting in the

Fig. 9.6. *Mature New Guinea impatiens can collapse if stressed repeatedly, in this case from insufficient water.*

spring and don't care that you may be too busy waiting on customers to water at the right time. I have found them to be more sensitive than other spring crops in this respect (fig. 9.6).

A couple of weeks after transplanting we like to have our drip tubes in place in each pot (fig. 9.7). The emitter we use delivers approximately one-half gallon (1.9 l) per hour or about an ounce (30-ml) a minute. I usually irrigate a zone of 5-inch (12.7 cm) pots for 2 minutes (60 ml), two ounces per pot. During February and March two or three waterings per week are sufficient. In May, as the crop matures, three to four waterings per day are common during sunny weather. It is difficult to even think of what it would be like to have to water by hand.

Many growers who are automating their watering systems for the first time try to save a few dollars by not installing a time clock to activate the system. The time clock is a critical part of the system and gives the grower the freedom to do other tasks without having to worry about turning zones on and off by hand. How many times have you forgotten to turn a valve off after an interruption? Today's clocks are reasonably priced and loaded with features to make the watering tasks easier.

I have gone a step further with my watering system in houses where I grow New Guinea impatiens. Hanging baskets of other crops, such as ivy geraniums, are often grown in the same house. These baskets require constant fertilization, while New Guinea impatiens require either no fertilizer, fertilizer at every other watering, or constant fertilization depending on their maturity. Two banks of solenoid valves have

Fig. 9.7. Drip tubes are placed into each pot approximately two weeks after transplanting.

been installed, one dedicated to fertilizer and the other to clear water. Each watering zone is tied to a pair of solenoids. Additionally, two clocks, one dedicated to each bank of solenoids, are in use.

As a result, each watering zone can be scheduled with a choice between fertilizer and clear water. One zone may be scheduled for two clear waterings and one fertilizer application, while another zone may be scheduled for constant fertilization on any given day. The cost of a second time clock and bank of solenoids is compensated for by the increased flexibility and higher quality that result.

Both ebb and flow and trough systems are also excellent for this crop. These systems are more expensive initially, but have been shown to pay for themselves in time. As my drip system ages I am considering replacing it with a trough system. My reasons for deciding on a trough system vs. an ebb and flow system include lower initial cost, ease of retrofitting into my existing greenhouses, and a smaller reservoir requirement.

Fertilization

The standard fertilization program used in my operation is constant fertilization at a concentration of 200 parts per million nitrogen. My injector is set up with two stock tanks; one supplying 150 ppm nitrogen from Peters' 15-15-15 and the second supplying 50 ppm nitrogen from Peters' 15.5-0-0. Additionally, 2 ounces (56 g) of Epsom salts (magnesium sulfate) are added to each 50-gallon (190 l) stock tank of 15.5-0-0. Because of the soil component in my growing medium I do not use Peat-Lite fertilizer formulations. My minor elements are supplied by the topsoil. Overapplication of minor elements to New Guinea impatiens should be avoided.

New Guinea impatiens have been shown to be light feeders, particularly during early stages of production. Fertilize quite sparingly during the first weeks following transplant. I use clear water only, no added fertilizer, during the first two weeks after transplanting. During the second two-week period, plants are fertilized lightly. This is accomplished in one of two ways. Either by fertilizing at half the normal rate or by using the full rate and alternating with clear water.

It is not feasible to change the concentration of the fertilizer in order to feed New Guinea impatiens more lightly than other crops. Ivy geranium, lantana, and fuchsia hanging baskets require the 200 ppm constantly. It is more realistic to alternate between the 200 ppm solution and clear water with each irrigation. During the fifth week the crop is on constant fertilization and is occasionally leached with clear water to prevent soluble salt levels from accumulating.

Temperature

Much has been written about temperatures for New Guinea impatiens, and while I agree with the recommendations, I must admit that they seem to behave similarly to most of my other spring crops. Namely, warm temperatures are nice, but January in New England can be rather nasty from time to time. Although I would like to say that if I set my thermostat on 63F (17C), I go to sleep knowing that the temperature will not dip below 63F (17C), but I cannot. I try to maintain night temperatures close to 65F (18C) for a week or two following transplant. In reality, temperatures may dip to 55F (13C) on a very cold night. I haven't had any serious problems, but if I were replanning my heating system, I would provide more heat for this crop.

Production

As mentioned earlier, after several years of growing in a 4¹/₂-inch (11.4 cm) pot, we switched to a 5-inch (12.7 cm). While we had no trouble producing a top quality plant in the smaller container, our customers were having trouble establishing them in their landscapes. After discussing the problem with many customers, we concluded that they were not providing enough water during the heat of the day for the plants to make a smooth shift from greenhouse to garden. New Guineas require more water during the period immediately following transplant into the garden than a geranium or most other bedding plants. Until the root system grows out into the garden soil, all of the water the plant needs must come from the original root ball of that 4¹/₂-inch (11.4 cm) pot.

When we realized this we made the decision to shift to a 5-inch (12.7 cm) pot. We did not want to produce a larger plant, just give the customer a larger root ball. It increased our production costs by the additional cost of the larger pot and additional growing medium. However, we feel that the move was a wise one and has made the crop easier for us to sell and easier for our customers to handle.

Pinching

Prior to 1992 we pinched all of our New Guinea impatiens, regardless of container size. We felt that the pinch contributed to increased branching and subsequent fullness and quality. Since 1992 we no longer pinch, as most of the new cultivars that we have put into production are free-branching. We used to license ourselves to take a top cutting for our June and July crops, but find it easier to also buy in those rooted cuttings.

Growth regulators

For the most part, New Guinea impatiens do not respond to chemical growth regulators in ways that would make them economical to use. An exception is Florel. This ethylene-releasing material stimulates branching and aborts flower initiation and development (CP 9.3). It is effective in eliminating premature flowering and can be used to synchronize and time the flowering of an entire crop. Research is ongoing and results to date are promising.

Pest control

The most serious pest concern with this crop is the threat of tomato spotted wilt (impatiens necrotic spot) virus, which is spread by thrips feeding. A carefully implemented integrated pest management program is necessary in order to control insect populations before they get out of hand. Once the virus is present in a crop, the only control measure is to rogue infected plants.

Other insect problems include fungus gnats and occasional spider mite outbreaks. Diseases that may be encountered include Botrytis and root rot complexes. These can be controlled with little or no fungicides if good culture and sanitation practices are followed.

Southeast

Bob Barnitz

Bob's Market and Greenhouse is located in Mason, West Virginia, on the Ohio River. It has 4¹/₂ acres (1.8 ha) of double poly greenhouses, with bedding plants and hanging baskets as the primary products. We sell 75% wholesale and also operate four retail locations in the area. The majority of our wholesale business is focused in the Carolinas and Georgia.

Bob's Market and Greenhouses has been growing New Guinea impatiens for 20 years. We have had our share of trials and tribulations growing New Guinea impatiens over the years, but now feel that our cultural techniques produce a premium quality product.

Production plan

Our 1994 production will include 16,250 10-inch (25.4 cm) hanging baskets (30% overall); 1,500 6¹/₂-inch (16.5 cm) pots (3% overall); 2,400

TABLE 9.2

Production schedule, Bob's Market and Greenhouses, spring 1994

Date planted	Container size	Number of containers	Sale date
1/15	10-inch (25.4 cm) basket	3,550	4/15—4/25
2/01	10-inch (25.4 cm) basket	4,600	4/25—5/10
2/01	4-inch (10.1 cm) pot	4,200	4/10—4/25
2/01	6½-inch (16.5 cm) pot	1,200	4/25—5/10
2/15	10-inch (25.4 cm) basket	4,600	4/25—5/10
2/15	4-inch (10.1 cm) pot	11,200	4/25—5/10
2/15	5-inch (12.7 cm) pot	800	4/25—5/10
2/15	6½-inch (16.5 cm) pot	300	5/01—5/20
3/01	10-inch (25.4 cm) basket	2,500	5/10—5/20
3/01	4-inch (10.1 cm) pot	11,200	5/01—5/20
3/01	5-inch (12.7 cm) pot	1,600	5/01—5/20
3/15	10-inch (25.4 cm) basket	1,000	5/25—6/15
3/15	4-inch (10.1 cm) pot	7,000	5/25—6/15

5-inch (12.7 cm) pots (4.5% overall); and 33,600 4-inch (10.1 cm) pots (63% overall). The 4-inch (10.1 cm) pots are packed in a 14-count shuttle tray, and the 5-inch (12.7 cm) pots are packed in an 8-count shuttle tray. By planting three cuttings per 10-inch (25.4 cm) basket, our required number of cuttings totals 86,250.

Since we experience an extended sales period throughout the spring and early summer, we stagger our production. For example, the southern states will have a demand for New Guinea impatiens in all sizes of containers beginning in April, but demand in our local area usually doesn't start until May 1st. Sales continue in the South through May and also in the Ohio Valley region until we are sold out sometime in June. Nearly half of our 10-inch (25.4 cm) basket production is sold during the week of Mother's Day. This demonstrates the selling power and beauty of big, full bloom 10-inch (25.4 cm) New Guinea impatiens during the year's biggest week for retail sales (CP 9.4).

Our production schedule is outlined in table 9.2. We have many plantings so we can maintain a much fresher product and provide the proper size finished plant for our customer.

We purchase only rooted cuttings, since both space and time for self-propagation are limited. A majority of the market in our area uses rooted cuttings as starting material. We prefer to grow Mikkelsens'

Lasting Impressions series since their close proximity in northern Ohio saves freight costs. This season we're also growing Ball FloraPlant's Celebration series and Paul Ecke Ranch's Kientzler Paradise and Pure Beauty series.

Cultural techniques ————————————

The cultural techniques that we follow have proven successful for us in our New Guinea impatiens production. These practices may not work for growers in other regions of the country or abroad, but they have worked well in the Ohio Valley.

Growing medium

Our base growing medium is Premier's Pro-Mix. It's a soilless medium consisting of sphagnum peat moss with perlite, vermiculite, a nutrient charge, and a wetting agent. We add styrofoam beads and pre-moisten the entire mixture prior to the filling process. Our unique media preparation method adds to the finished product's overall quality.

A stationary concrete-type ready mixer is used to loosen the compressed Pro-Mix and add the styrofoam beads. The medium is watered while it is tumbling in the mixer. Three mixers are used with an average capacity of 6 cubic yards (4.6 m³). We feel this gives us a completely consistent mix going to the filling machine.

Planting

The planting process begins with another one of our "little things" which we feel adds to the finished product's quality. We grade the cuttings by size when planted in 10-inch (25.4 cm) baskets. We use three cuttings per basket, and it's important that they are of the same size when planted. This is more important in the early stages of growth because of New Guinea impatiens' sensitivity to overwatering.

Once planted, the baskets are sent through a watering tunnel and placed on risers on the greenhouse floor. There are two reasons for positioning the baskets on the floor; first, temperatures at this lower level can be easily controlled; second and most importantly, the grower can see the soil while watering. New Guinea impatiens are susceptible to root rot, and by observing the soil you can allow it to dry completely between waterings. This helps establish a good root system before the basket is hung.

Temperature

Temperature is one parameter that I feel a lot of growers have trouble with when growing New Guinea impatiens. I learned years ago that you can't force a young cutting to grow fast in the low light or short days of winter. You have to be patient with the crop. At first it may not seem that the pot or basket will be ready for sales, but when the days become longer and the weather breaks there is a big change in their growth rate.

A three-stage temperature program is used when growing New Guinea impatiens hanging baskets. The first stage is when the rooted cuttings are stuck and the baskets taken to the greenhouse, where night temperatures of 62F to 65F (17C to 18C) are maintained for about two weeks. This allows the root system to establish in the new soil. Stage 2 is when the night temperature is dropped to 58F to 60F (14C to 16C) and maintained at this temperature until the baskets are hung. This second stage allows the small breaks to establish themselves.

Growers get into trouble trying to make young cuttings grow faster than required. Cool temperatures shorten the internodes and promote branching, which greatly enhances the finished product's quality. Once baskets are hung, they grow at a faster rate and 65F to 68F (18C to 20C) night temperatures are maintained for the crop's life.

The most important thing to remember about temperature is: Keep the temperature low when the light level is low. If warmer temperatures are maintained during this time, plant stretching will increase and plant quality will decrease. So keep the temperatures low, let the cuttings grow slowly, and watch your quality go up.

Humidity

Humidity is another important factor to consider when growing New Guinea impatiens. High humidity is needed when young rooted cuttings are first planted and establishing roots in the pot or basket. However, humidity should be reduced as the plant grows in the container. Susceptibility to Botrytis increases as more foliage develops on the plant.

Light

Light is a parameter over which the grower has limited control. We grow under 100% double poly with no trouble putting blooms on the plant. The temperate climate in our area, with natural increases in light and temperature in the spring, provides an excellent environment for finishing and establishing a beautiful presentation of blooms. All of our pots are finished on benches below hanging baskets. Because of the baskets overhead, we do not add any additional shade (fig. 9.8).

Nutrition

Proper nutrition can make or break a New Guinea impatiens crop. During the low light period of winter and early spring, it is critical that plants are not overfertilized. Excessive fertilizer, especially with warm

Fig. 9.8. *This is an overhead view of our 1993 finished crop. Photo taken May 1st.*

temperatures, results in stretched plants. We don't fertilize for the first two to three weeks after planting. The young cutting gets all that it needs from the nutrient charge in the soil.

When feeding begins, we pulse feed every third watering instead of constant feed at 200 ppm. We fertilize with Peters Excel 15-5-15 Cal-Mag. As size increases and the weather changes into spring, we feed with every other watering and increase the rate to 300 ppm. During finishing we alternate Peters Excel 21-5-20 All Purpose with Excel 15-5-15 Cal-Mag.

Irrigation

Proper watering of New Guinea impatiens can be the most confusing part of growing this crop. Although they are widely regarded as one of the most demanding plants for water, they certainly do not start out requiring a lot of water. It's critical for a young cutting just planted to get the proper amount of moisture. Root rot is common, and the grower should avoid excessive watering.

We water very lightly during the early stages of growth. It is important to keep the soil evenly moist but not overwet. Allow the soil to completely dry between waterings. On occasion we have gone a whole week between waterings for young crops if the light levels are low. If a relatively dry medium with lower temperatures can be maintained, a tremendous root system should develop. This will make the plant stronger and less susceptible to wilting as it gets older.

To reiterate, it is very important for the grower to be patient during the early stages of growth. This patience will pay off when the light levels and temperature increase in the spring. The plant will have a great foundation to support a beautiful display of foliage and color.

Insects and diseases

Insects most commonly encountered when growing New Guinea impatiens are aphids, spider mites, and thrips. They all can be dangerous to the well-being of your crop, however, thrips cause the most damage due to carrying tomato spotted wilt virus (TSWV). Our philosophy on insects is to take an aggressive approach toward prevention rather than cure.

If you can keep something from happening, you're much better off than trying to solve the problem once you already have it. We use a tank mix of Avid and Talstar applied as a heavy volume spray in the crop's early growth stage.

Once the baskets are hanging we'll apply the same chemicals using a low-volume fogger. We feel this type of spraying is very effective because of its ability to reach all parts of the plant.

The diseases (aside from TSWV) of greatest concern are root rot Pythium and Rhizoctonia and Botrytis. We take a preventative approach to root rot by applying Banrot seven to 10 days after planting at a rate of 9 ounces per 100 gallons (0.27 l/380 l) as a soil drench. This has been very effective in preventing several root, stem and crown rots, and other soil-borne diseases. This one application should provide six to eight weeks of protection from the major root rot diseases.

Botrytis is common during dark cloudy periods and high humidity. We apply Rhone-Poulenc's Chipco 26019 at a rate of 24 ounces per 100 gallons (0.72 l/380 l) as a spray against this pathogen. Use this chemical in the crop's younger stages because it can be phytotoxic to blooms and leaves.

Successful product

New Guinea impatiens have been our No. 1 hanging basket for years and our No. 2 crop in potted flowers behind geraniums. They're outstanding on retail display when in full color (CP 9.5). If the grower can produce a good quality plant, then New Guinea impatiens can be one of the most profitable items in the greenhouse.

—————— Midwest ——————

Heidi L. Tietz

Establishing cuttings

Starting with good plant material is of utmost importance with this crop. Obviously, plants should be insect and disease-free. Two potential problems to watch for on your starter material are:

1. Are the cuttings budded?

If yes, make sure there are vegetative nodes below the tips. Lack of vegetative nodes below budded tips results in poor branching and slow growth of the finished plant.

2. Have the cuttings been exposed to excessive cold?

Freeze damage to plant tops is obvious on New Guinea impatiens—the plants melt. While the plant tops appear to have minimal cold damage, the root ball may have become too cold. Plants with cold damage to the root ball will be very slow to take off, if they ever do.

New Guinea impatiens require a medium with good aeration. We use a mix containing peat, pine bark, vermiculite, and styrofoam. After planting, water well to moisten the soil. We then use a Banrot drench at a rate of 6 ounces per gallon (0.18 l/3.8 l).

The plants are now at their most critical stage in growing. Be sure not to keep the plants too wet! Allow them to dry out at this point. You can *almost* let them wilt. If your plants show signs of stress, mist lightly over the foliage. It is perfectly acceptable to plant rooted cuttings directly into the finished container such as three cuttings per 10-inch (25.4 cm) hanging basket. To prevent overwatering of small plants in large containers, some growers transplant to 4-inch (10.1 cm) pots first and then transplant into the larger containers.

Feeding and watering

New Guinea impatiens are **not** heavy feeders. You must be very careful not to overfertilize. We use clear water until plants are well established.

Once plants have a good root system and show some top growth, we use a general purpose fertilizer like 20-10-20 or 17-17-17 at a rate of 200 to 250 ppm. **Do not** use trace elements since New Guinea impatiens are very susceptible to minor element toxicity. The symptoms are very similar to tomato spotted wilt virus (TSWV). In some cases the plants will exhibit stunted growth at the plant tip and possibly some dieback. There are varietal differences associated with the fertilization program. Personal experience has shown that the older varieties (some recently discontinued) are the most susceptible to minor element toxicity. It also appears that Kientzler varieties (Paradise and Pure Beauty series) prefer more fertilizer than Mikkelsens varieties (Sunshine and Lasting Impressions series). In fact, I have had the Kientzler varieties bloom later when fed less.

The important message is that it's better to underfertilize New Guinea impatiens than to overfertilize (CP 9.6). We feed our New Guinea impatiens no more than four times with a maximum crop time of 14 weeks for our largest container.

Growth regulators aren't necessary on New Guinea impatiens grown in the Midwest. With the introduction of the newer varieties, pinching is not required either since it will only increase crop times.

Scheduling
Crop time varies depending on the season and the finished pot size. The schedule described in table 9.3 is based on an average spring season in the Midwest.

Variety selection
Variety selection is no easy task. Through breeding there have been significant improvements in plant habit, flower color, and size. At the time of this book's publication, there are over 100 cultivars with five breeding material sources available. Does this mean there are 100 different colors? No. First, choose your color classes and the percentages of each color your want to grow, and then begin to choose the varieties within each color class.

There are many colors that are unique to New Guinea impatiens. This is one of the traits that makes them so appealing to the general public. Don't assume that red will be your biggest seller, because it may not be with this crop. No one series has the entire color range, so choose the varieties that grow and sell well. There are seven series available at the time of this book's publication (see Chapter 19). I pick and choose the varieties from each series that perform best in my market.

Garden culture
New Guinea impatiens like cooler temperatures and high light. This is not a midsummer combination that exists naturally in the Midwest. Therefore, home gardeners will have the greatest success if they plant New Guinea impatiens in the following conditions:

TABLE 9.3

Midwest crop schedule

Finished pot size	Crop time (weeks)	Remarks
4-inch pot (10.1 cm)	8 to 10	Plant rooted cutting directly to finished container.
6-inch pot (15.2 cm)	10 to 12	Plant rooted cutting directly to finished container.
8- to 10-inch (20.3 to 25.4 cm) pot or tub	12 to 14	Two rooted cuttings per pot. May want to start in 4-inch (10.1 cm) then move up.
10-inch (25.4 cm) hanging basket	12 to 14	Three rooted cuttings per basket. May want to start in 4-inch (10.1 cm) then move up.

Minimum light: Full sun until 11:00 a.m. Low light levels reduce the number of blooms on the plant.

Maximum light: Full sun, but shaded the hottest two hours of the day.

Water: Lots of it.

Fertilizer: Really not necessary.

Garden uses

New Guinea impatiens can be used many ways as long as the above cultural conditions exist. They are wonderful specimen plants in individual pots and hanging baskets and do well in window boxes or mass ground beds. When planted in containers, consumers can move them until they find the right location for optimal growth. Mixing colors and complementing bicolor flowers with a solid color foliage is very effective. Consumers and landscapers should feel free to use New Guinea impatiens in mixed plantings but be prepared for them to steal the show with their colorful foliage and numerous blooms.

As long as appropriate cultural conditions are met, the home gardener's reward is New Guinea impatiens flower beds, pots, or hanging baskets that are self-flower cleaning, self-branching, and provide incredible color until the first frost.

CHAPTER 10

Seed New Guinea Impatiens—Seed to Plug to Finish

Brian Corr

The introduction of New Guinea impatiens from seed has enabled growers to include New Guinea impatiens in mass market sales in packs like other impatiens, as well as in larger containers. Seed propagation from seed also has the advantage that no stock plants are required, eliminating the risk of introducing diseases.

Cultivars

The first commercially significant New Guinea impatiens from seed was Tango, which won an All-America Selections award when it was introduced in 1989. Gardeners and growers were impressed with the large (2- to 3-inch/5- to 8-cm) bright orange flowers on vigorous plants. An improved Tango became available in 1994 with increased branching, a more compact habit, and brighter flowers. Tango foliage is bronze-green, which effectively sets off the flowers.

The second commercially significant New Guinea impatiens from seed was the Spectra series, introduced in 1991. Spectra is currently available as Light Pink Shades (see Color Plate section, CP 20.1), Lilac-Rose Bicolor, Red Shades, Rose Shades, Salmon Shades, White, and a formula mix. The cultivars are designated "shades" because flower color differs slightly within a cultivar. However, the colors are uniform enough for plants to be sold in the same pack or planted together in a hanging basket. The degree of foliage variegation differs by cultivar. Lilac Rose and Light Pink have the greatest amount of variegation, White has a lesser amount, Rose has almost none, and Salmon and

105

Fig. 10.1. *Optimal germination of New Guinea impatiens occurs between 75F to 80F (24C to 27C) with the seed covered lightly with vermiculite.*

Red seldom have variegation. Excessively variegated seedlings of some cultivars are occasionally produced and may be discarded at transplanting.

Uses of New Guinea impatiens from seed

The moderate cost of seed propagation allows New Guinea impatiens to be used in smaller containers. Spectra New Guinea impatiens are best produced in packs and pots with 3- or 4-inch (8 or 10 cm) diameters planted one plant per container. Tango requires at least a 4-inch (10-cm) diameter container. Hanging baskets with multiple plants per pot are also practical. A 10-inch (25-cm) diameter basket with three Tango or five Spectra plants works well.

Production requirements ⎯⎯⎯⎯⎯⎯⎯

New Guinea impatiens production from seed is in many ways similar to production of any bedding plant from seed. Attention to detail is essential to produce a high quality crop.

Germination and seedling production

The germination and seedling phase is the most critical. Any grower who successfully propagates other bedding plants, such as garden impatiens, from seed can succeed with New Guinea impatiens.

Although New Guinea impatiens and garden impatiens (*Impatiens wallerana*) are both produced from seed, there are significant differences in their culture. To reach optimum germination levels, growers must pay attention to the following.

Temperature. Temperature has a greater influence on germination success than any other factor. Optimum germination temperature for New Guinea impatiens is 78F (26C). Growers will have little success with germination if the soil temperature is below 75F (24C) or above 80F (27C) (fig. 10.1). Temperature control is less critical after Stage 1 (radicle emergence). Temperatures in the 70F to 75F (21C to 24C) range are acceptable from Stage 2 to transplant.

Timing. The timing of New Guinea impatiens germination is different from *I. wallerana*. While *I. wallerana* seedlings may be ready to remove from Stage 1 (radicle emergence) after three or four days, New Guinea impatiens require seven to 10 days. Maintain optimum temperature and moisture levels throughout this stage. New Guinea impatiens are ready to transplant from five-eighth-inch (1.6-cm) diameter plug cells (392 plug tray) approximately six weeks after sowing.

Light. Research has demonstrated that New Guinea impatiens germinate with a higher percentage and greater uniformity if light is available during germination (table 10.1). A light level of about 100 f.c. (1.1 klux) is sufficient. Seedlings develop quickest with moderately high levels, 4,000 to 5,000 f.c. (43 to 54 klux), from germination to transplant.

Seed covering. Although New Guinea impatiens have been shown to germinate better in light, covering the seed lightly with coarse vermiculite also has been shown to improve stands (table 10.1). Presumably sufficient light passes through the vermiculite to enhance germination. New Guinea impatiens seeds are larger than many bedding plant seeds (400 to 600 seeds per gram for New Guinea impatiens compared to 1,400 to 1,600 per gram for *I. wallerana*). Perhaps covering helps maintain sufficient moisture around these moderately large seeds.

Fertilization. Plugs of New Guinea impatiens should be fertilized with 50 to 100 parts per million nitrogen from a fertilizer such as 15-16-17 or 20-10-20 from full cotyledon expansion until transplant.

Since germination requirements for New Guinea impatiens are very specific, some growers can't provide the necessary environment for success. These growers may wish to purchase New Guinea impatiens plugs.

TABLE 10.1

Effect of light and vermiculite covering on Spectra New Guinea impatiens germination

Environmental conditions	Light Pink Shades	Rose Shades	Salmon Shades
	% germination 21 days after sowing		
75F (24C), vermiculite cover, light	90	96	94
75F (24C), vermiculite cover, dark	84	93	92
75F (24C), no cover, light	79	97	79
75F (24C), no cover, dark	59	92	87
80F (27C), vermiculite cover, light	91	96	96
80F (27C), vermiculite cover, dark	76	94	95
80F (27C), no cover, light	70	89	93
80F (27C), no cover, dark	58	90	85

Growing on

Transplant New Guinea impatiens seedlings as soon as they can be removed from the plug tray without damage to the root system (fig. 10.2).

Temperature and light. Always maintain temperatures above 60F (16C). Total light level has little effect on time to first flower, but does impact plant shape and number of flowers, which may influence time to sale (fig. 10.3). Plants grown at high light levels have more branches and flowers than those grown with less light. Grow seed propagated New Guinea impatiens with greenhouse light levels up to 7,000 f.c. (75 klux), provided temperatures can be maintained at a moderate level.

Fig. 10.2. *Spectra New Guinea impatiens plugs ready to transplant.*

Irrigation. New Guinea impatiens grown from seed differ substantially from *I. wallerana* in their response to drought stress. Some growers use drought stress to control height of *I. wallerana*. Drought stress of New Guinea impatiens will severely stunt the plant and may result in lower foliage yellowing. Strive to maintain a moderate moisture level, since overwatering can encourage root rot.

Fertilization. Contrary to some recommendations for vegetatively propagated New Guinea impatiens, seed propagated New Guinea impatiens should be fertilized throughout the crop cycle. Fertilization with 200-ppm nitrogen from a fertilizer such as 15-0-15, 20-10-20 or 15-5-15 with every other irrigation is appropriate. Maintain a pH of 5.8 to 6.5 in typical soilless media.

Height control. Spectra New Guinea impatiens are naturally compact with good basal branching. Under virtually all conditions they do not require any height control. Tango is a more vigorous grower and may require height control under some conditions. Studies have shown that B-Nine (daminozide) and A-Rest (ancymidol) do not have adverse effects on New Guinea impatiens when used at rates appropriate for bedding plants (B-Nine 1,500 ppm, A-Rest 67 ppm), but reduce height only slightly. Cycocel (chlormequat) at rates above 750 ppm resulted in chlorosis on the margins of Spectra foliage. Bonzi (paclobutrazol) and Sumagic (uniconazole) are effective for height control. Growers should

Fig. 10.3. *Time to first Spectra New Guinea impatiens flower is not affected by light level, but plant shape is improved by supplemental lighting during dark weather.*

test concentrations of 5 to 15 ppm for Bonzi and 2 to 5 ppm for Sumagic. Growers in cooler climates should try growing seed propagated New Guinea impatiens without growth regulators or test the lower rates. Growers in warmer climates should experiment with the higher rates. Note that plant growth regulators are usually unnecessary on Spectra New Guinea impatiens and may result in abnormally compact plants.

Crop timing. The time required to produce any greenhouse crop depends on the environment under which it is grown. Under most good greenhouse conditions, Tango New Guinea impatiens should be in flower and salable 15 weeks after sowing for early spring sales and 12 weeks after sowing for summer sales. Time to flower of Spectra New Guinea impatiens is 12 to 13 weeks from seed when grown at an average temperature of 65F (18C). Seed propagated New Guinea impatiens branch naturally and do not require pinching, which delays flowering. Temperature and light levels have the greatest influence on time to sale. While low light levels do not delay flowering, plant growth is reduced, increasing the time needed to produce a plant large enough to be appropriate for the container.

Diseases and insects. Seed propagated New Guinea impatiens are not immune to any of the common New Guinea impatiens diseases, but are initially disease-free. Good cultural conditions will usually limit disease development. Control insects with insecticides as needed. Dursban (chlorpyrifos), Kelthane (dicofol), and Vydate (oxamyl) have shown phytotoxicity in some instances.

Garden performance

Seed propagated New Guinea impatiens perform as well in the garden as those propagated vegetatively. Plants should be transplanted outdoors when the soil is warm and all danger of frost is past. For best bloom plant in partial shade. Tango and Spectra tolerate high light levels better in humid climates. Tango is more tolerant of high light levels than any other New Guinea impatiens.

Tango will reach a mature height of 18 to 24 inches (46 to 61 cm) and should be spaced 12 to 18 inches apart (30 to 46 cm) in the garden. Spectra will grow 10 to 14 inches (25 to 36 cm) tall and should be spaced 12 inches (30 cm) apart.

CHAPTER 11

Home and Landscape Use

Virginia L. Beatty

Well-grown New Guinea impatiens in full bloom are outstanding plants with tremendous decorative potential. The size, color range, and variety of their flowers, their foliage's beauty, their bloom's persistence, and their tidy, self-cleaning habit all combine to make them a very versatile plant. New Guinea impatiens were first introduced into cultivation in the 1880s as a conservatory plant. They were admired, but soon fell out of favor since their flowers persisted in growing under their foliage. Since the USDA brought them back in the 1970s, breeders have done much to coax the flowers out from under the leaves, to increase the range of flower colors, and to make plants more tolerant of water and temperature variations.

Today, if New Guinea impatiens are given the growing conditions that they need, they will bloom for months. New Guinea impatiens are sturdy, self-branching plants that don't change their basic form with time and don't have to be pruned, shaped, staked, or pinched back. Best of all, since New Guinea impatiens are self-cleaning, they don't need deadheading, greatly reducing maintenance time.

Match use to environmental conditions

The successful use of New Guinea impatiens depends, in part, on central heating and air conditioning and, in part, on geography. New Guinea impatiens are popular windowsill plants in northern European homes where outdoor night temperatures often run below the plant's range of preference. Depending on location in the United States, New Guinea impatiens are primarily used outdoors. They are used as bedding plants during the winter in the South and during the summer in the North. In other parts of the world, such as Veracruz, Mexico, New Guinea impatiens can be grown outdoors year-round if given some protection from the hot sun.

Environmental requirements

There are over 100 named cultivars of New Guinea impatiens. Some growth habits and environmental requirements vary by cultivar. To learn how specific cultivars perform in your area, grow plants in hanging baskets, other containers and/or flower beds around your sales area. In addition to providing specific information on their cultural preferences, these New Guinea impatiens will add beauty to your site and stimulate sales.

Light. New Guinea impatiens prefer bright light of 4,000 to 6,000 f.c. (43 to 65 klux) but not hot sun which wilts and scorches their foliage. In areas where the sun is hot, plant New Guinea impatiens where they will get shade during the heat of the day. New Guinea impatiens in the midwestern United States do well if they are shaded in the afternoon and provided with additional water when the temperature exceeds 80F (27C). They can also do well indoors in a window or under artificial light, providing that the temperature remains in the preferred range, and the light level does not exceed 6,000 f.c (65 klux). If indoor plants stop blooming, washing the windows is sometimes enough to restart blooming. A grimy film on the inside of a window can cut light transmission by as much as 40%. Artificial light, especially fluorescent tubes, can be used to supplement or extend day length.

Water. Many plants that originate in woods and jungles prefer to be kept evenly moist. These plants, including New Guinea impatiens, have hairlike roots that rot if they get too wet and shrivel and die if they get too dry. New Guinea impatiens should get enough water to remain turgid, but they are sometimes called "resurrection plants" because they will spring back after wilting.

Moisture holding resins added to the soil can help. Keeping the planting medium's surface area small in relation to its volume reduces moisture loss. In hanging baskets, you can mound the potting medium high in the container and cover the surface with moss, except where the plant stems emerge. For faster watering, sink a pot (with holes in it) in the center of the mound. Avoid high peat-based media which can become waterlogged and difficult to rewet once they have dried out. For thorough watering let a hose run on the ground under the plants or use drip irrigation.

Urban gardeners with small spaces and high disposable incomes are now computerizing their watering on roof gardens and balconies. They find that automatic watering pays in terms of convenience and a saving of both water and time. (For more information on watering, see Chapter 4.)

Temperature. New Guinea impatiens perform better within a temperature range of 60F (16C) to 80F (27C). A day/night differential is not as important as it is for some plants. More compact plants result when day and night temperatures are in the range of 65F (18C) to 75F (24C). When a high day temperature is combined with a low night temperature, the plants become leggy. Growth slows if the temperature falls below 60F (16C). Depending on the cultivar, plants will exhibit cold damage symptoms if the temperature falls below 50F (10C) or 55F (13C), yet other cultivars can survive a light frost.

Temperatures above 85F (29C) result in increased water demand, smaller and fewer flowers, and reduced growth rate. With extra water, New Guinea impatiens can withstand increased temperatures. They are an ideal indoor plant for people who maintain room temperatures between 68F (20C) and 72F (22C). Remind customers to pull pots back from windows when outdoor temperatures drop very low, and their window areas get cold. (For more information on temperature, see Chapter 5.)

Soil or potting mix. Outdoor plantings of New Guinea impatiens do best in a well-aerated, rich organic soil with a pH between 5.5 and 7. Place plants away from trees and shrubs to avoid competition for water and nutrients. Since New Guinea impatiens require more water than most plants, use an automatic irrigation system or be prepared for frequent watering. When planting next to a structure, extra watering may be required if planted beneath an overhang.

Soilless mixes are preferred in containers. These mixes are not as heavy as soil, do not compress, hold more air, and will provide more even moisture. However, high peat mixtures hold too much water and once they dry out are difficult to rewet. Since plants in containers dry out faster than plants in the ground, try to use containers that hold the largest amount of potting media per surface area.

Feeding. New Guinea impatiens are more easily stunted by overfertilizing than by underfeeding. They also are sensitive to soluble salts. Since most plants have been fertilized prior to sale, they can continue without additional feed for quite some time. More New Guinea impatiens suffer from overfeeding than starvation. This is especially true for plants grown in small pots and in containers where leaching is inadequate and salts build up. (For specific information on feeding, see Chapter 4.)

Pests and diseases. Spider mites can be a problem indoors and outdoors when the air is very dry. Avoid mites by increasing the humidity around the plant. Fungus gnats (small, black, flying insects) can be reduced by not overwatering and by making sure that plants don't stand in water. If customers receive clean, well-grown plants, the only disease to be concerned about is Botrytis (gray mold). This fungus often appears when plants get wet and cold at the same time. Botrytis can be reduced by keeping water off flowers and leaves during cool weather and removing dead leaves and flowers from the plant and container. (For more information on pests and diseases, see Chapters 12, 13, and 14.)

Ways to use New Guinea impatiens——

New Guinea impatiens are striking plants indoors in a bright window or outdoors in the ground, a container, or a hanging basket. Recommend that customers plant them in areas that need more color such as near an entrance or next to a structure or walk. When preparing mass plantings of New Guinea impatiens, such as in parks or other formal landscape plantings, precision is important. Customers should buy all their plants at one time, making sure they are all the same cultivar and age. If they are not, slight differences in growth habit can detract from the precise, formal appearance. Customers should purchase 10% more containers than the number calculated for the job. This assures perfection in the job, and the remainders will always find a spot in informal settings where variations in habit can be very attractive.

Containers

New Guinea impatiens are much easier to care for if grown in larger window boxes, containers, or hanging baskets. Plastic containers are lightweight and can be moved easily. Five-gallon buckets used for construction and cleaning products, with their labels removed, are great. These containers provide a sizeable volume for roots, don't dry out as fast as clay containers, and don't break. If plastic containers are too light, rocks or bricks can be placed in the bottom for stability. Drainage holes can be added with a drill or red-hot nail.

Terra-cotta containers are beautiful, and larger sizes are heavy enough so they don't tip over. However, they are more fragile and if left outdoors in winter are affected by freezing and thawing. Terra-cotta pots dry out faster and need to be watered more often than plants grown in plastic containers.

Size

When making recommendations to customers, it's important to find out how they intend to use the plants. Start with a plant that is close to the size needed for an instant show. Four-inch (10 cm) pots do well on a window sill, 6-inch (15 cm) pots and 8-inch (20 cm) tubs are ideal for window boxes or for bedding out. The 10-inch (25 cm) and 12-inch (30 cm) tubs are effective if planted in larger containers, as are plants bought in hanging baskets if the hangers are removed. Since New Guinea impatiens can grow quite large, it is important to make suggestions on the appropriate spacing for different effects. In a mass planting or a ribbon border, the plants should be close together; when used as accent plants, or "beads on a string," they should be spaced farther apart.

Design

Group the same cultivar or use harmonious or contrasting colors in mass plantings. Combine New Guinea impatiens with annuals or perennials, such as floribunda roses, that bloom all season. They can also be used as accent plants in a carpet of low-growing annuals. Consider the background—will the plants be viewed against a hedge, a fence or wall; how will they look against the colors of a building?

With their definite color and dependable form, New Guinea impatiens are becoming more popular in plantings that evoke the Victorian and Edwardian periods. The bright red and orange New Guinea impatiens are dramatic in Victorian plantings; the rose, white and lavender cultivars provide color all season in Edwardian plantings.

Inform customers for sales _____

Customers want long lasting color, plants that keep their place and require less fuss and maintenance. New Guinea impatiens can give people what they want. Offer customers suggestions on how to use them for maximum pleasure. Salespeople should give customers information on New Guinea impatiens' environmental requirements and how to modify the environment to match the plant's preferences. Most important, salespeople should share with the customer that all the hard work has already been done. Placing New Guinea impatiens in the garden or in a window, keeping them in bloom, and enjoying them for a whole season can be easy, rewarding, and great fun.

COLOR PLATE SECTION

Roy Larson

CP 1.1 Claude Hope, Linda Vista, Costa Rica, a pioneer New Guinea impatiens breeder.

Feeding and watering

David Hartley

CP 4.1 Enhanced growth at lower fertility levels was demonstrated at Southeast Missouri State University.

David Hartley

CP 4.2 Overfertilization may result in stunted, off-colored plants.

David Hartley

CP 4.3 Shiny, dark green leaves with wavy leaf surface indicate excessive fertility.

David Hartley

CP 4.4 Stunted growth and brown leaf tips are symptoms of overfertilization and/or high soluble salts levels.

Light and temperature

CP 5.1 Effect of day and night temperatures on growth of New Guinea impatiens.

CP 5.2 Effect of day and night temperature on New Guinea impatiens flower development.

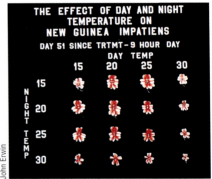

CP 5.3 Effect of day and night temperature on New Guinea impatiens plant and flower development.

Finishing

CP 9.1 A spring crop of New Guinea impatiens pots with hanging baskets above.

CP 9.2 Mature moss baskets of New Guinea impatiens.

Finishing

CP 9.3 Effect of Florel on New Guinea impatiens. Treated plant (right), untreated (left).

CP 9.4 Full New Guinea impatiens baskets stand out in the garden center.

CP 9.5 New Guinea impatiens are our No. 1 hanging basket and No. 2 potted plant.

CP 9.6 Effect of overfertilization.

Thrips

Michael Parrella

CP 12.1 Western flower thrips egg.

CP 12.2 Western flower thrips first instar larva.

CP 12.3 Western flower thrips second instar larva.

CP 12.4 Western flower thrips prepupa.

CP 12.5 Western flower thrips pupa.

CP 12.6 Western flower thrips female (upper), male (lower).

Jan Hall

CP 12.7 Thrips feeding damage on New Guinea impatiens.

TSWV/INSV symptoms

CP 12.8 Necrotic ringspots.

CP 12.9 Interveinal necrosis.

CP 12.10 Leaf necrosis.

CP 12.11 Leaf mosaic.

CP 12.12 Leaf necrosis.

CP 12.13 Necrotic ringspots in flower.

TSWV/INSV symptoms

CP 12.14 Stem necrosis with leaf distortion.

CP 12.15 Plant stunting.

Diseases

CP 13.1 Rhizoctonia infection at the stem base leads to leaf scorch, stunting, wilting, and death.

CP 13.2 Thin black streaks often appear at the base of a stem affected by Pythium crown rot.

CP 13.3 Brown leaf spots caused ◄ by *Myrothecium roridum*.

Diseases

CP 13.4 Sporulation of *Myrothecium ror-idum* on the underside of a leaf spot.

CP 13.5 Leaf spot on upper surface caused by *Botrytis cinerea.*

CP 13.6 Leaf spot on lower surface caused by *B. cinerea.*

CP 13.7 Bacterial leaf spot caused by *Pseudomonas syringae* seen from upper surface.

CP 13.8 Bacterial leaf spot caused by *Pseudomonas syringae* seen from underside of leaf.

CP 13.9 A powdery mildew *(Oidium* sp.) on New Guinea impatiens.

Diseases

Ruth Welliver

CP 13.10 Stunting and leaf distortion in a New Guinea impatiens infected with tobacco mosaic virus (TMV).

Steve Nameth

CP 13.11 New Guinea impatiens infected by both TMV and impatiens necrotic spot virus (INSV).

Insects

CP 14.1 Aphid adult and nymph.

CP 14.2 Fungus gnat larva.

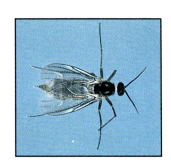

CP 14.3 Fungus gnat adult.

Insects

CP 14.4 Shore fly adult.

CP 14.5 Two-spotted spider mite adult.

CP 14.6 Cyclamen mite adult.

Merchandising

CP 17.1 Informative garden center displays increase sales.

New cultivars

CP 19.1 Ball Seed Co. field trial of commercially available varieties.

CP 19.2 Bora-Bora, Paradise Series.

CP 19.3 Celebration Raspberry Rose, Celebration Series.

CP 19.4 Rhapsody, Lasting Impressions Series.

CP 19.5 Sunregal, Mikkel Sunshine Series.

New cultivars

CP 19.6 Celebration Light Lavender II, Celebration Series.

CP 19.7 Flamenco, Danziger Series.

CP 19.8 Celebration Pure White, Celebration Series.

CP 19.9 Samoa (Improved), Paradise Series.

CP 19.10 Kallima, Pure Beauty Series.

CP 19.11 Impulse, Lasting Impressions Series.

New cultivars

CP 19.12 Aglia, Pure Beauty Series.

CP 19.13 Celebration Electric Pink, Celebration Series.

CP 19.14 Martinique, Paradise Series.

CP 19.15 Celebration Apple Star, Celebration Series.

CP 19.16 Ambience, Lasting Impressions Series.

New cultivars

CP 19.17 Pago Pago, Paradise Series.

CP 19.18 Prepona, Pure Beauty Series.

CP 19.19 Celebration Red, Celebration Series.

CP 19.20 Blazon, Lasting Impressions Series.

CP 19.21 Karina, Bull Series.

CP 19.22 Ambrosia, Lasting Impressions Series.

New cultivars

CP 19.23 Celebration Deep Coral, Celebration Series.

CP 19.24 Celebration Salmon, Celebration Series.

CP 19.25 Bonaire, Paradise Series.

CP 19.26 Cameo, Lasting Impressions Series.

CP 19.27 Danova, Danziger Series.

Genetics

CP 20.1 Light Pink Shades, Spectra Series.

CP 20.2 Canon, Twice as Nice Series.

Robert Quené

CP 20.3 Variation in F₁ progeny of New Guinea impatiens cross among cultivars.

Robert Quené

CP 20.4a Variation in leaf shape, size, and color.

Robert Quené

CP 20.4b Variation in leaf variegation patterns.

Genetics

Robert Quené

CP 20.5 Variation in flower color, size, and shape available in New Guinea impatiens germplasm.

Breeding potential

CP 21.1 *Impatiens platypetala aurantiaca.*

CP 21.2 *Impatiens auricoma.*

CP 21.3 *Impatiens hawkeri.*

CP 21.4 *Impatiens grandis.*

CHAPTER 12

Thrips and TSWV/INSV

James W. Moyer, Margaret E. Daub, and Karen L. Robb

Tomato spotted wilt virus (TSWV) was first described in Australia about 1910 and was found in the United States during the 1930s. For the next 50 years this virus remained a curiosity [5]. It was only occasionally isolated from crops along the California coast and in Louisiana. Although the virus was of intellectual interest, it received little serious attention during that period. In fact, it was not until the late 1960s that scientists discovered what the virus looked like, and not until the past three to five years have all of this virus's properties been fully appreciated [13].

The virus

TSWV is very unusual among plant viruses—it has a complex virus particle, it is transmitted in nature by thrips and in propagative material, and it has a broad host range [13]. The virus can be transmitted experimentally by sap transmission, but the efficiency of transmission varies with isolate and host. Thus, the virus is difficult to manipulate compared to many other plant viruses. Until the mid-1980s, the difficulty in investigating the virus and the lack of any economic importance resulted in only one or two virology groups around the world studying this virus. TSWV was considered a unique virus and was classified in a category by itself. Even though there were many anomalies associated with individual virus isolates, it was widely accepted among the virology community that there was only one "tomato spotted wilt virus." The so-called anomalies were attributed to its unusual characteristics and the lack of understanding of the virus and how it caused disease. We now know that the diseases of floral crops that were once considered to be caused by a single virus (TSWV), are in fact caused by at least two, related yet distinct viruses—TSWV and impatiens necrotic spot virus (INSV) [19, 20].

Progress in understanding the floral crop diseases caused by members of this virus group resulted from the floral crop industry's interest and the support provided to researchers investigating these diseases. The diseases became prevalent in the floral crop industry and in several field crops (e.g., peanut, tomato, and tobacco) from 1984 to 1986. A Sanibel Island Conference sponsored by individual companies and the American Floral Endowment was held during this time to examine the current status of TSWV. Conference goals were to assess the extent of the problem, to determine appropriate control measures based on available information, and to recommend areas in need of research. Although understanding the complexity of the disease at that time can only be considered primitive by current standards, several recommendations were made that are the basis of current control strategies. These recommendations primarily consisted of measures designed to control the thrips vector and to eliminate the virus from the production cycle. Research since then has made it possible to implement these control recommendations and forms the basis for the next generation of control strategies.

As a consequence of the Sanibel Island Conference, intensive TSWV research efforts were initiated to improve virus detection for indexing and to identify resistance to the virus in many crops. As in most other crops, no sources of high levels of virus resistance to TSWV have been found, although there is considerable variation in susceptibility among cultivars of many crops. Recent efforts using new technologies from biotechnology research have resulted in opportunities for resistant cultivars. Progress in this area will be discussed later in this chapter under the section, Genetic engineering for virus resistance.

Virus detection ⸻

Efforts to improve virus detection have resulted in major advancements in TSWV and INSV disease control as well as providing fundamental knowledge for designing new control strategies. TSWV can cause many different symptoms, many of which mimic other diseases (see Color Plate section, CP 12.8 to 12.15). Depending on the host and environmental stresses, diagnosis has always been a problem. In contrast to other diseases and injuries where the symptoms are diagnostic, the symptoms of these diseases have been easily confused even by the most experienced diagnostician. For example, symptoms on gloxinia are similar to those caused by Phytophthora, on exacum they look like bacterial diseases, and on tomato leaves they can be easily confused with chemical injury. Each of these problems requires a different control measure and thus the need for a virus-specific diagnostic test. In addition to being efficient and reliable, the test must be sufficiently routine to be commercially available and used by personnel with minimal training.

As in medical diagnoses, serological assays are currently the assay of choice. They are less expensive and often more reliable than the traditional transfer of virus onto indicator hosts (biological assay), particularly for the large numbers of assays required in indexing programs. The disadvantage of serological assays is that they will only detect the virus(es) for which they are designed. Serological assays are only reliable when based upon a thorough knowledge of the viruses that are present and involved in the disease syndrome. Any gaps in that knowledge can yield errors in diagnosis.

One of the first discoveries was the isolation and characterization of the second TSWV-like virus. This virus, which we named impatiens necrotic spot virus (INSV) [20], is now known to be responsible for many of the false negative or questionable results obtained in the early efforts to diagnose the cause of the disease. The confusion was due to the differences in the two viruses' host range and in the virus particle's composition. Because of host range differences, only *Nicotiana benthamiana* (a tobacco host sensitive to all isolates of TSWV and INSV) is now used when testing for both viruses, as opposed to one of the traditional TSWV hosts that is not as sensitive to INSV. The difference in particle composition is the reason the TSWV antisera failed to detect INSV. Only two of the three predominant proteins are sufficiently related between the two viruses to react with antisera made to whole virions of the viruses. Unfortunately these two proteins are the least abundant of the three proteins and thus result in many false negative or ambiguous results. Many antisera are made to only one of the viral proteins, the nucleocapsid (N) protein. The N protein antisera does not cross-react between these viruses, again resulting in false negative results.

The recognition of INSV's distinguishing characteristics resulted in the production of antisera to this virus that is now widely used in the industry [20, 21]. Additional research designed to clarify the relationship between these two viruses has resulted in isolation of a monoclonal antibody that recognizes both viruses [15]. This finding may ultimately lead to a single test for the two viruses. Since the discovery of INSV, research by ourselves and others has resulted in the discovery of at least five additional TSWV-like viruses [11]. None of these other viruses are as yet recognized as major problems in floral crops, and several are only known to occur in Asia, Africa, or South America. Importing plant material from these areas means a constant vigil to reduce the probability that these (or other viruses) are inadvertently introduced into the production cycle of floral crops. One research component in our labs is now designed to identify parts of the TSWV-like viruses that are common to all of the viruses [16, 22]. Our research goal is to develop a scheme that would detect all TSWV-like viruses. Since control strategies for all these viruses are the same, a single diagnostic test would be highly efficient and useful.

Thrips as TSWV and INSV vectors

TSWV and INSV are only transmitted by a few species of thrips; no other vectors have been identified. Unlike other insect vectors, thrips must feed on infected plant tissue as larvae to acquire the virus [3, 4]. There is a three- to 10-day latency period before thrips become infective. After they acquire the virus as larvae, infective adults can transmit the virus for the remainder of their lives. A minimum of 15 to 30 minutes of feeding is required for transmission to healthy plants [30, 31].

Western flower thrips, *Frankliniella occidentalis* (Pergande), is one of the six thrips species known to transmit these viruses [31]. Currently, it is the primary vector associated with this disease on North American floriculture crops.

Damage from WFT feeding

In addition to transmitting TSWV, western flower thrips also damage plants through feeding. The type of damage caused by this insect depends on the development stage and plant species attacked. Western flower thrips have a tremendous host range, including many floriculture crops, other agricultural crops, native plants, and weeds [6, 7].

Western flower thrips feeds by inserting its modified mandible into plant tissue and withdrawing the cell fluids via a hypodermic-like stylet, resulting in the cell's death. When a thrips feeds on developing foliage, the injury is not usually apparent until the affected leaves expand. Then the inability of the dead cells to expand causes foliage deformation. Western flower thrips will also feed on fully expanded leaves. The dead plant cells are filled with air, causing the leaves to take on a silvery appearance (CP 12.7).

Thrips feeding on open flowers results in a characteristic petal scarring. This damage is most apparent on darker flowers, where white streaks are particularly noticeable. In addition to scarring, flowers become deformed when thrips feed on unopened flower buds.

Western flower thrips development____

This insect is usually found in flowers, although it is occasionally found on the foliage of some plants (fig. 12.1). Eggs are deposited within plant tissue, and first instar larvae begin feeding upon hatching (CP 12.1, 12.2). Second instar larvae are also active feeders (CP 12.3). Both larval instars are most commonly located in the protection of the flower perianth or within developing terminal foliage. Second instars become whitish in color just prior to the next molt and usually move down the plant to pupate in the soil or plant litter (fig. 12.1). Prepupae and pupae are quiescent non-feeding stages whereas the adult resumes feeding (CP 12.4, 12.5). Adult females are larger than males and can vary in coloration from yellow to dark brown while males are always pale yellow (CP 12.6).

Western flower thrips development, as with all insects, is influenced

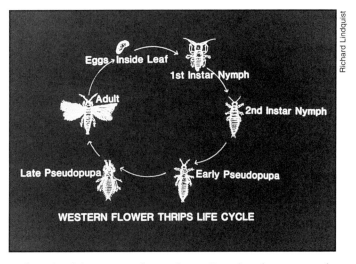

Fig. 12.1. Life cycle of the western flower thrips. Note that the two pseudopupal stages occur off of the plant.

strongly by temperature. The insects develop slowly at cooler temperatures and more quickly at warmer temperatures, until upper and lower temperature thresholds are reached. Temperatures of 80F to 85F (27C to 29C) are optimal for western flower thrips development; an egg can develop into an adult in less than 10 days at these temperatures [26].

Female thrips do not need to mate with a male in order to produce viable eggs, but all unfertilized eggs become males. After mating, the female can produce both males and females. Adult females live longest at cooler temperatures and expire quickly at constant high temperatures (greater than 85F/29C). Females live approximately 30 days at temperatures between 58F and 85F (14C to 29C) and produce the greatest number of offspring (120 to 225 offspring per female) at these temperatures [26].

Relationship between TSWV and thrips

Research has illustrated that feeding on TSWV-infected leaves shortens western flower thrips larval development times compared to larvae-fed healthy plant material. Exposure to TSWV-infected chrysanthemum leaves throughout the entire larval period exacted a high mortality of immature thrips [26]. All surviving adult western flower thrips, which had been reared on infected chrysanthemums as larvae, transmitted the virus to healthy plants.

The relationship between TSWV and western flower thrips in floriculture greenhouses is very complex and is mediated by several factors. Many weeds and crops can serve as reservoir hosts for both virus and vector, and adult thrips can migrate from these hosts into the greenhouse. The inoculative potential of western flower thrips may be affected by the virus titer present in the reservoir plants [10]. The attraction of the plant to western flower thrips may influence the TSWV transmission rate [1] as well as the cultivar's sensitivity to TSWV [7]. Indeed, even the presence of TSWV in a plant may alter its attractancy. For example, thrips were found in greater numbers on infected *Emilia sonchifolia* [9] and on infected lettuce [35] than on healthy plants.

Control strategies ─────────────

Control of these virus' diseases depends on reducing or eliminating the viruses in the production cycle in concert with reducing or eliminating thrips. Since a single thrips can inoculate one or more plants with the virus, the economic threshold for thrips as a virus vector is significantly lower than the threshold for thrips as a plant pest. The threshold in some areas may require extreme measures, such as the screening of production areas and restricting access to the production areas. The difficulties in controlling thrips dictates that stringent measures are needed to eliminate the viruses from production material. The thrips can't spread the virus if it isn't present.

Virus control

The first line of defense is to eliminate the virus from propagation material in the vegetatively propagated crops. Mother blocks of source plants should be established from material that has been thoroughly tested for viruses and repeatedly shown to be free of the known viruses. It is essential that these mother blocks be isolated from commercial production areas to reduce the probability of reinfection. When possible, stocks should be renewed annually from tissue culture material where the probability of reinfection by viruses and other pathogens is the lowest.

Propagators should monitor for the presence of virus at each cycle of multiplication so that if reinfection occurs, the infected plants can be removed from propagation, avoiding additional increase of infected material. Growers, especially those who have a persistent problem with these viruses, should monitor production areas routinely (not less than weekly) for symptomatic plants and remove them from production areas (roguing). It's important to recognize the many different symptoms of INSV/TSWV infections on New Guinea impatiens. Symptoms may range from leaf and flower spotting or distortion to stem blackening and overall plant stunting (CP 12.8 to 12.15).

Infected plants should be placed in bags or other containers at the bench to avoid spreading viruliferous thrips to other greenhouse areas. Rogueing should be conducted in both seed and vegetatively propagated crops. Perennial plants exhibiting mild symptoms can be as good a source of virus as some of the more severely affected plants. Any plant that is maintained in the production area where these viruses are a persistent problem should be examined as a possible virus inoculum source. Remember these viruses have one of the most extensive host ranges of any of the plant viruses encompassing both monocotyledonous and dicotyledonous plants.

Thrips control strategies

Chemical control of western flower thrips can be extremely difficult for many reasons. Good contact of thrips with pesticides is hard to achieve due to its secretive behavior. Its propensity to develop insecticide resistance [17, 26] is another factor, as well as reinfesting populations through thrips migration.

Based on a knowledge of this pest's biology and behavior, several management strategies have been developed. An integrated approach incorporates strategies for the reduction/prevention of western flower thrips in the greenhouse, without relying solely on insecticides for control. While all of these strategies may not be appropriate for every situation, many can be used by almost every grower.

Thrips exclusion. The most effective strategy for thrips control is prevention [27]. Many greenhouse structures have open sides or vents for increased ventilation. This offers no impediment to thrips movement into these greenhouses. A significant proportion of pest infestations result from insects moving into greenhouses from surrounding areas [24, 27]. Screening vents and doorways can greatly reduce thrips movement into greenhouses and reduce or eliminate the need for pesticide applications. Exclusion screening is being utilized by growers in Europe, Israel, and North America. Many growers are reporting 50% to 90% reductions in pesticide use as a result.

One-hundred percent exclusion is warranted when virus-susceptible propagative material is being produced, as there are no pesticides available which give continual protection from one pesticide application to the next. Thus, exclusion is a more effective virus control strategy than chemical control of western flower thrips.

Many growers have achieved significant reductions in pest problems and reduced pesticide applications without 100% exclusion. Several growers with naturally vented greenhouses that could not be retrofitted for complete exclusion screened only the side of the greenhouse facing the prevailing wind. These growers effectively restricted the migration of a majority of thrips. Certainly this strategy does not exclude all the insects from the greenhouse; monitoring and pesticide applications are still required. However, most growers using this technique have reported significant reductions in pest levels. These smaller populations are easier to manage and require fewer pesticide applications.

Screening for insect exclusion, however, is not simply a matter of placing a fine screen over vents and air intakes. There are several important considerations in the design of exclusion screening for greenhouses. The grower must determine all the avenues that could be used by potential pests to gain entry into the greenhouse. Is it a retrofit of an older structure or new greenhouse construction? How is the greenhouse cooled? How to compensate for reduced airflow? How to maintain the system?

The National Greenhouse Manufacturers Association has developed a set of recommendations for using insect screens in mechanically vented greenhouse structures. Screening greenhouses to exclude thrips is no small undertaking, but there are several measures that will help ensure success. It is important to start with clean, thrips-free greenhouses, select proper screening material, assure adequate air flow, and prevent the introduction of infested plant material [23, 29]. An in-depth analysis of insect screening is reviewed in Chapter 15.

Control weeds in and around greenhouses. Western flower thrips has a broad host range, including many weeds. Weeds, however, are not usually targeted for pesticide applications and can serve as a refuge during pesticide applications. Weeds can also act as a reservoir for TSWV.

Dispose of unused plants. Once a crop has been harvested, it is a good practice to get rid of the leftover plants immediately. Like weeds, these plants have no commercial value, but are still capable of supporting large populations of thrips that may move on to new plants.

Avoid contiguous cropping. Many flower crops are grown in very large, contiguous greenhouses. All stages of production may be present under one roof. As crops are harvested, mobile adult populations can move from an older planting to a newly planted area. Thus, a constant food supply is available to the thrips, and populations will continue to flourish. Whenever possible, large growing areas should be broken into smaller units to reduce this problem.

Monitor thrips population levels. Greenhouse conditions are often suitable for western flower thrips development throughout the year, including winter. It is clear from its short generation time and high reproductive rate that large populations of western flower thrips can quickly build up in greenhouses. Other factors, including reinfestation from outside sources, also influence thrips numbers. Once established in a greenhouse, control may be difficult to obtain, so early detection is important. The short time required for transmission of TSWV to healthy plants makes early detection of this pest even more imperative.

Although both blue and yellow traps are attractive to western flower thrips [8, 26, 34, 35], yellow sticky traps are also attractive to other pests of ornamental crops [18, 25]. Yellow sticky traps provide early detection of western flower thrips, permitting remedial action before populations reach damaging levels. An average of five traps per hectare (2.47 acres) is usually sufficient to estimate western flower thrips populations in greenhouses [26].

Chemical control. When monitoring indicates that chemical control is necessary, certain strategies help to maximize the treatment efficacy.

Two applications made five days apart are recommended to reduce high populations of western flower thrips since chemical controls are not effective against eggs, and sprays are not usually directed against pupae in the soil. The interval between sprays is based on thrips development at greenhouse temperatures ranging from 70F to 85F (21C to 29C). This interval should be shortened at higher greenhouse temperatures and lengthened during cooler temperatures. *Good coverage and penetration into flowers, buds, and terminal foliage is essential and is enhanced with smaller droplet sizes.*

The development of insecticide resistance is a serious concern with western flower thrips control, so it's important to rotate classes of insecticides. A rotation of classes every four to six weeks, based on two to three generation times of western flower thrips, has been suggested.

There is no single best solution for dealing with the problem of insecticide resistance; the best approach is to integrate various management strategies, including cultural, physical, and biological control alternatives.

Growers who have implemented control recommendations and have followed them faithfully have significantly reduced losses from these viruses. These viruses, however, remain a serious threat to the industry and although losses have been reduced, these recommendations are labor intensive and expensive. As chemical controls are not available for these or any other plant viruses, development of resistant cultivars remains the only alternative. Although there is considerable difference in the tolerance level to these viruses between cultivars, commercially usable sources of resistance have not been identified in any of the crops that are susceptible to TSWV. (Some recent tomato cultivars show promise, but it isn't known if the resistance will survive over time.) Little progress has been made in any of the crops using naturally derived sources of host resistance, but pathogen-derived resistance sources are showing promise [14].

Genetic engineering for virus resistance

Pathogen-derived resistance refers to the strategy of isolating a portion of the virus' genome and genetically engineering this gene into the plant's genome. This strategy was initially based on a phenomenon called "cross-protection," where infection of a plant with a mild strain of a virus can protect against subsequent infection by a more virulent strain. It was discovered some eight to 10 years ago that this protection could be duplicated by transferring specific viral genes into plants. Although the mechanism is not understood, lines resistant to many viruses have been developed and are ready for commercialization in some food crops such as squash. Traits such as those that slow the ripening process have been transferred to other crops such as tomato (e.g., Flavr-Savr).

The genetic engineering strategy of developing resistant cultivars has two requirements. First, each of the target viruses must be sufficiently characterized at the molecular level so that the right viral gene may be isolated. Second, the procedures must be developed for engineering the gene into the plant. These techniques and the gene transfer process are collectively referred to as "plant transformation." The plant transformation process consists of inserting the gene into individual plant cells and then selectively regenerating the cells that contain the viral gene into whole plants. The techniques for transformation of many model species such as tobacco, carrot and petunia have been available for over 10 years. However, in general, these techniques are species and sometimes cultivar specific, so standard protocols must be modified, often significantly, for each crop.

Only recently has significant progress been made in floral crops. The first chrysanthemum plant transformation and regeneration has been reported [32]. This work is in the process of being extended to other cultivars and for use in virus resistance [33]. Other lab work has extended these efforts to other crops such as gloxinia. The transformation protocols being developed for virus resistance should also be applicable for introducing other traits, such as delayed senescence, flower color, or fungal resistance. Most of the research in our lab will be focused on strategies for plant transformation and on identifying plants that express the virus resistance. Extending these techniques to other crops will depend on the availability of transformation techniques for individual crops and an ongoing knowledge of the prevalent viruses in the commercial production areas.

References

[1]   Allen, W.R., and A.B. Broadbent. 1986. Transmission of tomato spotted wilt virus in Ontario greenhouses by *Frankliniella occidentalis. Can. J. Plant Pathol.* 8:33-38.

[2]   Bailey, S.F. 1933. A contribution to the knowledge of the western flower thrips, *Frankliniella occidentalis. Can. J. Plant Pathol.*

[3]   ———. 1935. Thrips as vectors of plant disease. *J. Econ. Entomol.* 28:856-863.

[4]   Bald, J.G., and G. Samuel. 1931. *Investigations on "spotted wilt" of tomatoes II.* Aust. Counc. Sci. Ind. Res. Bull. 54.

[5]   Best, R.J. 1968. Tomato spotted wilt virus. In *Advances in virus research.* Ed. K.M. Smith, M.A. Lauffer. 13:65-145. New York: Academic Press.

[6]   Bryan, D.E., and R.F. Smith. 1956. The *Frankliniella occidentalis* (Pergande) complex in California (Thysanoptera:Thripidae). *Univ. Calif. Publs. Entomol.* 10:359-410.

[7]   Broadbent, A.B., J.A. Matteoni, and W.R. Allen. 1990. Feeding preferences of the western flower thrips, *Frankliniella occidentalis* (Pergande) (Thysanoptera: Thripidae), and incidence of tomato spotted wilt virus among cultivars of florist's chrysanthemum. *Can. Entomol.* 122:1111-1117.

[8]   Brodsgaard, H.F. 1989. Coloured sticky traps for *Frankliniella occidentalis* (Pergande) (Thysanoptera:Thripidae) in glasshouses. *J. Appl. Entomol.* 107:136-140.

[9]   Carter, W. 1939. Populations of Thrips tabaci, with special reference to virus transmission. *J. Anim. Ecol.* 8:261-276.

[10]   Cho, J.J., W.C. Mitchell, R.F.L. Mau, and K. Sakimura. 1987. Epidemiology of tomato spotted wilt disease on Crisphead lettuce in Hawaii. *Plant Dis.* 71:505-508.

[11]   De Avila, A.C., P. de Haan, R. Kormelink, R. de O. Resende, R.W. Goldbach, and D. Peters. 1993. Classification of tospoviruses based on phylogeny of nucleoprotein gene sequences. *Journal of General Virology* 74:153-159.

[12]   Francki, R.I.B., C.M. Fauquet, D.L. Knudson, and F. Brown. Ed. 1991. *Classification and nomenclatures of viruses.* Rep. ICTV Arch. Virol. 5th Suppl. 2. New York: Springer Verlag.

[13]   German, T.L., D.E. Ullman, J.W. Moyer. 1992. Tospoviruses: diagnosis, molecular biology, phylogeny, and vector relationships. *Annu. Rev. Phytopathol.* 30:315-348.

[14]   Gielen, J.L., P. de Haan, A.J. Kool, D. Peters, M.Q. van Grinsven, J.W. Moyer, R.W. Goldbach. 1991. Engineered resistance to tomato spotted wilt virus, A negative-strand RNA virus. *Bio-Technology* 9:1363-1367.

[15]   Hall, J.M., S. Geske, and J.W. Moyer. 1993. An epitope map of conserved and monospecific domains on the nucleocapsid protein of *Tospoviruses.* Abst. IXth Int. Cong. of Virol. Glasgow. Aug. 1993.

[16]   Hickey-Tiani, C.M., S. Geseke, J.M. Hall, and J.W. Moyer. 1993. Molecular analysis of the diversity between the tomato spotted wilt *Tospovirus* M. RNAs. Abst. APS Mtg. Nashville. Nov. 1993.

[17]   Immaraju, J.A., T.D. Paine, J.A. Bethke, K.L. Robb, and J.P. Newman. 1992. Western flower thrips (Thysanoptera:Thripidae) resistance to insecticides in coastal California greenhouses. *J. Econ. Entomol.* 85:9-14.

[18]   Jones, V.P., and M.P. Parrella. 1986. The movement and dispersal of Liriomyza trifolii (Diptera:Agromyzidae) in a chrysanthemum greenhouse. *Ann. Appl. Biol.* 109:33-39.

[19]   Law, M.D., and J.W. Moyer. 1989. Physicochemical analysis of a serologically distinct tomato spotted wilt virus strain. *Phytopathology* 79:1157.

[20]   ———. 1990. A tomato spotted wilt-like virus with a serologically distinct N protein. *J. Gen. Virol.* 71:933-938.

[21]   Law, M.D., J. Speck, and J.W. Moyer. 1991. Nucleotide sequence of the 3' non-coding region and N gene of the S RNA of a serologically distinct tospovirus. *J. Gen. Virol.* 72:2597-2601.

[22]   ———. 1992. The nucleotide sequence and genomic organization of the impatiens necrotic spot tospovirus MRNA. *Virology* 188:732-741.

[23]   Mears, D.R. 1991. Screen out bugs... without knocking out your ventilation system. *Greenhouse Grower,* Nov. 1991.

[24] Neal, K. 1992. Screen pests out, reduce chemical use. *Greenhouse Manager,* Apr. 1992.

[25] Roach, S.H., and J.A. Agee. 1972. Trap colors: preference of alate aphids. *Environ. Entomol.* 1:797-798.

[26] Robb, K.L. 1989. Analysis of *Frankliniella occidentalis* (Pergande) as a pest of floriculture crops in California greenhouses. Ph.D. diss., University of California, Riverside.

[27] Robb, K.L. 1993. Screening for insect exclusion: the nuts and bolts. In *Proceedings.* Ninth Conference on Insect and Disease Management on Ornamentals, Del Mar, Calif.

[28] Robb, K.L., and M.P. Parrella. 1988. Chemical and non-chemical control of western flower thrips. In *Proceedings.* Fourth Conference on Insect and Disease Management on Ornamentals, Kansas City, Mo.

[29] Roberts, W.J. 1992. Screening for insect control in greenhouses. *Center for Controlled Environment Agriculture.* June 15, 1992.

[30] Sakimura, K. 1962a. Frankliniella occidentalis (Thysanoptera: Thripidae), a vector of the tomato spotted wilt virus with special reference to the color forms. *Ann. Entomol. Soc. Am.* 55:387-389.

[31] Sakimura, K. 1962b. The present status of thrips-borne viruses. In *Biological transmission of disease agents.* New York: Academic Press.

[32] Urban, L.A., J.M. Sherman, J.W. Moyer, and M.E. Daub. 1992. Regeneration of *Agrobacterium*-mediated transformation of chrysanthemum. International Society of Horticultural Science symposium, Invitro culture and Horticulture Breeding, Baltimore, Md.

[33] ———. 1994. High frequency shoot regeneration and *Agrobacterium*-mediated transformation of chrysanthemum (*Dendranthema grandiflora*). Plant Science. In press.

[34] Vernon, R.S., and D.R. Gillespie. 1990. Response of Frankliniella occidentalis (Thysanoptera:Thripidae) and *Trialeurodes vaporariorum* (Homoptera:Aleyrodidae) to fluorescent traps in a cucumber greenhouse. *J. Entomol. Soc. Br. Columbia.* 87:38-41.

[35] Yudin, L.S., W.C. Mitchell, and J.J. Cho. 1987. Color preference of thrips (Thysanoptera: Thripidae) with reference to aphids (Homoptera: Aphididae) and leafminers in Hawaiian lettuce farms. *J. Econ. Entomol.* 80:51-55.

CHAPTER 13

Other Diseases
and Their Control

Margery Daughtrey

Although New Guinea impatiens growers are most concerned with avoiding the Tospovirus diseases, impatiens necrotic spot (INSV) and tomato spotted wilt (TSWV), there are several other disease problems which are troublesome occasionally. Rhizoctonia stem rot and web blight, Pythium root rot, Myrothecium leaf spot, Botrytis leaf spot and dieback, bacterial blight caused by *Pseudomonas syringae*, an unidentified powdery mildew, cucumber mosaic virus (CMV), turnip yellow mosaic virus (TYMV), and tobacco mosaic virus (TMV) have all caused crop injury. A *Verticillium* sp. that is not a problem in production has caused wilt symptoms in the landscape. Additionally, a fungus (*Phoma* sp.) has been frequently isolated from foliage and stems. None of these problems is unique to New Guinea impatiens, but growers may find the diseases tricky to identify the first time they encounter them on this crop. The diseases caused by these pathogens are minor in comparison to the tospovirus diseases, but production of a high quality New Guinea impatiens crop will require that they be kept in check.

Rhizoctonia ———————————————————

The *Rhizoctonia solani* fungus is a common damping-off and crown rot pathogen on bedding plants. Rhizoctonia is often seen on *Impatiens* x *wallerana*, and is also encountered on New Guinea impatiens.

133

Symptoms

R. solani attacks stems of New Guinea impatiens at the soil line. Crown rot caused by Rhizoctonia has a dry, brown appearance, and the affected stem tissue may develop cracks. Superficial black streaking of the lower stem, 2 to 2.8 inches (5 to 7 cm) long, sometimes accompanies Rhizoctonia infections, but this symptom is more often seen with Pythium infections. Yellowing and browning of the lower leaves may be the first indication of Rhizoctonia crown rot; further progression of symptoms may involve leaf scorch, stunting, wilting, and death of plants (see Color Plate section, CP 13.1). Under humid conditions, the fungus may grow a short distance up the stem and cause web blight of lower leaves. Leaf tips in contact with the growing medium during propagation are also sometimes directly infected, resulting in irregularly shaped, watersoaked leaf lesions.

Disease management considerations

Either infested cuttings or accidental introduction of contaminated soil can be the source of a Rhizoctonia infestation. Symptoms may develop a number of weeks after the inoculum has been introduced. Careful sanitation to avoid introducing Rhizoctonia to the growing medium is the most critical practice for minimizing losses from this common pathogen. Rhizoctonia is likely to be associated with soil particles, which are most easily splashed or blown into uncovered piles of stored growing mix, or into pots or baskets grown at the greenhouse floor level. There are no environmental controls for Rhizoctonia; the correct temperature and humidity for healthy crop production are also conducive to Rhizoctonia growth.

Careful cultivar selection, coupled with careful sanitation, may allow a grower to reduce dependency on fungicide drenches. In a comparison of 13 New Guinea impatiens cultivars [1], Gemini and Milky Way showed the greatest disease resistance; inoculation did not result in plant death for these two cultivars. Other cultivars (Astro, Aurora, Nova, and Sunset) showed as much as 60% mortality when inoculated with *R. solani.*

Fungicides for Rhizoctonia control may be drenched or sprayed onto the growing medium at transplanting [5]. Products containing thiophanate-methyl, iprodione, quintozene, or triflumizole are effective against Rhizoctonia. See Chapter 16 for a list of fungicides containing these active ingredients. Where treatment for Pythium is also desirable, note that thiophanate-methyl may be used as a drench at a two-week interval for Rhizoctonia suppression, while Pythium controls that might be used in combination treatments usually require a four-week interval [8]. Fungicide usage may have some drawbacks: One study detected some stunting of New Guinea impatiens that were successfully protected against Rhizoctonia by a Terraclor drench [1], while another observed stunting with high rates of Banrot application at transplant [9].

Pythium root rot

Root rot throughout the root system as is seen in Pythium-infected poinsettias and geraniums, is not usually observed in New Guinea impatiens. Symptoms are generally concentrated in the root crown and sometimes extend into the lower stem.

Symptoms

Infection by *Pythium* species commonly causes stunting of New Guinea impatiens. Crown rot caused by *P. ultimum* generally appears wetter and blacker than crown rot due to Rhizoctonia [1]. Infections tend to be concentrated in the upper part of the root system and lower stem; black streaking at the stem base typically accompanies the Pythium infection. A second species of *Pythium, P. irregulare*, has also been isolated from wilting New Guinea impatiens [7]. Black streaks (CP 13.2) and discolored xylem near the stem base are typical of *P. irregulare* infection; black streaks are at times also visible in the upper roots. *P. irregulare* is often observed on New Guinea impatiens that have been transplanted too deeply. Since blackening of stem portions is frequently cited as a symptom of INSV, take care to discriminate between the relatively thin black lines at the stem base associated with fungal crown rots and the larger blackened areas anywhere along the stem commonly associated with INSV or TSWV infection.

Disease management considerations

Pythium infestations may originate from infected cuttings or from crop contact with contaminated soil containing the fungus spores. Fungus gnats and shore flies (see Chapter 14) have been identified as potential vectors of Pythium, which may serve to move inoculum from the greenhouse floor to the crop level or from infected to healthy plants. Cultivar choice may help to reduce Pythium disease losses. In a New Jersey study comparing disease susceptibility of 13 New Guinea impatiens cultivars [1], a wide range of disease susceptibility was observed. The cultivar Milky Way was the most resistant to *P. ultimum*, followed by moderately susceptible Columbia, Red Planet, Sunset, and Twinkle. All of the cultivars tested, except for Milky Way, showed some mortality following Pythium inoculation. For the highly susceptible cultivars—Aurora, Cosmos, and Twilight—inoculation almost always resulted in plant death. Sprays and drenches with Aliette and drenches with Subdue reduced stunting and eliminated mortality in the moderately susceptible Astro cultivar in this trial.

Pythium diseases of flowering potted plants generally do not cause dramatic losses when crops are grown in carefully stored, well-drained mixes in a greenhouse with a good sanitation program. General sanitation efforts and fungus gnat and shore fly control (see Chapter 14) will help to keep Pythium in check. High soluble salts have been shown to predispose poinsettias to Pythium infection, and New Guinea impatiens are known to be intolerant of high salts [10, 11]. Keeping soluble salts levels below 1.0 to 1.5 mmho/cm (by the 1:2 soil:water extract method) may help in maintaining a healthy, disease-free root system on a New Guinea impatiens crop [11]. These plants are particularly sensitive to both salts and fungicides during the first two weeks after transplanting. In one study, Banrot 40W drenches at transplant resulted in a 10% to 28% growth reduction (dry weight) in Nebulous, Sunburst, and Rosetta, whereas drenches delayed until two weeks after transplant were not injurious [9]. Excessive (greater than labeled) application rates caused more pronounced growth reduction.

Fungicides containing etridiazole, fosetyl-Al, metalaxyl or propamocarb are effective against Pythium crown rot.

Myrothecium leaf spot

The *Myrothecium roridum* fungus is a common pathogen of wounded tissues in hot, humid environments. This fungus has occasionally been observed on New Guinea impatiens.

Symptoms

M. roridum causes brown leaf spots with a "camellia flower" shaped pattern on New Guinea impatiens (CP 13.3). Sporulation of the fungus is often clearly visible on the underside of a lesion (CP 13.4). Spots develop on both wounded and unwounded New Guinea impatiens leaves under moist conditions [7]. Fruiting bodies of *M. roridum* have also been observed on blackened stem bases of cuttings that had wilted during propagation, but a cause-and-effect relationship has not been established. Myrothecium has distinctive fruiting bodies that appear first as white tufts of mycelium and later exhibit a wet-looking, greenish-black spore mass at the center of each tuft (sporodochium).

Disease management considerations

For control of Myrothecium leaf spot, practice careful sanitation and maintain good air circulation around plants and cuttings. Avoid circumstances that would allow leaves to sit wet for extended periods of time. Terraguard (triflumizole) drenches or Chipco 26019 (iprodione) sprays for Rhizoctonia control will also reduce Myrothecium disease. Growers should note that there is a label precaution against drench applications of iprodione to impatiens.

Botrytis blight ─────────────────────────

Botrytis cinerea is common on New Guinea impatiens. Leaf spots and dieback from cutting wounds due to Botrytis infection are particularly likely to occur during winter greenhouse conditions.

Symptoms

The leaf spots are generally oval to irregular in outline, tan in color, and may show several concentric growth rings within the lesions. Leaf infection may occur after flower petals fall onto leaf surfaces. These petals provide an excellent nutrient source for Botrytis (CP 13.5, 13.6). Botrytis may also attack through cutting wounds on stock plants. Black discoloration may develop in the area of a Botrytis stem infection. Stem blackening is not specific to Botrytis injured tissue; this tissue reaction is seen in cases of INSV, Pythium, or Rhizoctonia infection as well. Areas infected by Botrytis often develop a fuzzy, tan-to-gray mass of spores under humid conditions.

Disease management considerations

B. cinerea spores germinate and infect when a film of moisture on the plant surface persists for four to 12 hours. The necessary moisture often happens when condensation occurs following temperature drops. Heating and ventilating the greenhouse at sunset is an important management practice, as this drives the moisture-laden warm air out of the greenhouse and reduces the possibility of condensation. Techniques for maintaining good air circulation, including the use of fans to provide horizontal air flow, and adequate spacing between plants, reduce Botrytis blight. Fungicides containing chlorothalonil, copper, iprodione, mancozeb, or vinclozolin (see Chapter 16) may be used to supplement a grower's ongoing environmental control program. Benzimidazole fungicides (including thiophanate-methyl) are generally not effective for Botrytis control on greenhouse crops due to widespread resistance.

Bacterial blight caused by
Pseudomonas syringae

This New Guinea impatiens disease was first reported in California in 1989 [6]. The disease has also been observed on New Guinea impatiens in Florida and Massachusetts [A.R. Chase and R.L. Wick, personal communications].

Symptoms
The symptoms of this bacterial blight are large, watersoaked or brown to dark gray necrotic lesions that occur both at the leaf margins and between the veins (CP 13.7, 13.8). Leaves are sometimes deformed. The *P. syringae* from New Guinea impatiens in California appeared to be host-specific, while the isolates studied in Florida could cause disease on other flower crops, including *Impatiens* x *wallerana* [A.R. Chase, personal communication]. Bacterial leaf spots on *I.* x *wallerana* also occur between veins as well as centered around hydathodes at the edge of the leaf. The *P. syringae* strain isolated from New Guinea impatiens in California was resistant to copper, but exhibited some sensitivity to streptomycin [6]. Florida isolates from impatiens were susceptible to weekly copper treatment (Kocide 101) at 2 pounds per 100 gallons (0.91 kg/3,800 l) and to Agribrom at 25 ppm [2, 4]. Trials on *I.* x *wallerana* indicate that high fertilization rates are conducive to bacterial leaf spot [3]. Since there are no registered controls for this disease, avoiding extended periods of leaf wetness is critical for preventing outbreaks.

Powdery mildew

Powdery mildew is not common on New Guinea impatiens, but it has occasionally been observed in North America [J. Matteoni, M. Klopmeyer, personal communications]. The causal agent is *Oidium* sp. Red-flowered varieties appear to be most susceptible.

Symptoms
Airborne conidia are produced in chains on fungal mycelium that grows on both leaf and stem tissue (CP 13.9). Because the powdery mildew growth may be thinly spread over the leaf rather than taking the form of distinct white colonies, it might easily be overlooked or mistaken for spray residue.

Disease management considerations

Monitor carefully for outbreaks of this disease: Early detection will allow roguing out of inoculum and prompt fungicide application. A hand lens will help a scout to visualize the fringed margin of powdery mildew colonies and the upright conidiophores.

Since powdery mildew has been seen so rarely on this host, no mildicides have been tested for effectiveness or for their safety to New Guinea impatiens, and few fungicides are labeled for such a use. Thiophanate-methyl products, however, are registered for powdery mildew control and for application to herbaceous ornamentals.

Phoma sp. ─────────────────────

New Guinea impatiens submitted to plant disease diagnostic labs occasionally show tiny, elliptical brown cankers at the extreme base of the stem. When these cankers or other necrotic areas on stems or leaves are cultured, a fungus in the genus *Phoma* is often isolated. No studies have been conducted to establish whether this fungus is indeed a pathogen. In many cases in the past, New Guinea impatiens from which *Phoma* sp. was isolated were also affected with impatiens necrotic spot virus, so it has been difficult even to speculate on the possible impact of this fungus on the plant's health. Inoculation trials under controlled conditions will be required to establish whether this fungus poses a significant disease threat to New Guinea impatiens.

Viruses ────────────────────────

Impatiens necrotic spot virus (INSV) is the virus most frequently encountered in New Guinea impatiens crops in the United States (see Chapter 12), but other viruses have been detected occasionally. Tomato spotted wilt virus (TSWV) causes symptoms similar to those of INSV; currently it is more commonly detected in Europe than in the United States. Up to this time, viruses other than the two tospoviruses (INSV and TSWV) have not presented a production problem for the grower. Tomato ringspot and tobacco ringspot viruses, as well as turnip yellow mosaic and an unidentified carlavirus, have occasionally been detected in some New Guinea impatiens cultivars [M. Tiffany and G. Grüber, personal communications].

Symptoms

New Guinea impatiens infected with cucumber mosaic virus (CMV) (vectored by aphids) may show twisted, distorted leaves. Tobacco mosaic virus (TMV) (CP 13.10) has been detected in plants showing stunting, and leaf distortion has been observed in combined infections of TMV and INSV (CP 13.11).

Disease control considerations

New Guinea impatiens producers should buy cuttings only from propagators with virus indexing programs. Growers should also monitor for virus disease symptoms (ring spots, leaf distortion, black stem discoloration, etc.) and monitor for and control potential insect vectors (particularly western flower thrips and aphids). Plants showing symptoms of virus should be rogued out promptly.

References _____

[1]   Castillo, S., and J.L. Peterson. 1990. Cause and control of crown rot of New Guinea impatiens. *Plant Dis.* 74:77-79.

[2]   Chase, A.R. 1990. Control of some bacterial diseases of ornamentals with Agribrom. In *Proceedings*, Fla. State Hort. Soc. 103:192-193.

[3]   ———. 1990b. *Effect of Osmocote rate on growth of* Impatiens wallerana *and severity of pseudomonas leaf spot.* Apopka Res. Rept. RH-90-19. Central Fla. Res. and Educ. Ctr., Univ. of Fla., CFREC.

[4]   ———. 1992. *Bacterial disease control on ornamentals using Aliette, Kocide, GreenShield and ASC-66825.* Apopka Res. Rept. RH-92-10. Central Fla. Res. and Ed. Ctr., Univ. of Fla, CFREC.

[5]   ———. 1993. *Fungicides to replace Benlate for some diseases of ornamentals.* Apopka Res. Rept. RH-93-1. Central Fla. Res. and Ed. Ctr., Univ. of Fla, CFREC.

[6]   Cooksey, D.A., and S.T. Koike. 1990. A new foliar blight of impatiens caused by Pseudomonas syringae. *Plant Dis.* 74:180-182.

[7]   Daughtrey, M., and M. Macksel. 1991. *Impatiens inoculation trials.* Long Island Horticultural Research Laboratory 1990 Annual Report, Cornell University.

[8]   ———. 1992. *Combined pythium and rhizoctonia control on New Guinea impatiens.* Long Island Horticultural Research Laboratory 1991 Annual Report, Cornell University.

[9]   Han, S.S. 1993. *Reduction in growth of New Guinea impatiens from fungicide applications.* Research Report #3. Massachusetts Flower Growers' Association.

[10]   Judd, L.K., and D.A. Cox. 1992. Growth of New Guinea impatiens inhibited by high growth-medium electrical conductivity. *HortScience* 27:1193-1194.

[11]   ———. 1992. Watch out for soluble salts. *Greenhouse Grower.* February.

CHAPTER 14

Other Insects, Mites and Their Control

Richard K. Lindquist

This chapter will cover the major insect and mite pests of New Guinea impatiens, other than thrips. Fortunately, the list of "other" pests is quite short, and that is the good news. The bad news is that this short list of pests can cause growers some very serious problems. The following section discusses these other pests. Only general concepts related to pest management are covered in this chapter, but specific pesticide control recommendations are found in Chapter 16. A discussion of biological controls is included with each pest group for those wishing to consider alternatives to pesticides. However, this section is mostly for information, because not enough is known at this time to suggest specific biological control programs. Growers wishing to use biological controls on New Guinea impatiens will need to experiment with the different biological control agents available to determine what will or will not succeed in any production situation. Excellent information is available from insectaries that supply the biological control agents.

Aphids

There are more than 4,000 aphid species worldwide. On New Guinea impatiens, the most common aphids are the green peach aphid, *Myzus persicae*, and melon/cotton aphid, *Aphis gossypii* (see Color Plate section, CP 14.1).

Biology

Aphids are small, generally less than one-eighth inch (3 mm) long, soft-bodied, slow-moving insects. They have piercing-sucking mouthparts that are inserted into the phloem tissue of plants and remove fluids. Aphids can be many colors, including black, brown, pink, red, or white, although they most often are green. There can be color variation within the same species. Aphids have "honey tubes," or cornicles, on the rear end of the abdomen. The tubes resemble exhaust pipes and make aphids appear as if they are jet-propelled.

In greenhouses and tropical areas, all aphids are usually females that produce live young, called nymphs. Each female can produce about 50 or more nymphs, and the nymphs can begin reproducing in seven to 10 days. The reproduction period may continue for about one month. Adult aphids may be winged or wingless. Depending on population density and/or condition of the host plant, winged individuals are sometimes formed. Winged aphids can fly and can appear on a crop very suddenly (e.g., from an outdoor crop). Winged aphids are also able to spread within a crop. Host plant quality and nutrition have considerable effect on aphid reproduction. Temperatures are also very important (fig. 14.1).

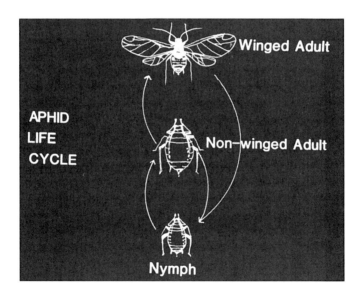

Fig. 14.1. Life cycle of aphids in greenhouses. Note that adults may or may not have wings.

Economic impact

Large numbers of aphids are necessary to actually affect plant growth. Much of the potential to cause problems depends on when the infestation occurs. The same number of aphids will have a greater effect on younger plants. Heavily infested plants will be shorter than non-infested plants. Usually an aphid infestation is a nuisance, because the insects, or their white cast-off skins, detract from a plant's value. As a by-product of feeding on plant fluids, aphids excrete a sugary liquid called honeydew, which can cover leaves and flowers with a sticky layer. If humidity is high enough, a black sooty fungus forms on the honeydew. These conditions commonly occur within plantings of New Guinea impatiens. If the honeydew and resulting sooty fungus deposits are heavy, leaves will then begin to fall off the plants.

Pest management

Detection. Winged aphids are attracted to yellow sticky traps, and these can be used to monitor for them. However, keep in mind that most aphids do not have wings, so plant inspection is the best way to detect aphids. Pay special attention to lower leaves, terminal shoots, and flower buds before flowers open. Examine both upper and lower leaf surfaces. Look for the white skins left on plants by aphids during molting. Inspect plants every week. Also inspect new plant shipments and the entire planting the day following high winds or thunderstorms produced by weather fronts. After thunderstorms or windy weather is also a good time to inspect sticky traps, because winged aphids can be carried on wind currents. Ants can be another clue to aphids being present. Some ant species "tend" aphids for their honeydew. In return the ants protect aphids from predators and parasites.

How many plants need to be inspected to detect aphids? No one knows for sure. The best that can be said is to look at plants in all areas of the greenhouse. Do the best you can with the time available. If you hire a pest management scout, this will, of course, be done for you. Some growers place colored markers in aphid-infested areas so that those persons doing the spraying (or releasing natural enemies) will know where to concentrate their efforts.

Cultural and physical control. Weeds often contain aphid populations that can infest, or reinfest, the crop. An obvious cultural control method is removal of weeds from around the plant production area, including the areas just outside of the greenhouse. Plant nutrition can be important in aphid development. High nitrogen levels may promote larger aphid populations. Although the relationship between plant nutrition and insect population development is very complex, it is safe to say that fertilizer management is very important. There sometimes can be a fine line between adequate and overfertilization. Unfortunately, this line has not yet been determined.

Screening or other barriers, as well as positive air pressure, can be used as physical control methods. Determine first before installing such equipment that aphid movement into the greenhouse from outside is occurring. This movement will most likely be via winged aphids. Sticky traps placed toward and away from prevailing winds, fan intakes, doorways, etc., will provide some of the answers.

Pesticides. Aphids can be difficult to control for several reasons including small size, high reproductive capacity, occurrence on lower leaf surfaces or deep within plant canopies or in flowers, and pesticide resistance. Pesticide resistance among green peach aphid and cotton/melon aphid populations is quite widespread. Because pesticide resistance among aphid populations varies, there is no guarantee which, if any, of the registered pesticides will provide control. The most important aspect of control is detecting the infestation before numbers build. Apply the same insecticide at least twice before changing to another class of chemicals. If a systemic insecticide is being used, make two applications three to four weeks apart. Nonsystemic insecticides should be applied three or four times at weekly intervals. Do not apply the same pesticide four times in sequence. It is better to make two applications in sequence, using pesticides from two different chemical classes.

Biological control. Parasites, predators, and fungi can *potentially* be used to manage aphids on some ornamental crops, including New Guinea impatiens. Both predators and parasites are available from commercial insectaries. Predators include the predatory midge *Aphidoletes aphidimyza* and lacewing *Chrysoperla* spp. Ladybird beetles (*Hippodamia convergens*) are also available, but their actual effectiveness as biological controls in greenhouses has not been determined. Parasites available commercially include *Aphidius matricariae* and *A. colemani.*

Parasitized aphids appear as light brown "mummies" on leaves. Other parasite species will usually invade an aphid-infested area if no pesticides are being used, or the insecticides are harmless to the parasites. This invasion, although eventually quite effective at reducing the aphid population, usually occurs too late for satisfactory control on a commercial greenhouse crop. The fungus *Verticillium lecanii* is effective in controlling some aphid species, but no commercial product is available in North America. It is presently used in Europe. Other fungi may soon be available in North America.

Fungus gnats ─────────────────────────

Fungus gnats are insects that can be found nearly everywhere that plants are grown or maintained. New Guinea impatiens certainly are no exception. The most common species in greenhouses in North America are called dark winged fungus gnats. There are several species in the genus *Bradysia,* including *B. coprophila*, *B. impatiens* and *B. paupera.*

Biology

The life cycle consists of egg, larva, pupa, and adult. Adults are dusky gray flies that resemble mosquitoes and are about one-quarter inch (6 mm) long, with long legs and antennae. The adults are often seen running across the growing medium surface or flying around plants. Females lay eggs in cracks and depressions in the growing medium surface. Each female may lay more than 100 eggs. In five or six days the eggs hatch into white, translucent larvae with shiny black heads. The larvae pass through four instars and are about one-quarter inch long when fully developed. Late instar larvae turn milky white. They are often seen on the growing medium surface, and most larvae occur in the top inch or so of the medium. After 10 to 14 days the larvae pupate within silky chambers in the growing medium. Several days later adults emerge. Two to four weeks are necessary to go from egg to adult (CP 14.2, CP 14.3, fig. 14.2).

Economic importance

Fungus gnat larvae feed on fungi, decaying organic matter, and healthy plant tissue. Direct injury to seedlings and transplants by larval feeding sometimes occurs that stunts or kills young plants during rooting, etc. Feeding on healthy plant tissue apparently occurs when there is no fungal food source, so damage may be more severe when the potting mix or soil has been pasteurized.

In addition to direct feeding injury, there are links between fungus gnats and several plant pathogens, including Pythium, Verticillium, Cylindrocladium, Sclerotinia, and Thielaviopsis. Both adults and larvae may carry pathogens from diseased to healthy plants. A good sanitation, environmental control, and fungicide program will be of great help here.

Whether or not fungus gnats are directly damaging plants, neither growers producing nor customers receiving infested plant shipments are enthused about these insects. Customers' tolerance for fungus gnat adults is very low.

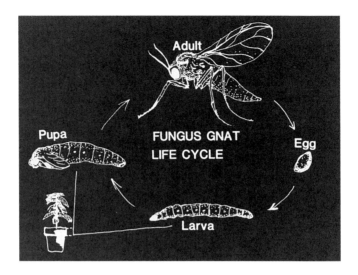

Fig. 14.2. *Life cycle of fungus gnats.*

Pest management

Detection. Yellow sticky traps can be used to detect fungus gnat adults. Vertical or horizontal traps can be used, but horizontal traps will be more effective, especially early in the crop, before the canopy thickens. Place horizontal traps sticky surface up on the potting mix. Vertical traps should be placed among plants within the crop canopy, with the trap tops extending slightly above crop height. Place some traps underneath greenhouse benches and near doorways to get some picture of what is happening in these areas. Check the traps weekly for fungus gnat adults. It is not necessary to count all of the adults on the traps, but you do need to estimate whether numbers are increasing or decreasing.

Fungus gnat larvae can be detected by placing 1-inch (2.5-cm) diameter, one-quarter-inch (6-mm) thick potato slices on the growing medium surface. The slices should remain a minimum of 24 hours to attract larvae, and they may be left in place up to a week. Examine the slices for larvae, as well as the potting mix surface just below the potato slices. Potato wedges inserted into the potting mix may be more effective.

We don't know how many yellow traps or potato slices to use for accurate fungus gnat sampling. One sampling program using potato slices to detect larvae places 10 slices per 1,000 square feet (90 m²) of greenhouse bed or bench area. We also do not know how many adults or larvae constitute a damaging population. The point is to have a monitoring program to detect these insects, especially when starting young plants. Probably a simple presence or absence classification can be used where the mere sighting of fungus gnats will cause a problem.

Cultural and physical control. Potting mixes vary in their attractiveness to fungus gnats and/or their capacity to sustain these insects. Mixes with high amounts of microbial activity (eg, those containing bark, immature compost) will be more attractive to and yield greater numbers of fungus gnats. The significance of this related to plant injury and pathogen transmission is variable. Producing plants in potting mixes with low levels of microbial activity may actually increase plant injury by fungus gnat larvae. The reduced amount of fungal growth in the mix may "force" fungus gnat larvae to feed on plant roots. Conversely, plant pathogen suppressive composts with a great deal of microbial activity may reduce plant injury by fungus gnat larvae, but will have more fungus gnats. Either way, there will be problems.

Pesticides. Most pesticide applications are directed at the larvae in the growing medium. Applications are made as drenches or coarse sprays to the surface. For best results, the application should be repeated in three to four weeks. Aerosols, fogs, smoke generators, etc. (space treatments) will be effective against adults. These need to be repeated frequently (every four to five days). Some growers also treat areas under benches with hydrated lime or copper sulfate.

Biological control. Of all the insect and mite pests affecting New Guinea impatiens, fungus gnats probably offer the best opportunity for biological control. There are several such methods available commercially. The microbial pesticide *Bacillus thuringiensis* H-14 (Gnatrol) has been somewhat effective when applied as a drench. Because Gnatrol is not persistent, applications need to be repeated weekly for best results.

Entomopathogenic nematodes are being sold for fungus gnat control. The nematodes are not plant pests, but are specialized for attacking insects. The nematodes carry bacteria that they release after invading their insect hosts. The bacteria, harmless to non-insects, multiply and kill the host. The nematodes also reproduce inside the insect, finally moving on to seek or await other victims. The nematode *Steinernema carpocapsae* is most widely used in the United States, but other species including *Heterorhabditis bacteriophora* are available. Another *Steinernema* species, *S. feltiae*, has provided excellent control. This species became commercially available in 1994. Nematodes are applied as drenches, using hand watering or mechanical injectors. It is very important to make the applications soon after planting to avoid a possible damaging peak of fungus gnats.

Predatory mites in the genus *Hypoaspis* have controlled fungus gnat larvae in several commercial greenhouses. These tiny mites are available from some insectaries and are released onto the growing medium. The mites can exist in the growing medium on other food sources (mainly other insects, including thrips), so they can be introduced very early in the crop.

Shore flies

Shore flies are usually found in the same general areas as fungus gnats and are often confused with them. However, they are a completely separate group of flies. The species found in greenhouses are in the genus *Scatella.*

Biology
There are four development stages—egg, larva, pupa, and adult. There is very little known about the details of their biology in greenhouses. Adult shore flies are nearly all black, have reddish eyes, white spots on the wings, and short antennae. They resemble fruit flies and leafminer adults. Adults sometimes gather in large numbers on surfaces of pots, flats, and irrigation matting, wherever algae are found. The larvae are maggot-like and light tan in color. There are breathing tubes on the posterior end to enable the larvae to get air. Both adults and the brown larvae feed on several species of algae (CP 14.4).

Economic importance
Direct injury to plants is rare, although larvae have been reported to injure roots of plants grown in substrates such as rock wool. There is evidence that shore fly adults and larvae can aid in the spread of some plant pathogens. Large numbers of adults create a nuisance and also leave "fly specks" on leaves and pots. As with fungus gnats, there are few people who would appreciate receiving these insects along with their plants.

Pest management
Detection. Adults are attracted to yellow traps, so these can be used as monitoring tools. Horizontal traps seem to be more effective than vertical traps. Use them in the same way as for fungus gnats. Shore flies often appear after fungus gnats begin to decline later in the crop, after algae populations have increased.

Physical and cultural control. Shore fly control is accomplished by eliminating large areas of algae with either physical (irrigation mat covers) or chemical (bromine, quaternary ammonium salts) methods.

Pesticides. There are pesticides that will provide at least some control, but there are few products specifically registered for shore fly control. Pesticide applications against shore flies must be applied to areas other than pots and flats, because these insects are found in areas with algae—on benches, floors, etc.

Biological control. Shore flies offer similar opportunities for biological control as do fungus gnats, but with distinct differences because of where these insects live. Results of applications of nematodes and predatory mites for shore fly control have been more variable than have results against fungus gnats. This may be partially because of the essentially aquatic habitat where shore flies develop. Neither nematodes nor predatory mites can survive well in these environments. Also, the fact that shore flies often develop in areas away from the pots or flats themselves makes targeting the treatments difficult.

This problem was mentioned in connection with insecticides. The microbial pesticide *Bacillus thuringiensis* H-14 (Gnatrol), as with fungus gnat control, has reduced shore fly numbers when applied as a drench. Shore fly larvae are sometimes heavily parasitized by a wasp in the genus *Hexacola*. These wasps invade areas where no harmful pesticides (to the wasp) have been applied. Normally, these invasions occur well after shore fly numbers have increased to the point where they are causing problems. However, if the pesticides used to control fungus gnats and shore flies are harmless to the parasites, this additional control factor can be utilized.

Spider mites _____

Spider mites are among the most common and serious pests of greenhouse crops worldwide. These tiny creatures have a very wide host plant range. Small size, rapid development, and pesticide resistance all contribute to their pest status. The most important spider mite species affecting New Guinea impatiens is *Tetranychus urticae*, the two-spotted spider mite.

Biology
Although both males and females can be found in spider mite populations, females are in the majority. Adult females are about one-fiftieth

inch (0.5 mm) long and are variable in color, ranging from light yellow or green to dark green, straw-brown, and black. Two dark spots are usually visible on either side of the abdomen. Spider mite females lay between 50 and 200 eggs, usually on leaf undersides. Eggs hatch in four to seven days into six-legged larvae. The remaining stages are protonymph, deutonymph, and adult. The total development time for the immature stages is seven to 14 days. The length of time for development from egg to adult depends on temperature, age of plant, plant nutrition, etc. All development usually occurs on undersides of leaves. Spider mites develop extremely high populations during hot, dry conditions. Spider mites produce large amounts of webbing, which is usually visible during moderate to heavy infestations (fig. 14.3, CP 14.5).

In northern latitudes some spider mites will diapause (hibernate) in greenhouses during the winter months. At about the latitude of Chicago, for example, mites begin diapause in November and emerge from diapause in mid-February. Diapausing spider mites are reddish and are sometimes confused with predators or the carmine spider mite. Diapausing mites do not feed and are less susceptible to pesticides. Not all spider mites within a greenhouse will diapause. Some will remain active the entire year.

Economic impact
Heavy spider mite infestations can kill plants or cause severe leaf drop. Mites pierce leaf surfaces with stylet-like mouthparts and suck out cell

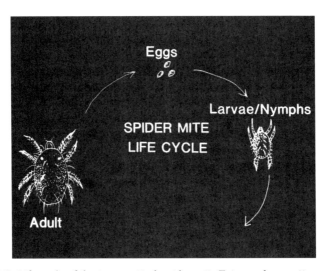

Fig. 14.3. *Life cycle of the two-spotted spider mite* Tetranychus urticae.

contents. Injured areas have no chloroplasts, giving the leaves a chlorotic, stippled look. Webbing produced by the spider mites can cover foliage and flowers.

Pest management

Detection. Monitoring involves frequent (weekly) plant inspections, looking for feeding injury or webbing. A hand lens of 10 or 15X will be very useful in detecting spider mites themselves. On New Guinea impatiens, spider mite infestations are most likely to occur when the mites move onto the plants from adjacent crops. Be especially alert for spider mites during hot, dry weather periods. Trap crops or indicator plants (plants more attractive to spider mites than the main crop) such as bean, may also have some potential as early warning devices.

Cultural and physical control. Spider mite populations are often higher on moisture-stressed plants. Proper irrigation can help keep these high populations from developing. High nitrogen is also associated with severe mite outbreaks. Ensuring that no weeds are growing within the production area, or immediately around it, is another pest management tool. Try and keep workers from moving from known spider mite-infested areas to areas without them, because mites can disperse by clinging to clothing. Visit known spider-mite-infested areas last.

Pesticides. Frequent pesticide applications are required to control spider mites. When using pesticides, make at least two applications, about five days apart, to significantly reduce a spider mite population. Application technique is important, because most mites will be found on undersides of leaves. A New Guinea impatiens crop will present special problems for applicators because of foliage thickness. Some pyrethroid insecticides can stimulate spider mite reproduction and/or cause the mites to become more active, forming additional colonies in other areas of a crop.

Biological control. There are several species of predatory mites used on greenhouse and outdoor crops to help manage spider mites. The best known of these predators for greenhouse use is *Phytoseiulus persimilis*. Other species being used include *Mesoseiulus (Phytoseiulus) longipes*, *Neoseiulus (Amblyseius) californicus* and *Galendromus (Typhlodromus) occidentalis*. There are major differences among the species in their abilities to survive in different environmental conditions.

Pesticide management is extremely important if predators are going to be introduced. Many pesticides remain harmful for weeks after application. Predators with some pesticide resistance are available, but this resistance is not broadly based and does not extend to pyrethroid insecticides.

Tarsonemid mites

Mites in this family are very tiny, microscopic animals. The two best-known members of this group for greenhouse crop producers are the cyclamen mite, *Stenotarsonemus pallidus*, and broad mite, *Polyphagotarsonemus latus*. Both species are widely distributed with large host plant ranges. The broad mite has been most often associated with impatiens.

Biology

The general life cycles of both the broad and cyclamen mites are similar. In contrast to spider mites, tarsonemid mites do best in cool, moist environments. The adults are less than 1/100 inch (0.3 mm) long and are colorless or tinted brown. Female cyclamen mites lay eggs on upper leaf surfaces, whereas broad mites lay eggs on undersides of leaves and/or dark, moist places on plants. After two to 11 days eggs hatch into whitish larvae, which develop for three to seven days, and then pass through a quiescent stage and molt into adults. The approximate development time from egg to adult for cyclamen mites is 18 days and for broad mites 10 days (CP 14.6).

Dispersal is often on infested plants or cuttings. Broad mites have been found on winged and non-winged green peach aphids, so insects already in the greenhouse may carry them around.

Economic importance

Tarsonemid mite feeding can distort plant growth, stunt plants, and prevent flowering. A toxin is injected into the plants, causing these varied symptoms. No webbing is produced. Infested plants probably will be unsalable.

Pest management

Detection. Injury caused by tarsonemid mites is the best way to recognize an infestation. They are too small to see without a microscope. Injury symptoms include leaf distortion, stunting, bronzing, and plant death. During the initial symptoms of an infestation, leaves tend to be hardened with the margins rolled underneath. Plant growth distortion, stunting, etc., then occurs as the infestation increases. The symptoms resemble those caused by either pesticide injury, viruses such as impatiens necrotic spot virus (INSV), or nutritional problems. Tarsonemid mite injury symptoms tend to be localized rather than occuring everywhere in the crop.

Physical and cultural control. If only a few plants are affected, the best way to deal with the problem is to remove the affected plants from the planting.

Pesticides. There are a few pesticides registered for broad and cyclamen mite control. Several applications at weekly intervals will be required. Pesticide applications are best used along with plant removal.

Biological control. Very little is known about biological control of tarsonemid mites on greenhouse crops. The predatory mite *Neoseiulus barkeri* has been used with some success against the broad mite in experiments. These predators are also introduced for thrips control.

References

[1]   Gaugler, Randy, and Harry K. Kaya. 1990. *Entomopathogenic nematodes in biological control.* Boca Raton, Fla.: CRC Press.
[2]   Gill, Stanton. 1994. Take control with bio-controls. *Greenhouse Grower* 12(2):20-24.
[3]   Jeppson, Lee R., Hartford H. Keifer, and Edward W. Baker. 1975. The Tarsonemidae. In *Mites injurious to economic plants.* Berkeley: University of California Press.
[4]   Petit, Fred L. 1993. Biological control in the integrated pest management program at The Land. *IOBC Bulletin* 16(2):129-132.
[5]   Powell, C.C., and R.K. Lindquist. 1992. *Ball pest and disease manual.* Batavia, Ill.: Ball Publishing.

CHAPTER 15

Insect Screening

James R. Baker, James A. Bethke, and Edwin A. Shearin

Chemical control of greenhouse pests is becoming increasingly difficult. A reduced arsenal of pesticides due to government regulations and increased pest resistance is threatening the role of chemicals in greenhouse pest management. Costs of developing new pesticides have escalated as have reregistration costs making pesticides more expensive than in the past.

Growers may soon be forced to make major changes in the way they deal with pests. Although pesticides will remain important tools, other methods of suppression incorporated in a comprehensive, integrated pest management approach [12, 19] must be used to slow the buildup of resistance and conserve the usefulness of the dwindling supply of legally registered pesticides. This includes the use of predators, parasitoids, insect-resistant plants, cultural controls (sanitation, proper fertilization, and watering), and physical controls such as insect screening [8, 18]. Indeed, screening is now more cost-effective than in the past [16].

Greenhouses are often plagued by one or more relatively small insect pests. Sealing those portions of the greenhouse open to the external environment with insect screening can effectively prevent insect pests moving into these production areas [19]. Pest exclusion coupled with the introduction of insect-free plants will markedly reduce the need for pesticide applications [1, 2, 9].

Covering greenhouse openings with screening will not necessarily exclude every pest, but screening may help decrease the need for frequent insecticide applications. It is now feasible to fit screens on existing greenhouses, and certainly screening will become a major factor in future greenhouse design [21].

Screening specifications, descriptions ___

With the new popularity of screening as a control measure [12], a variety of new screening materials are available on the market (table 15.1). Screens can be manufactured using a number of different types of materials. However, the most practical for use in greenhouse production are the woven polyethylene and polyester fiber screens. They may not last as long as a metal screen, but they have other benefits. Polyester (polymeric resin fabric) screens have small holes that can exclude small insects, but they break down more quickly in sunlight than do polyethylene (thermoplastic resin) screens. Both can be chemically treated to inhibit structural breakdown, but inhibitors appear to benefit polyethylene more than polyester. Also the greater strand thickness typically used in polyethylene screen manufacture makes them stronger than polyester fabrics.

Styles and types of screening material are constantly changing, and selection of the screen most beneficial to a particular grower requires a well-informed purchaser. Therefore, independent laboratory and field studies at our respective universities have characterized a variety of screen types for their abilities to exclude pest insects and their effects on air flow restriction.

Efficacy of selected screens ___

Most of the serious greenhouse crop pests, such as aphids, leafminers, thrips, and whiteflies, are likely to be excluded by screens with hole sizes smaller than the insects' thoracic width [6, 7]. The thorax is usually the widest and least flexible part of the insect's body. Projecting body parts, such as the legs of aphids and wings of whiteflies, prohibit their ability to penetrate many microscreens (table 15.2). Unlike other insects, aphids hold their wings in an unusual position—perpendicular to and above the abdomen. This characteristic may further inhibit aphids from passing through certain screens.

Some barrier screens that could be used for excluding insect pests were examined (table 15.3). Adult stages of the melon aphid, *Aphis gossypii* Glover; the green peach aphid, *Myzus persicae* (Sulzer); the

TABLE 15.1

Screening materials commercially available

Common name	Source	Description
Polyethylene sheet		
Vispore[a] 400, 1600	Tredegar	Sheet of high-density polyethylene film with formed holes.
Visqueen	Tredegar	Solid sheet film that will not allow any air flow, but can be used as a solid barrier.
Spunbonded filters		
Flybarr	Hygrogardens	An unwoven polyester filter.
Tybar	Reemay	An unwoven polypropylene fabric.
Reemay	Reemay	An unwoven polyethylene fabric.
Polyester woven materials		
Bug Bed 85, 123	NazDar	Regular weave polyester screens with small holes.
Protex 1, 2	Perifleur	Warp net knitted polyester screens. Protex 1 is metalized.
50062-280	Lumite	A 52 x 52 mesh high-density screen with a small hole size.
50094-435	Lumite	2-1-twill weave screen with 42 x 42 mesh.
50060-435	Lumite	A 32 x 32 mesh with relatively large hole size.
Econet L	L.S. Americas	High-density polyethylene fiber with a relatively large hole size and a polyester yarn interwoven.
Econet M	L.S. Americas	A regular weave high-density polyethylene fiber screen.
Econet T	L.S. Americas	High-density polyethylene fiber with a relatively small rectangular hole and a polyester yarn interwoven.
No-Thrip	Green-Tek	A regular weave high-density polyethylene screen with small fiber widths and a relatively small hole size.
Anti-virus Net	Green-Tek	A high-density polyethylene regular weave with large fiber width for strength and longevity.

[a] No longer available.

silverleaf whitefly, *Bemisia argentifolii* Bellows and Perring; the greenhouse whitefly, *Trialeurodes vaporariorum* (Westwood); the western flower thrips, *Frankliniella occidentalis* (Pergande); and the thrips, *Frankliniella minuta* Moulton, were placed in cages designed to test the insects' ability to pass through [7]. Cages were placed in environmental chambers with light and food above the caged insects. In order to reach the attractive sources of light and food, the insects were required to penetrate the barrier screens of the test cages. The number of insects that were able to penetrate the screen in a 24-hour period was recorded (table 15.4).

Berlinger [4] states that using screens in actual practice has proved better than testing in the laboratory. Reduced disease incidence [1, 2, 3, 4, 5], reduced pest population [1, 3, 4, 5, 19], and reduced pesticide

TABLE 15.2

Specifications of selected microscreens (listed from smallest hole width to largest)

Screen	Hole size (width x length) Micrometers	Inches	Longevity (in years [b])	Fiber width [a] Micrometers	Inches [a]
No-Thrip	134 x 134	0.0053 x 0.0053	3	175	0.0069
Bug Bed 123	135 x 135	0.0053 x 0.0053	3	75	0.0030
Econet T	150 x 450	0.0059 x 0.0177	5	175	0.0069
Bug Bed 85	200 x 200	0.0079 x 0.0079	3	112	0.0044
AntiVirus Net	239 x 822	0.0094 x 0.0324	8	300	0.0118
Protex 1	267 x 738[c]	0.0105 x 0.0291	—	—	—
50062-280	296 x 296	0.0117 x 0.0177	5-7	225	0.0089
Protex 2	313 x 511[c]	0.0123 x 0.0201	—	—	—
50094-435	340 x 340	0.0134 x 0.0134	5-7	275	0.0108
Econet M	470 x 470	0.0185 x 0.0185	—	250	0.0098
50060-435	546 x 546	0.0215 x 0.0215	5-7	275	0.0108
Econet L	659 x 659	0.0259 x 0.0259	5	212	0.0083

[a] As determined in the laboratory by microscope.
[b] As determined by the source.
[c] Triangular shaped hole (base x height).

applications [3, 10, 19] have been documented. Demonstration trials comparing the incidence of impatiens necrotic spot virus (tomato spotted wilt virus) on gloxinias, infestation levels of western flower thrips on African violets, and sweet potato whitefly infestation levels on gerbera daisies revealed that Vispore screening worked impressively well.

TABLE 15.3

Average sizes of greenhouse pests (arranged by thorax size, smallest to largest)

Insect pest Common name	Scientific name	Width (micrometers/inches) Thorax [a]	Widest width [b]	Length (micrometers/inches) Head to wing tip
—	*Frankliniella minuta*	145/0.0057	220/0.0087	1,320/0.0520
Western flower thrips	*Frankliniella occidentalis*	215/0.0085	265/0.0104	1,260/0.0496
Silverleaf whitefly	*Bemisia argentifolii*	239/0.0094	565/0.0222	1,070/0.0421
Greenhouse whitefly	*Trialuerodes vaporariorum*	288/0.0113	708/0.0279	1,283/0.0505
Melon aphid	*Aphis gossypii*	355/0.0140	2,394/0.0549	2,369/0.0933
Green peach aphid	*Myzus persicae*	434/0.0171	2,295/0.0904	3,525/0.1270
Citrus leafminer	*Phyllocnistis citrella*	435/0.0171	810/0.0319	2,560/0.1008
Serpentine leafminer	*Liriomyza trifolii*	608/0.0239	850/0.0335	1,775/0.0463

[a] The thorax is measured at its widest point in resting position.
[b] Edges of wings were measured for all whiteflies and leafminers. Body width was measured for thrips. Leg width was measured for aphids.

TABLE 15.4

Average numbers of the following insects passing through tested screens: *Frankliniella minuta* (FM), western flower thrips (WFT), silverleaf whitefly (SLW), greenhouse whitefly (GHW), melon aphid (MA), and the green peach aphid (GPA). Screens are listed from smallest hole width to largest.

Screen	FM	WFT	SLW	GHW	MA	GPA
No-Thrip	10.1	10.0	0.0	0.0	0.0	—
	(115) [a]	(358)	(127)	(158)	(64)	(0)
Bug Bed 123	2.1	8.4	0.0	0.0	0.0	0.0
	(166)	(339)	(160)	(189)	(84)	(12)
Econet T	37.9	20.7	0.1	0.2	0.0	0.0
	(194)	(182)	(177)	(147)	(33)	(11)
Bug Bed 85	43.1	21.0	0.2	0.6	0.0	0.0
	(135)	(300)	(155)	(181)	(65)	(12)
AntiVirus Net	34.5	14.3	0.0	0.4	0.0	0.0
	(256)	(337)	(266)	(210)	(128)	(10)
Protex 1	24.5	12.4	0.4	0.6	0.0	—
	(172)	(358)	(202)	(194)	(59)	(0)
50062-280	30.0	11.4	0.0	0.1	0.0	0.0
	(493)	(332)	(217)	(204)	(88)	(94)
Protex 2	29.0	8.9	0.0	0.5	0.0	—
	(211)	(236)	(200)	(165)	(120)	(0)
50094-435	25.5	20.0	0.0	0.2	0.0	0.0
	(122)	(340)	(388)	(204)	(171)	(88)
Econet M	—	—	3.0	4.0	1.6	0.0
	(0)	(0)	(66)	(72)	(71)	(3)
50060-435	28.6	38.0	6.1	1.3	9.1	0.0
	(147)	(238)	(226)	(204)	(100)	(128)
Econet L	26.8	16.0	7.2	2.5	2.2	—
	(213)	(246)	(169)	(271)	(79)	(0)
Flybarr	—	58.4	65.9	—	44.3	0.0
	(0)	(101)	(0)	(0)	(131)	(83)

[a] Total number of insects tested in cages are in parenthesis.

Essentially, some screening is much better than none [1, 2].

Appreciably less infection by impatiens necrotic spot virus occurred on gloxinia when caged with Vispore 400 even in close proximity to heavily infected plant material. Crop losses due to the virus were greater in the unscreened areas than screened ones. In another case, after two months, gerberas inside cages covered with Vispore 400 or Reemay had significantly fewer whiteflies than those outside the cages [1].

Baker and Jones [1] found that almost twice as many thrips entered unscreened greenhouses compared to the number of thrips entering the screened house (fig. 15.1) and that impatiens necrotic spot virus (tomato spotted wilt virus) occurred first in the unscreened houses causing greater losses. In 1990, Baker and Jones [2] fitted four small

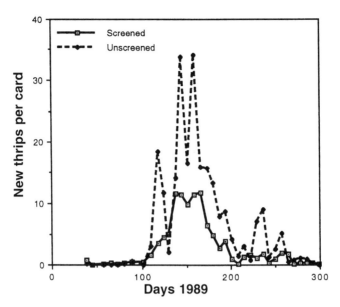

Fig. 15.1. Numbers of thrips caught on sticky cards in the screened house (solid line) and in unscreened houses (dash line).

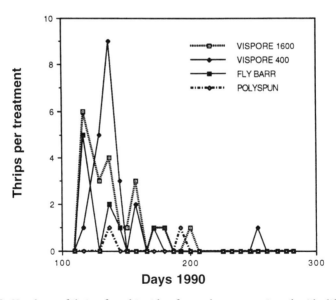

Fig. 15.2. Numbers of thrips found inside of greenhouses equipped with different insect screens.

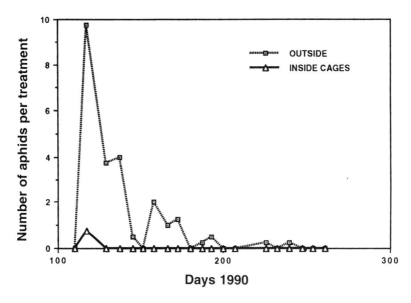

Fig. 15.3. *Numbers of aphids found inside and outside of the screened greenhouses. (The number of aphids found inside the greenhouses was so small that the data were pooled to make the numbers show more clearly.)*

(8 x 8 foot) (2.44 x 2.44 m) greenhouses with Vispore (400 and 1,600 holes per square inch) (62 and 246 holes/cm²), Reemay (spunbonded polyester), and Flybarr (reinforced spunbonded polyester). All of the screening materials were effective in excluding thrips (fig. 15.2) and aphids (fig. 15.3).

Proper selection of screening ⎯⎯⎯⎯

The first and most important question is: What are the most serious insect pests in the crop that need to be excluded [5, 6, 8, 13, 14, 20]? Once this has been decided, a screen must be chosen with the appropriate hole size to exclude those pests [6, 7]. For instance, screens with larger hole sizes can exclude the serpentine leaf mining fly, *Liriomyza trifolii*, but the smaller western flower thrips is only excluded by a much smaller screen hole size.

If the western flower thrips is the only pest of concern, a slightly larger screen than one needed for total exclusion may be enough. However, if the reason for excluding thrips is to prevent the transmission of tomato spotted wilt virus and impatiens necrotic spot virus, then nearly complete exclusion is necessary, and screens with smaller hole sizes are essential. Although it may seem advantageous to purchase and use screens with the smallest hole size, there are tradeoffs involved. As the screen hole size decreases, the effort to move air through it increases, and greater screening area is required to maintain adequate air flow.

When exhaust fans are running, a noticeable pressure drop occurs inside the greenhouse. Growers notice that the doors are harder to open, and gusts of air whoosh through opened doors as the greenhouse pressure equalizes with the outdoor pressure.

The drop in pressure inside a greenhouse is called static pressure. If one end of a U-shaped tube filled with liquid (manometer) is inserted into the greenhouse, the level of the liquid inside the house rises as the fans come on and static pressure drops (like sucking soda up a straw). Static pressure is usually measured in tenths or hundredths of inches of water. If the static pressure drop is too great, the fans will not be able to move enough air to properly ventilate the greenhouse and will use excessive power [15] or the plastic film covering may pull loose from the staples.

In either case, the greenhouse will overheat during hot, bright summer days. Johnson [11] suggested not using screening materials that create a static pressure over 0.05 inch (1.3 mm) of water at 250 feet (75 m) per minute air velocity. Sase and Christianson [21] recommend 0.032 inch (0.8 mm) of water pressure drop for clean screening materials, and the total pressure drop should not exceed 0.1 inch (2.5 mm) with dirty screening. In North Carolina, we rarely measure pressure drops in unscreened greenhouses above 0.03 inch (0.8 mm). We agree with Sase and Christianson [21] that a pressure drop of 0.1 inch (2.5 mm) should be the maximum for a screened greenhouse.

For determining static pressure drop, an inexpensive manometer such as the Dwyer Mark II, Model 25 is a good value, but you must make sure that the flexible tubes are free of any drops of liquid, that the tubes are not kinked, and that the tube-to-manometer connections are tight. Otherwise, you may obtain inaccurate measurements. The Mark II, Model 25, is available from Dwyer Instruments, Inc. (P.O. Box 373, Michigan City, Ind. 46360).

To check if a greenhouse is adequately ventilated, estimate the amount of air moving through the greenhouse with all the fans running and all unscreened doors and windows closed. Use a manometer to measure the difference in static pressure in the structure with the fans shut off and with the fans running. Use that pressure drop when consulting a fan specification chart given in various greenhouse supply catalogs. Look across the line from the model of each fan at the volume of air moved by that fan at that static pressure drop.

Interpolate between the 0.0 inch (0 mm), 0.05 inch (1.3 mm) and 0.1 inch (2.5 mm) volumes given for the various fans and motors. (For example, if the pressure drop is 0.025 inch [0.6 mm], that is halfway between 0 inch [0 mm] and 0.05 inch [1.3 mm]. Thus the volume of air moved by the fans would be about halfway between the volumes given for 0 inch [0 mm] and 0.05 inch [1.3 mm]). Add all the volumes of each fan together.

By dividing the total volume by the number of square feet (square meters) of the greenhouse, the quotient should equal an air exchange of 11 to 17 cubic feet per minute per square foot (0.33 to 0.51 m^3 per minute per m^2) (recommended by Willits [22]). This recommendation is higher than Nelson's recommendation [17] of 8 cubic feet per minute per square foot (0.24 m^3 per minute per m^2). If the volume of air exchange is below 8 cubic feet (0.24 m^3) per minute, the structure is likely to overheat during hot, bright weather. If your total volume of air exchange is well above 17 cubic feet per minute per square foot (0.51 m^3 per minute per m^2), the selection of screening fabrics may be limited, and you may have excessive transpiration and evaporation.

Adding an exclusion screen ——————————

Caution: *Any screening retrofitted to a greenhouse without other changes will decrease air flow and increase greenhouse temperatures.*

The steps outlined in this section should help avoid serious ventilation problems. *An additional consideration:* if you start with pests already inside or bring pests in on plants or clothing, screening will keep them inside. Other management practices can directly affect the efficiency of screening such as a pest management strategy—quarantine new plant material, wear red, brown, black, or dark gray clothing, and carefully inspect new plant material to avoid introducing pests into the screened greenhouse.

Pest exclusion structures do not need to be constructed of heavy timbers nor do they necessarily need to be elaborate. Screening fabrics are relatively light and strong and do not require much support. Most retrofitted screens are placed outside the ventilation windows and entry doors. Pest exclusion will be much more effective if greenhouse workers can be trained to keep the doors closed as much as practical, especially during ventilation.

When building an exclusion structure, be sure to incorporate easy access to the inside to facilitate cleaning of the screening material. Make it easy to clean as clean fabrics have less resistance to air flow. According to D.H. Willits [personal communication], as resistance to air flow increases, the volume of air moved by a fan decreases proportionally to a certain point. At that point there is a sudden and drastic decrease in air volume moved. The fan then churns uselessly expending energy, but moving little or no air. It is a good idea to have a manometer convenient to check static pressure in each screened greenhouse on a regular basis, especially in hot, dry weather when screening is likely to be fouled by dust.

Do not clean the screening material while the ventilation fans are running! Water can fill the openings in the material by capillary action and completely stop air flow. On a hot day, temperatures inside the greenhouse would rise swiftly, and unscreened windows and doorways would have to be opened to prevent heat damage to plants before the water in the screen evaporates. Opening the windows and doors to prevent heat damage defeats the whole exclusion effort.

Steps for retrofitting

Step 1.   Measure the pressure drop inside the greenhouse using a manometer: _____ inches (mm). (If the pressure drop is close to 0.1 inch [2.5 mm] without screening, consider enlarging the ventilation window. If the fans stay the same, enlarging the ventilation windows will reduce static pressure.)

Step 2.   Subtract the pressure drop in Step 1 from 0.1 inch (2.5 mm). (Or, 0.1 inch minus _____ inch from Step 1 equals _____ inches.)
This difference is a guide to how much additional resistance to air movement can be tolerated. For example, if your pressure drop in Step 1 is 0.025 inch (0.6 mm), then you can use a screen that adds up to an additional 0.075 inch (1.9 mm) of pressure drop without exceeding our maximum recommended pressure drop.

Step 3.   Now calculate an estimated total air movement at 0.1 inch (2.5 mm) by consulting a fan specification chart given in various greenhouse supply catalogs. Determine the volume of air moved by each fan by looking across the line from the fan model to the static pressure drop (from Step 1). Then add all the fan volumes together: _____ cfm (m^3/minute). (Now you can check if the volume of air that will move through the house after screening exceeds Nelson's [17] or Willits' [22] recommendations. If not, your houses may become too hot during July and August. Consider using larger motors on the fans or adding additional fans.)

Suggested air exchange per minute:

Nelson's:

> Greenhouse area x 8 cfm (0.24 m^3/minute) = _____ cfm (m^3/minute).

Willits' low:

> Greenhouse area x 11 cfm (0.33 m^3/minute) = _____ cfm (m^3/minute).

Willits' high:

> Greenhouse area x 17 cfm (0.51 m^3/minute) = _____ cfm (m^3/minute).

Step 4. Calculate the area of the ventilation windows. Total ventilation window area (length x width) = _____ sq. ft. (m^2).

Step 5. Calculate the approach velocity of the air moving through the ventilation windows. Total air volume after screening (Step 3) divided by the ventilation window area (Step 4) = _____ ft./min. (m/min).

Step 6. Find the approach velocity from Step 5 on the horizontal axis (fig. 15.4 to 15.6). Those fabrics whose curves do not exceed the pressure drop level (calculated in Step 2) at this approach velocity (from Step 5) can be used directly over the ventilation window. If the resistance curve for the fabric you wish to use exceeds the pressure drop level (from Step 2), then move to the left along the velocity axis until you reach a velocity for that fabric at which the resistance does not exceed Step 2 pressure drop. Divide the velocity through the ventilation window (from Step 5) by the lower velocity on the chart. This quotient is the number you must multiply the area of the ventilation window by to arrive at the required area of the screening material = multiplication factor:

> _____.

Origin of the resistance curves

The resistance curves presented in figures 15.4 to 15.6 were generated in a small wind tunnel. Air was pulled through the 8-inch metal wind tunnel by a 0.75-hp squirrel cage fan. Velocity was measured with a Pitot tube using a Dwyer Mark II, Model 25, manometer. A Dwyer Durablock Model 102.5 manometer was used to measure the pressure drop across the fabric under test. The fabrics were stretched on stiff foam forms and introduced into the wind stream by bolting them between air-tight flanges. Most of the fabrics we tested are shown in figures 15.4 to 15.6. Each fabric was tested at a number of pressure drops and velocities. The curves presented in these figures were obtained by fitting fabric pressure drop versus air velocity data for each fabric to a second degree polynomial equation.

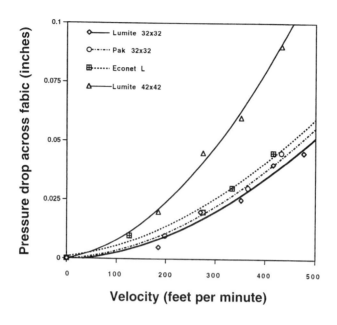

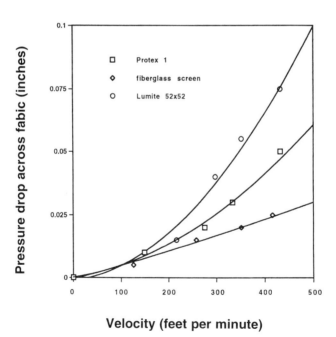

Fig. 15.4A and 15.4B. *Resistance factors for seven screening materials with relatively low resistance to air flow shown as functions of velocity in feet per minute and static pressure in inches of water.*

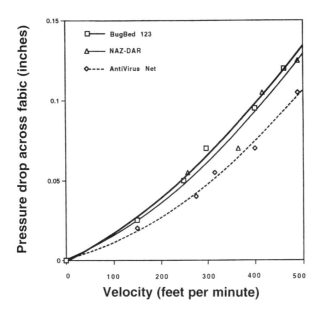

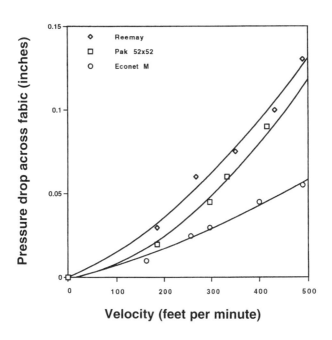

Fig. 15.5A and 15.5B. *Resistance factors for six screening materials with moderate resistance to air flow shown as functions of velocity in feet per minute and static pressure in inches of water.*

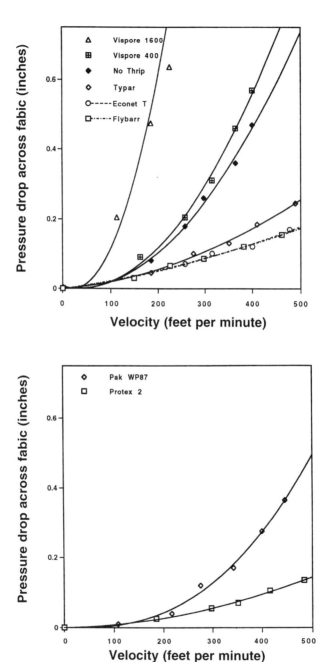

Fig. 15.6A and 15.6B. Resistance factors for eight screening materials with high resistance to air flow shown as functions of velocity in feet per minute and static pressure in inches of water.

Use of the second degree polynomial equation rather than the theo-retically predicted "Pressure Drop = Resistance Factor x Velocity Squared" function provided a better fit both to our data and to data published for some of the fabrics. (For some reason, the Pak WP87 data points had to be fitted to a third degree polynomial equation.)

Although our results do not agree perfectly with other published results, we believe these curves are within reasonable limits of error. It is very difficult to measure velocities between 0 and 100 feet (30 m) per minute, but it is unlikely that most greenhouses can be properly venti-lated at air exchange velocities of less than 100 feet (30 m) per minute. Our advice is to "round up" when rounding off and slightly overbuild rather than have a screen that works well except in late July and August.

Screening in production greenhouses —

Growers may choose to economize by selecting specific crops or areas to screen with the more effective and costly screens and design. Plants highly susceptible to tomato spotted wilt virus and impatiens necrotic spot virus could be isolated from the rest of the greenhouse environ-ment by screening.

The impact of using insect screens on greenhouse function can be significant. Insect screens reduce air flow through greenhouses and may, depending on position, reduce light levels. Screens must be kept clean to minimize reductions in air flow and light levels.

If greenhouses are to be retrofitted with screen barriers, modifica-tions may be made in order to maintain adequate air flow and cooling. Such modifications may include enlarging or physically modifying the vents, adding more vents, and adding additional fans or cooling sys-tems. Prior to installing screen barriers, growers are strongly urged to consult their nearest horticultural farm advisor, Cooperative Extension agent, an environmental engineer, or their greenhouse manufacturer for information regarding the impact of pest exclusion barriers upon greenhouse ventilation.

References ————————————

[1]   Baker, J.R., and R.K. Jones. 1989. Screening as part of insect and disease management in the greenhouse. *N.C. Flower Grower's Bulletin.* Dec. 34(6):1-9.

[2]   ———. 1990. An update on screening as part of insect and disease management in the greenhouse. *N.C. Flower Grower's Bulletin.* Dec. 35(6):1-3.

[3]   Berlinger, M.J., Alla M. Gol'berg, R. Dahan, and S. Cohen. 1983. The use of plastic covering to prevent the spread of Tomato Yellow Leaf Curl virus in greenhouses. *Hassadeh* 63(9):1862-1865.

[4]   Berlinger, M.J., S. Leblush-Mordechl, D. Fridja, and N. Mor. 1992. *The effect of types of greenhouse screens on the presence of western flower thrips: A preliminary study.* Agricultural Research Organization. Volcani Center, No. 3716-E. Bet Dagan, Israel.

[5]   Berlinger, M.J., S. Mordechl, A. Leeper. 1991. Application of screens to prevent whitefly penetration into greenhouses in the Mediterranean basin. In *Proceedings.* Working Group Integrated Control in Protecting Crops under Mediterranean Climate. Bull. IOBC/WPRS, 1191/14/5. 29 Sept. 2-Oct. 1991. Alassio, Italy.

[6]   Bethke, J.A. 1994. Screening for the exclusion of insect pests: the first step. *Greenhouse Manager* April, Vol. 13(1):34-38.

[7]   Bethke, J.A., and T.D. Paine. 1991. Screen hole size and barriers for exclusion of insect pests of glasshouse crops. *J. Entomol. Sci.* 26(1):169-177.

[8]   Bethke, J.A., and R.A. Redak. 1994. New screens with potential for whitefly exclusion. *California Florists.* January-March.

[9]   Bethke, J.A., R.A. Redak, and T.D. Paine. 1994. Screening material evaluated for pest exclusion in protected culture. *California Agriculture.* May-June: 48(3):37-40.

[10]   Hall, J. 1992. *The poinsettia: special whitefly edition.* Vol. 3. Encinitas, California. Poinsettia Growers Association.

[11]   Johnson, G.B. 1990. *Insect barrier.* Coolair Bull. 90-6. Jacksonville, Fla.: Amer. Coolair Bull.

[12]   Mears, D.R. 1990. Screening for insect control. *Horticultural Engineering Newsletter* January 5(1):6.

[13]   ———. 1990. Screening for insect control. *Horticultural Engineering Newsletter* March 5(2)5-6.

[14]   ———. 1991. Screen out bugs...without knocking out your ventilation system: Part II. *Greenhouse Grower.* November: 52-58.

[15]   National Greenhouse Manufacturers Association. 1993. *Recommendations for using insect screens in greenhouse structures.* Addendum to NGMA ventilation and cooling standards.

[16]   Neal, K. 1992. Screen pests out, reduce chemical use. *Greenhouse Manager.* April: 54.

[17]   Nelson, P.V. 1985. *Greenhouse operation and management.* 3rd ed. Virginia: Reston Pub.

[18]   Parrella, M.P., and V.P. Jones. 1987. Development of integrated pest management strategies in floricultural crops. *Bull. Entomol. Soc. Am.* 33:28-34.

[19]   Robb, K.L., and M.P. Parrella. 1988. Chemical and non-chemical control of western flower thrips. Ed. A.D. Ali, J. Hall, and M.P. Parrella. In *Proceedings.* Fourth Conference on Insect and Disease Management on Ornamentals. Kansas City, Mo.

[20]   Roberts, W.J. 1992. Screening for insect control. *Horticultural Engineering Newsletter.* July 7(4):2-5.

[21]   Sase, S., and L.L. Christianson. 1990. Screening greenhouses, some engineering considerations. Ed. T.D. Carpenter. In *Proceedings.* American Greenhouse Vegetable Growers Association Conference. Jacksonville, Fla.

[22]   Willits, D.H. 1993. Greenhouse cooling. *N.C. Flower Grower's Bulletin.* 38(2):15-18.

CHAPTER 16

IPM Programs

Jan Hall

There are a number of potential pests of New Guinea impatiens, but using an integrated pest management (IPM) program will help you produce a clean crop free of insect, mite, and disease pests. The first step in developing an IPM program is to recognize and understand the pests most likely to attack the crop. It's important to know when and where the pests are most likely to occur, their biology, and to recognize the damage they can cause. The more knowledge you have about the enemy the better you will be able to plan your strategy for control. Chapters 12 through 14 provide detailed information about the most important New Guinea impatiens pests. By understanding the potential pests, you can develop an IPM program to manage them.

An IPM program means just that, integrating various control measures into a complete program. You need to evaluate the various possible components and determine how each can be implemented in your greenhouse. IPM program components may include: sanitation, exclusion, environmental/cultural practices, monitoring, biological and chemical controls. Putting together all these pieces will give better control than relying solely on one control method, such as chemical control.

As I go through the various components of an IPM program for New Guinea impatiens I'll mention those components that have been beneficial to us at the Paul Ecke Ranch. Our situation is a little different from most growers in that we produce New Guinea impatiens cuttings rather than a blooming product; however, the same IPM principles apply.

Sanitation ───────────────────────────

Begin good sanitation practices before the New Guinea impatiens arrive and continue these practices throughout the crop. The greenhouse and all equipment used with the crop (benches, knives, hands, etc.) should be cleaned and disinfected with a product such as Clorox, Green-Shield, or Physan 20. Keep the greenhouse free of weeds and plant debris as they can serve as hosts for insect and disease pests. Ideally, the greenhouse should be emptied of all plant material, disinfected, and kept closed up for seven to 14 days before the start of the New Guinea impatiens crop to avoid transferring pests from previous crops.

Some pests can survive in the absence of a plant host. For example, western flower thrips pupate in soil. The pupal stages could occur in the crop pots, debris on bench tops, or even the soil under benches. Robb [4] showed that WFT take two to four days to pupate at 80F (26C). A longer time is required at cooler temperatures, and there is minimal survival of WFT pupae at constant temperatures below 50F (10C).

Winter and spring temperatures in much of the country will enable growers to eliminate WFT pupae by keeping their clean, empty greenhouses at constant cold temperatures prior to the arrival of the New Guinea impatiens crop. Our climate in southern California does not allow us to use cold temperatures to kill WFT pupae. However, we can take advantage of hot temperatures to speed up any WFT pupation in the soil under the benches and starve the emerging adults in the absence of a crop.

Steam all native soil and sand used for the potting mix, or use a clean, ready-to-use soilless mix. Keep the end of the hose off the ground to avoid introducing soilborne pests to the crop. The removal of plant debris on a daily basis will help prevent the buildup of Botrytis populations. Good sanitation practices should be a routine part of your greenhouse operation.

Exclusion ───────────────────────────

The best way to avoid a pest buildup is to stop the pests from entering the greenhouse. Inspect all incoming plant material. If 100% of all incoming plants cannot be inspected, randomly check a minimum of 10% to 15% of the plants in each shipment. Insects and diseases will generally occur in a sporadic rather than uniform distribution, so be sure to check the shipments thoroughly. It is much easier to remove a few leaves or cuttings at the door rather than treating the entire crop once the pests have become established.

WFT carrying tomato spotted wilt virus or impatiens necrotic spot virus may transmit them to healthy New Guinea impatiens within 30 minutes of feeding. Wherever possible, use insect screening barrier to exclude WFT in locations where populations exist outdoors. There are several considerations before starting a screening project, such as the level of control needed, production requirements, target pests to be excluded, and compensation for reduced air flow.

The most effective strategy for insect control is 100% exclusion. However, this can be difficult to achieve and may not be warranted for some operations. In greenhouses where the thrips are only entering the greenhouse from a particular spot, it might be feasible to use partial screening. If sticky card counts show that the thrips are only entering the greenhouse through the doors and vents on the side with the prevailing wind, screening any openings on this side may result in significant reductions in thrips populations and still minimize the cost of screening.

You should also consider production requirements prior to beginning a screening project. In order for barrier screening to work, greenhouse access must be limited. Screening might not be practical for a retail operation with a constant influx of traffic. Even in a production greenhouse, it is important to consider ways to maintain the exclusion system's integrity while still allowing production procedures. We have found that including the packing area within our screened environment allows packing ease without compromising our exclusion system.

The type of screen needed for pest exclusion depends on the pests to be excluded. The screen chosen must have holes small enough to exclude the smallest pests of concern. If thrips are excluded, the other insect and mite pests of New Guinea impatiens will also be excluded. According to Bethke and Paine [1], the maximum hole size to exclude WFT is 192 microns. If the screen has holes small enough to exclude insects, it will also reduce the air flow into the greenhouse. Increasing the surface area for the vents or adding fans will help to compensate for this air flow reduction. See Chapter 15 on Insect Screening.

Greenhouses at the Paul Ecke Ranch are cooled by natural ventilation. We have installed the screen materials gutter-to-gutter inside the greenhouses to increase air flow. Horizontal air flow fans help circulate the air. Inside installation also protects the screens, helps keep them clean, and increases their longevity. The screens are inspected on a regular basis, and any rips are immediately repaired. We have limited the access to our greenhouses, and each entrance contains a double door to avoid thrips blowing into the greenhouse as doors are opened. In addition, employees must put on clean suits over their street clothing to keep thrips from entering the greenhouse on clothing.

Environmental/cultural practices ———

A grower's environmental and cultural practices will affect pest management. Adequate crop spacing, avoiding wetting foliage during irrigation, watering early in the day, heating and venting the greenhouse at sunset, and the use of horizontal air movement fans will help prevent the buildup of Botrytis blight and other disease pests. Conditions that stress the crop will encourage pest problems. For example, New Guinea impatiens are very sensitive to overfertilization. High salt levels in the potting medium (2.0 millimhos/cm or higher) can predispose the crop to root and stem rots. Once a New Guinea impatiens crop is established and actively growing, it'll require frequent watering; however, overwatering the crop prior to establishment will result in soggy media and increased risk of fungus gnat development. (See Chapter 4 on Feeding and Watering.)

New Guinea impatiens cultivars may differ in susceptibility to various pests. This type of information can be gathered as a grower works with the crop and will be helpful in making future crop decisions such as which cultivars to grow and each cultivar's placement within the greenhouse. For example, cultivars most resistant to Botrytis blight should be placed in the areas with the poorest air movement.

A grower may want to place the cultivars most susceptible to a particular pest together to make control measures more convenient. Growers should consider the potential pests of surrounding crops that may move onto the New Guinea impatiens. Avoid landscaping the area surrounding the greenhouse with plants that might attract pests to the New Guinea impatiens. We also avoid the use of blue in and around the greenhouses as this color attracts WFT.

Monitoring ————————————

Monitoring or scouting should be a cornerstone of any IPM program. Regular monitoring will enable a grower to track pest occurrence and location. Monitoring for New Guinea impatiens should consist of both sticky cards and plant samples. Some growers use blue sticky cards as they're attractive to WFT, however, we use yellow sticky cards because they not only attract WFT, but also fungus gnats and shore flies which might be in the crop. The sticky cards should be hung in a grid pattern every 1,000 square feet (90 m^2) just above the crop. Sticky cards should be checked at least once a week and changed whenever they become dirty or are no longer sticky. These cards are the best monitoring tool for WFT as thrips tend to hide in flowers and apical tissue.

In addition to sticky cards, the crop itself should be randomly inspected each week. It's important to check plants from all sections of the greenhouse and to check roots, stems, and foliage for insect, mite, and disease pests. Walk down each aisle and randomly select plants from both the aisle and the center of the benches. In addition to the random inspection, any plants that appear abnormal will require a thorough inspection. For example, yellow foliage might signal a nutritional disorder, root or stem rot, spider mite injury, etc.

Once the New Guinea impatiens crop begins to flower, check for thrips in the blooms by blowing gently into the flower. The warm air will excite any thrips, and they'll be more visible as they move. Some growers will flag a few plants once a pest has been found and use them as indicator plants. These flagged plants can then be checked after a biological or chemical control has been applied to see if the control measure was effective.

Good records for both monitoring results and control measures allow a grower to determine trends and the most effective controls for each pest. Some growers include environmental information as well. The crop should be monitored on the same day each week to give consistent records. It's important that a scout be well trained in pest identification, pest biology, as well as the biology of any biological control agents used. In addition to formal scouting, take time to train all employees about the potential New Guinea impatiens pests. Employees handle the crop on a frequent basis and may find pests missed by random scouting.

Biological control

Biological control can be an important component of a New Guinea impatiens IPM program, but it should be used in conjunction with other control measures. Before beginning to use biological control agents, it is important to understand not only the crop's potential pests but also the control agents' biology. TSWV and INSV complicate the use of biological controls, as even low WFT levels can be devastating if these viruses are present in the greenhouse. We currently apply biological control agents for fungus gnat control, use different IPM components to control WFT, and pesticides to control other pests on New Guinea impatiens.

Before beginning a biological control program, make lists of the pests to be controlled, the potential control agents, the pesticides used in the greenhouse during the last two to three months, and the pesticides that are expected to be used in the future. Some pesticides have a long residual effect on biological control agents.

When selecting the best control agents for the job, it's also important to review the environmental conditions in the greenhouse (temperature, relative humidity, light intensity and duration), and make sure that they are acceptable for the control agents. For example, *Orius tristicolor*, which feeds on thrips as well as aphids and spider mites, goes into a diapause or resting stage under short day conditions. This probably wouldn't be the best agent to use for thrips control during winter and early spring conditions unless supplemental lighting is provided.

Biological control agent suppliers may be good sources of information about their control agents. The selection of biological control

■■■ TABLE 16.1 ■■■

Biological control agents used on greenhouse grown floriculture crops

Pest	Biological control agent
Aphids	*Aphidius colemani*
	Aphidius matricariae (aphid parasite)
	Aphidoletes aphidimyza (aphid predator)
	Chrysopa spp., *Chrysoperla* spp. (lacewings)
	Hippodamia convergens (ladybugs)
Fungus gnats	*Bacillus thuringiensis* (H-14, Gnatrol)
	Heterorhabditis bacteriophora
	Hypoaspis miles (predatory mite)
	Steinernema carpocapsae (exhibit)
	Steinernema feltiae
Shore flies	*Bacillus thuringiensis* H-14 (Gnatrol)
Spider mites	*Amblyseius (Neoseiulus) californicus*
	Amblyseius fallacis
	Phytoseiulus (Mesoseiulus) longipes
	Phytoseiulus persimilis
	Typhlodromus (Galendromus) occidentalis
Thrips	*Amblyseius barkeri*
	Amblyseius cucumeris
	Orius tristicolor (minute pirate bug)

agents available is increasing rapidly. As shown in table 16.1, there are several biological control agents available for each of the insect and mite pests commonly found on New Guinea impatiens [2]. Using more than one agent may give better control than relying on just one.

Determine pest thresholds which are the maximum allowable levels of the various pests, in advance. The control agents should be applied to low levels of pest populations or on a preventative basis. Keep in mind that biological control agents tend to control pests more slowly than pesticides. Monitoring is crucial for well-timed releases, evaluating the program, and adjusting release rates. Incoming shipments of biological control agents should also be monitored for viability.

If pesticides are required, select chemicals with minimal effect on the biological control agents. Consider spot sprays and timing the applications to minimize impact on biological control agents. Compatibility charts are available from suppliers of biological controls.

Chemical control _____

Chemical control is still an important IPM component for most New Guinea impatiens growers. It is becoming more and more difficult to use pesticides due to increased government regulations and reentry intervals, pesticide resistance, and removal of pesticides from the ornamentals market. Use of the IPM components previously discussed will help minimize the need to apply pesticides. Monitoring after each application will help evaluate pesticide coverage, effectiveness, and the best timing for future applications.

Table 16.2 lists the fungicides federally labeled for use on New Guinea impatiens, and Table 16.3 lists the insecticides and miticides. Before applying a pesticide for the first time or when making an application to a new cultivar, treat a few plants and evaluate for phytotoxicity for three to five days before treating the entire crop. Whenever possible, apply pesticide prior to bloom, as New Guinea impatiens flowers are more susceptible than foliage to pesticide injury. Applications made to plants under stress from water, temperature, or nutrition are also likely to injure. Check the pesticide label and application equipment directions for any specific instructions on recommended environmental conditions.

Several pesticides are available to control each of the New Guinea impatiens pests. Take advantage of rotating pesticides from different chemical classes to delay resistance. For insect and mite control, rotate chemicals approximately every one to two pest generations.

TABLE 16.2

New Guinea impatiens federal disease control chart—1994

Disease/causal organism	Common name	Product name	Formulation	Dose/ 100 gallons	Comments
Botrytis blight/ *Botrytis cinerea*	Chlorothalonil	Exotherm Termil	Fumigator	3.5 oz./1,000 sq. ft.	Thermal dust. Apply at 7-day intervals to foliage only. Don't apply when greenhouse temperatures are above 75F (24C).
	Copper complex	Phyton 27	21.36%	13-15 fl. oz.	Foliar spray as needed.
	Iprodione	Chipco 26019	50WP	16-32 oz.	Foliar spray at 7- to 14-day intervals.
	Thiophanate-methyl	Cleary's 3336	F	10 fl. oz.	Foliar spray at 10- to 14-day intervals.
		Cleary's 3336	50WP	12 oz.	Foliar spray at 7- to 10-day intervals.
		Domain	FL	10 fl. oz.	Foliar spray at 10- to 14-day intervals.
		Fungo Flo	F	10 fl. oz.	Foliar spray at 10- to 14-day intervals.
		SysTec 1998	F	10 fl. oz.	Foliar spray at 10- to 14-day intervals.
	Thiophanate-methyl plus Mancozeb	Zyban	75W	24 oz.	Foliar spray at 7-day intervals.
		Duosan	75W	24 oz.	Foliar spray at 7-day intervals.
	Vinclozolin	Ornalin	FL	8-16 fl. oz.	Foliar spray at 10- to 14-day intervals. Also labeled for thermal fogger use.
Pythium root rot/ *Pythium* **spp.**	Etridiazole	Terrazole	5G	10 oz./cu. yd.	Incorporate in potting mix.
		Terrazole	35WP	4-6 oz.	Drench at 4- to 8-week intervals.
		Truban	25EC	3-4 fl. oz.	Drench at 4- to 8-week intervals.
		Truban	5G	5 oz./cu. yd.	Incorporate into potting mix.
		Truban	30WP	4-6 oz.	Drench at 4- to 8-week intervals.
	Etridiazole plus	Banrot	8G	8 oz./cu. yd.	Incorporate in potting mix.
	Thiophanate-methyl	Banrot	40W	4-8 oz.	Drench at 4- to 8-week intervals.
	Fosetyl-Al	Chipco Aliette	80WDG	20-64 oz.	Spray to wet using no more than 400 gal./acre. Don't apply more than once every 30 days.
		Chipco Aliette	80WP	20-64 oz.	Spray to wet using no more than 400 gal./acre. Don't apply more than once every 30 days.

TABLE 16.2 continued

Disease/causal organism	Common name	Product name	Formulation	Dose/100 gallons	Comments
Pythium root rot/ *Pythium* spp. (cont.)	*Gliocladium virens* GL	GlioGard	G	1-1.5 lb./cu. yd. of soil	Incorporate in potting mix and wait one day before transplanting. Don't use with other fungicides.
	Metalaxyl	Subdue	2E	0.5-2 fl. oz.	Drench at 1- to 2-month intervals. Don't apply 1.5 to 2 fl. oz. more than once every 6 weeks.
		Subdue	2G	15-30 oz./1,000 sq. ft. or 4-8 oz./ cu. yd. of soil	Drench at 1- to 2-month intervals. Don't apply 22 to 30 oz. more than once every 6 weeks.
	Propamocarb	Banol	66.5%	20 fl. oz.	Drench at 3- to 6-week intervals.
Rhizoctonia stem rot and web blight/ *Rhizoctonia solani*	Etridiazole plus	Banrot	8G	8 oz./cu. yd.	Incorporate in potting mix.
	Thiophanate-methyl	Banrot	40W	4-8 oz.	Drench at 4- to 8-week intervals.
	Gliocladium virens GL	GlioGard	G	1-1.5 lb./cu. yd. of soil	Incorporate in potting mix and wait one day before transplanting. Don't use with other fungicides.
	Iprodione	Chipco 26019	50WP	16-32 oz.	Apply as a spray every 7 to 14 days.
	Quintozene	Terraclor	75W	4-8 oz.	Apply at time of transplant. One repeat application can be made 4 to 6 weeks later.
		Turfcide	10% G	15 lb./1,000 sq. ft.	Apply over soil surface then mix thoroughly.
	Thiophanate-methyl	Cleary's 3336	F	20 fl. oz.	Drench at 2- to 4-week intervals.
		Cleary's 3336	50WP	12 oz.	Drench at 2- to 3-week intervals.
		Domain	FL	20 fl. oz.	Drench at 2- to 4-week intervals.
		Fungo Flo	F	20 fl. oz.	Drench at 2- to 4-week intervals.
		SysTec 1998	F	20 fl. oz.	Drench at 2- to 4-week intervals.
	Triflumizole	Terraguard	50WP	4-8 oz.	Drench at 3- to 4-week intervals.

E = Emulsifiable concentrate
EC = Emulsifiable concentrate

F = Flowable
FL = Flowable

G = Granular
W = Wettable powder

WDG = Water dispersible granules
WP = Wettable powder

Read and follow the instructions on the label before using any pesticide. Some fungicides are not available in all states. Before using a fungicide on the crop for the first time or on a new cultivar, treat a few plants and check for phytotoxicity.

TABLE 16.3

New Guinea impatiens federal insect and mite control chart—1994

Pest	Pesticide class	Common name	Product name	Formulation	Dose/100 gallons	Comments
Aphids	Botanical	Azadirachtin	Azatin	EC	12-16 fl. oz.	Acts as an insect growth regulator. Apply at 10-21 fl. oz./acre.
		Nicotine	Margosan-O	L	40-80 fl. oz.	Acts as an insect growth regulator.
			Nicotine	Smoke	12 oz./20,000 cu. ft.	Foliage and blooms must be dry at the time of application.
		Pyrethrum	PT 170 (X-Clude)	ME	50-200 fl. oz.	Direct spray to open blooms may cause petal drop.
			PT 1100	Aerosol	1 lb./3,000 sq. ft.	May spot open blooms.
			PT 1600A (X-Clude)	ME	5-10 sec./100 sq. ft.	Don't apply to plants in bloom.
	Carbamate	Bendiocarb	Dycarb	76WP	12-20 oz.	
			Turcam	WP	3-6 oz.	Apply at 3-week intervals.
		Methiocarb	PT 1700	Aerosol	1 lb./3,000 sq. ft.	Use 1 lb./1,500 sq. ft. for the control of green peach aphid.
			Grandslam	75WP	1-2 lb.	Apply up to 4 applications per season. Don't apply with foliar fertilizer applications.
		Oxamyl	Oxamyl	10G	60-80 lb./acre or 1.4-1.9 lb./1,000 sq. ft.	
	Chlorinated hydrocarbon	Endosulfan	Thiodan	50WP	16 oz.	
				3EC	21.3 fl. oz.	
				Smoke	6 oz./10,000 cu. ft.	Foliage and blooms must be dry at the time of application.
	Chloronicotinyls	Imidacloprid	Marathon	1G	3 lb./cu. yd. media	Label also gives rates per pot.
	Insect growth regulator	Kinoprene	Enstar	5E	6-20 fl. oz.	Apply at 7- to 14-day intervals.
			Enstar II	5E	3-10 fl. oz.	Apply at 7- to 14-day intervals.
	Insecticidal soap	Insecticidal soap	M-Pede	L	250 fl. oz.	Test for phytotoxicity.
	Organophosphate	Acephate	PT 1300 (Orthene)	Aerosol	1 lb./3,000 sq. ft.	Phytotoxicity has been reported for impatiens.
		Chlorpyrifos	Dursban	50W	8 oz.	For outdoor use only. May cause phytotoxicity.
				L	8 fl. oz.	Phytotoxicity has been reported for impatiens.
			Pageant	DF	8 oz.	
			PT 1325 (DuraGuard)	ME	25-50 fl. oz.	Direct spray to open blooms may cause petal drop.

TABLE 16.3 continued

Pest	Pesticide class	Common name	Product name	Formulation	Dose/100 gallons	Comments
Aphids (cont.)	Organophosphate	Diazinon	PT 1500R (Knox Out)	ME	5-10 sec./100 sq. ft.	May spot petals.
		Dichlorvos	DDVP	Fumigator	5.1 oz./10,000 cu. ft.	Foliage and blooms must be dry at the time of application.
		Sulfotep	Dithio	Smoke	7 oz./20,000 cu. ft.	Foliage and blooms must be dry at the time of application.
			Plantfume 103	Smoke	7 oz./20,000 cu. ft.	Foliage and blooms must be dry at the time of application.
	Pyrethroid	Bifenthrin	Talstar	F	8-40 fl. oz.	
				10 WP	6.4-32 oz.	May leave a residue.
			PT 1800 (Attain)	Aerosol	1 lb./3,000 sq. ft.	
		Cyfluthrin	Decathlon	20WP	1.9 oz.	
		Fenpropathrin	Tame	2.4EC	10.7 fl. oz.	Add 12 oz. of Orthene/100 gal.
		Fluvalinate	Mavrik	Aquaflow	4-10 fl. oz.	May cause nose and throat irritation if respirators do not fit properly.
		Permethrin	Astro	3.2EC	4-8 fl. oz.	
		Resmethrin	PT 1200	Aerosol	1 lb./3,000 sq. ft.	
	Botanical	Azadirachtin	Azatin	L	8 fl. oz.	Acts as an insect growth regulator. Apply 10-21 fl.oz./acre.
		Pyrethrum	PT 170 (X-Clude)	ME	50-200 fl. oz.	Direct spray to open blooms may cause petal drop.
			PT 1100	Aerosol	1 lb./3,000 sq. ft.	May spot open blooms.
			PT 1600A (X-Clude)	ME	5-10 sec./100 sq. ft.	Don't apply to plants in bloom.
	Carbamate	Oxamyl	Oxamyl	10G	60-80 lb./acre or 1.4-1.9 lb./1000 sq. ft.	
		Fenoxycarb	Precision	WP	4 oz.	Repeat applications on a 10- to 14-day schedule. Also labeled for control of shore flies.
	Insect growth regulator	Kinoprene	Enstar	5E	6-20 fl. oz.	Apply at 7- to 14-day intervals.
			Enstar II	5E	3-10 fl. oz.	Apply at 7- to 14-day intervals.
	Microbial	Bacillus thuringiensis H-14	Gnatrol	L	2-8 pt.	Don't combine with fertilizers or fungicides.
		Steinernema carpocapsae	Exhibit	Gel	1 container/10,000 cu. ft.	Three weekly applications are required.
Fungus gnats	Organophosphate	Chlorpyrifos	PT 1325 (DuraGuard)	ME	25-50 fl. oz.	Direct spray to open blooms may cause petal drop.
		Diazinon	PT 1500R (Knox Out)	ME	5-10 sec./100 sq. ft.	May spot petals.

TABLE 16.3 continued

Pest	Pesticide class	Common name	Product name	Formulation	Dose/100 gallons	Comments
Fungus gnats (cont.)	Pyrethroid	Bifenthrin	Talstar	F	8-40 fl. oz.	
				10 WP	6.4-32 oz.	May leave a residue.
		Cyfluthrin	Decathlon	20WP	1.3 oz.	
		Permethrin	Astro	3.2EC	4-8 fl. oz.	
		Resmethrin	PT 1200	Aerosol	1 lb./3,000 sq. ft.	
			SBP-1382	2EC	1 pt.	
Spider mites	Botanical	Pyrethrum	PT 170 (X-Clude)	ME	50-200 fl. oz.	Direct spray to open blooms may cause petal drop.
			PT 1100	Aerosol	1 lb./3,000 sq. ft.	May spot open blooms.
			PT 1600A (X-Clude)	ME	5-10 sec./100 sq. ft.	Don't apply to plants in bloom.
	Carbamate	Bendiocarb	Dycarb	76WP	20-40 oz.	
		Methiocarb	PT 1700	Aerosol	1 lb./3,000 sq. ft.	
		Oxamyl	Oxamyl	10G	60-80 lb./acre or	
					1.4-1.9 lb./1,000 sq. ft.	
	Insecticidal soap	Insecticidal soap	M-Pede	L	250 fl. oz.	Test for phytotoxicity.
	Macrocyclic lactone	Abamectin	Avid	0.15EC	4 fl. oz.	Apply 8-16 fl. oz./acre.
	Organophosphate	Acephate	PT 1300 (Orthene)	Aerosol	1 lb./3,000 sq. ft.	Phytotoxicity has been reported for impatiens.
		Chlorpyrifos	Dursban	50W	8 oz.	For outdoor use only. May cause phytotoxicity.
			Pageant	L	8 fl. oz.	Phytotoxicity has been reported for impatiens.
			PT 1325 (DuraGuard)	DF	8 oz.	Direct spray to open blooms may cause petal drop.
		Diazinon	PT 1500R (Knox Out)	ME	25-50 fl. oz.	May spot petals.
		Dichlorvos	DDVP	ME	5-10 sec./100 sq. ft.	Foliage and blooms must be dry at the time of application.
		Sulfotep	Dithio	Fumigator	5.1 oz./10,000 cu. ft.	Foliage and blooms must be dry at the time of application.
			Plantfume 103	Smoke	7 oz./20,000 cu. ft.	Foliage and blooms must be dry at the time of application.
				Smoke	7 oz./20,000 cu. ft.	

TABLE 16.3 continued

Pest	Pesticide class	Common name	Product name	Formulation	Dose/100 gallons	Comments
Spider mites (cont.)	Pyrethroid	Bifenthrin	Talstar	F	12-40 fl. oz.	Also labeled for broad mite control.
			PT 1800 (Attain)	10 WP Aerosol	9.6-32 oz.	Also labeled for broad mite control. May leave a residue.
		Fenpropathrin	Tame	2.4EC	1 lb./3,000 sq. ft.	
		Fluvalinate	Mavrik	Aquaflow	8-16 fl. oz.	
					4-10 fl. oz.	May cause nose and throat irritation if respirators do not fit properly.
		Resmethrin	PT 1200	Aerosol	1 lb./3,000 sq. ft.	
Thrips	Botanical	Azadirachtin	Azatin	EC	12-16 fl. oz.	Acts as an insect growth regulator. Apply at 10-21 fl. oz./acre.
			Margosan-O	L	40-80 fl. oz.	Acts as an insect growth regulator.
		Nicotine	Nicotine	Smoke	12 oz./20,000 cu. ft.	Foliage and blooms must be dry at the time of application.
	Carbamate	Bendiocarb	Dycarb	76WP	12-20 oz.	
			Turcam	WP	11 oz.	Apply at 3-week intervals.
		Oxamyl	Oxamyl	10G	60-80 lb./acre or 1.4-1.9 lb./1,000 sq. ft.	
	Chloronicotinyls	Imidacloprid	Marathon	1G	3 lb./cu. yd. media	Label also gives rates per pot.
	Insecticidal soap	Insecticidal soap	M-Pede	L	250 fl. oz.	Test for phytotoxicity.
	Organophosphate	Acephate	PT 1300 (Orthene)	Aerosol	1 lb./3,000 sq. ft.	
		Chlorpyrifos	Dursban	50W	16 oz.	Phytotoxicity has been reported for impatiens.
				L	16 fl. oz.	For outdoor use only. May cause phytotoxicity.
			Pageant	DF	16 oz.	Phytotoxicity has been reported for impatiens.
			PT 1325 (DuraGuard)	ME	25-50 fl. oz.	Direct spray to open blooms may cause petal drop.
		Diazinon	PT 1500R (Knox Out)	ME	5-10 sec./100 sq. ft.	May spot petals.
			Dithio	Smoke	7 oz./20,000 cu. ft.	Foliage and blooms must be dry at the time of application.
		Sulfotep	Plantfume 103	Smoke	7 oz./20,000 cu. ft.	Foliage and blooms must be dry at the time of application.

TABLE 16.3 continued

Pest	Pesticide class	Common name	Product name	Formulation	Dose/100 gallons	Comments
Thrips (cont.)	Pyrethroid	Bifenthrin	Talstar	F	12-40 fl. oz.	
		Cyfluthrin	Decathlon	10 WP	9.6-32 oz.	May leave a residue.
		Fluvalinate	Mavrik	20 WP	1.9 oz.	
				Aquaflow	4-10 fl. oz.	May cause nose and throat irritation if respirators do not fit properly.
		Resmethrin	PT 1200	Aerosol	1 lb./3,000 sq. ft.	

DF = Dry flowable
E = Emulsifiable concentrate F = Flowable
EC = Emulsifiable concentrate
G = Granular
L = Liquid
ME = Microencapsulated
W = Wettable powder
WP = Wettable powder

Read and follow the instructions on the label before using any pesticide. Some pesticides are not available in all states. Before using a pesticide on the crop for the first time or on a new cultivar, treat a few plants and check for phytotoxicity.

Organophosphates and carbamates have similar modes of action and should not be rotated back to back.

For disease control, rotate fungicides or fungicide mixtures with every application. Moorman and Lease [3] collected *Botrytis cinerea* from 13 greenhouses in Pennsylvania and found that all were resistant to Benlate and six were also resistant to Ornalin. Since fungicides containing thiophanate-methyl act like Benlate, they shouldn't be used by themselves for Botrytis control. Ornalin and Chipco 26019 also have a similar mode of action and should not be used in back-to-back applications. Tank mixtures of two dissimilar fungicides will give better control of *Botrytis cinerea* than single applications. Reduced rate tank mixtures of two fungicides may provide as good protection as full rate mixtures.

Also take advantage of the various application methods available. Pesticides registered for use on New Guinea impatiens come in smoke, aerosol, granular, as well as sprayable formulations. Consider the possibility of low volume pesticide application equipment that reduces the amount of water applied and the time needed for application.

Try to use as many IPM components as possible rather than relying on only one or two control methods. Pay attention to details. For example, leaving doors open can negate the benefit of exclusion screening. Pest control should be part of every employee's job—everyone should follow good sanitation practices and help scout. The pest problem is dynamic and so should be the control program. Continually reevaluate your IPM program as you try to improve control methods and the level of control.

References

[1]   Bethke, J.A., and T.D. Paine. 1991. Screen hole size and barriers for exclusion of insect pests of glasshouse crops. *J. Entomol. Sci.* 26: 169-177.
[2]   Matteoni, J.A., and M. Steiner. 1992. Successful biological control of insect pests in floricultural crops. In *Proceedings*. Eighth Conference on Insect and Disease Management on Ornamentals.
[3]   Moorman, G.W., and R.J. Lease. 1992. Benzimidazole and dicarboximide resistant *Botrytis cinerea* from Pennsylvania greenhouses. *Plant Dis.* 76: 477-480.
[4]   Robb, K.L. 1989. Analysis of *Frankliniella occidentalis* (Pergande) as a pest of floricultural crops in California greenhouses. Ph.D. diss. University of California, Riverside.

CHAPTER 17

Marketing and Merchandising

Steven Elliott

Color sells

"Color sells" is a dictum to which our industry owes its very existence. The introduction of New Guinea impatiens to our product line has made it easy to provide long-lasting color on a truly unique plant. Additionally and perhaps more importantly for the continued growth of our industry, New Guinea impatiens create an opportunity for diversification in our selection of plants suitable for a wide range of garden styles. Provided with soils that drain adequately and ample light, New Guinea impatiens can be recommended for everything from borders in the cottage garden, to patio planters, or even to stand-alone mass plantings.

In recent years I have honestly wondered just how much more can the breeders provide? The selection of geraniums, annuals, and now New Guinea impatiens is nothing short of amazing. With such a fantastic array of New Guinea impatiens, our sales teams have the opportunity to sell specific varieties that will accent a customer's color scheme and garden style.

Creating profit potential

Examining current retailing trends, we find that more and more outlets are selling products that had previously been another retailer's specialty. This has accelerated the conversion of so many of the bread and butter products in our mix to so-called "commodity item" status selling at reduced prices. Fortunately these large volume sales are helping us "Colorize America," and this is triggering increased demand. However, many segments of our industry can't survive on the reduced profit margins of "commodity item" sales.

We have found in our garden center that New Guinea impatiens offer a unique opportunity to combat these trends and capture a better profit margin. With New Guinea impatiens, we have been able to promote ourselves as industry leaders, bringing our customers the best current varieties from breeders and botanists around the world. New Guinea impatiens help us demonstrate different ideas to our customers. We have shown them how to grow more beautiful gardens and planters with less labor. With our new palette of colors to choose from, we have attracted additional customers who have witnessed the striking commercial and residential gardens that our landscape crews have created with New Guinea impatiens.

Perhaps even more importantly, our current customer base has found new and additional gardening activities that use various sizes of New Guinea impatiens. We have found New Guinea impatiens a very effective tool to retain necessary profit margins, expand our customer base, and increase our present customers' interest in gardening.

Build your company business image —

A less tangible but very important bonus of creatively promoting New Guinea impatiens is enhanced company image. New Guinea impatiens offer consistent color from the day of purchase and throughout the entire season. Try to find more than a handful of annuals that truly will perform that well! What a simple way to satisfy your valuable customers.

Let your customers know it was your store that suggested New Guinea impatiens to them and that you are, in large part, responsible for their beautiful summer. A trained sales team can satisfy a gardener's specific needs by selling the variety with the correct growth habit for his intended use. With the selection of colors available you can help your customer enjoy a more pleasing landscape color combination. Let New Guinea impatiens help you build a company image that says, "This is a professional retailer with expert salespeople selling superior plants."

Marketing strategy

Complement your overall business promotion

New Guinea impatiens marketing should involve many of the same techniques you use to promote your business. We believe a better informed customer will develop keener interests in our products. Once there is excitement we can stimulate the imagination by demonstrating uses of New Guinea impatiens with companion plants or other products.

Hobbies that are not rewarding don't last long. Our customers' success with our plants is largely our responsibility. We all hope that success will lead to customer loyalty and the best form of advertising we could ever have—word of mouth. Join in the celebration of success along with your customer—after all (and we can appropriately remind our customers of this) was it not our creative display and helpful assistance that helped create "Your Beautiful Summer"? Slogans such as this help create an image, and there are many ways to say thank-you to customers to remind them that it was your company that fulfilled that image. This is our four-part marketing strategy:

1. Create interest and enthusiasm about New Guinea impatiens.
2. Explain and demonstrate the many possible uses and benefits of growing New Guinea impatiens.
3. Provide cultural advice to ensure a successful growing season for our customers.
4. Share in the success.

1. **Create interest and enthusiasm.** Hobby gardeners often enjoy background information on their plant choices. We used a newsletter to tell our customers about the impatiens before they arrived. The article explained the advantage of compact growth and higher light tolerance than bedding impatiens, but when the customers arrived they wanted more information about these new New Guinea impatiens. Frequently we were asked, "Why are these called New Guinea impatiens?" "Where is New Guinea, anyway?" "Will New Guinea impatiens grow in the same place I have grown geraniums for so many years?" By just listening, these questions enabled us to quickly define our marketing plan. Dr. Cathey's chapter on the history of New Guinea impatiens (see Chapter 2) readily provides the background information needed to create newsletter articles, handouts, radio talk programs, or public presentations that you might use to help build customer interest.

It's fascinating to see how few years it has taken to bring wild plants from the hillsides of a country in the Southern Hemisphere, improve them for commercial use, build stock programs, and introduce so many outstanding new varieties to the public. Informing gardeners about the important work being done by breeders all around the world also gives you the opportunity to tell your customers that you are constantly seeking better performing varieties for their gardens. Let them know that you are part of a larger industry with substantial behind-the-scenes technology.

There is also an opportunity for you to inform the public that our green industry is leading the way regarding various environmental issues. Work being done by breeders to enhance natural pest and disease resistance within a wide range of crops, both ornamental and edible, is a strong selling point for you, your plants, and our industry.

2. **Explain and demonstrate uses and benefits.** We grow and offer New Guinea impatiens in 11 different pot sizes so that we can fill many different customer needs. These include 4-, 6- and 8-inch (10, 15 and 20 cm) azalea pots, 8-, 10-, and 12-inch (10, 25 and 30 cm) hanging baskets, 10-inch (25 cm) hanging gardens, 10-inch (25 cm) wall pots, 16-inch (40 cm) moss baskets, basket packs, and "Basket Buddies." Suggest that your customers choose a container size that is closest to the finish size plant they expect. Maximum color will then be enjoyed from the start. Also the care, especially watering and fertilizing, will not change significantly during the season. The instructions that you send home with the customer should suit the plants' needs consistently all season long (See Color Plate section, CP 17.1).

Stress the benefits of New Guinea impatiens to your customers. They are self-cleaning and require no pinching, pruning, or staking. Point out that "Beyond watering and fertilizing, New Guinea impatiens are carefree in any garden" (suggested signage phrase). Another benefit provides you with an opportunity to promote your expertise in garden design trends: Color coordination of landscape plantings to the surrounding architecture is easy with the broad color selection in New Guinea impatiens. Demonstrate that New Guinea impatiens are available in several cool colors, or if preferred, striking clear colors, such as red or orange, that carry the eye to a more distant garden. Often it is pleasing to add white, which makes the other colors stand out.

3. **Provide cultural advice.** Design a system for your garden store that provides the necessary cultural advice and instructions to

ensure your customers' success with New Guinea impatiens. Incorporate cross-selling into this system and do your customer a favor at the same time. For example, Mikkelsens' cultural guide for New Guinea impatiens suggests using a fertilizer ratio of 2-1-2. Promote a fertilizer of this formulation along with your New Guinea impatiens. Take-home handouts and cultural guides should have your store's phone number and hours on it, too.

4. **Share the success.** When your customers grow outstanding New Guinea impatiens, let them know that you, too, are enjoying their gardens. Special recognition programs or thank-you notes mailed to your customers lets them know just how interested and dedicated you are to their success with your plants. Pictures displayed in your garden center of your customers' flower beds help you share ideas with all of your customers.

Programs can be designed to start promoting the next season as well. For example, in the North, you might suggest a follow-up planting to New Guinea impatiens with hardy pansies or mums. Win new customers by recognizing outstanding gardens of those who are not currently buying from your garden center. An unexpected compliment is sure to set your operation apart and bring in new business.

Merchandising New Guinea impatiens

Retail display opportunities for New Guinea impatiens vary with the type of retail outlet. Mass merchants need simple signage and displays that make a strong visual impact, promote price, and offer cultural advice. I was very impressed with a display I saw in Florida that was two-tiered, with colorful picture signs on the front of the second shelf just above the canopy of flowers on the first level. These signs were descriptive and informative. A separate, highly visible price sign appeared above the second level. Plants were grown in round pots and displayed in shuttle trays and were easier for customers to reach than the pot tight, square pot, and tray systems. Hanging baskets and 4- and 6-inch (10 and 15 cm) pot sizes appear most often at mass merchandisers and will be the most competitively priced. A retail garden center has more opportunity to expand the market for New Guinea impatiens.

Customize your display

Since there are so many uses for New Guinea impatiens, there is a wide range of sizes to sell. Building a custom display just for New Guinea impatiens should include these important elements and design concepts:

1. **Make the display say "wow!"** Upscale the display with show-stopper pieces such as large moss baskets. The perceived value of all items in the display will be boosted, and the display will stimulate other ideas. Mass merchandisers use masses of color to draw attention. Retail garden centers can use creations to do the same, but with a different technique.

2. **Show plants in a range of containers.** Display finished planters along with the suggested pot size for customers to plant on their own. Offer both the finished planter and the new materials for sale. This might also be a place to post those garden pictures from your successful customers.

3. **Accommodate transplanting.** If room allows, provide a selection of various planters and a potting bench so that a customer or salesperson can repot while the idea is still fresh in their minds.

4. **Let signs deliver the message.** Create signs that educate and create interest. Point out the outstanding features of New Guinea impatiens explaining why they will be enjoyed. Explain the growth habit so they know what they can expect of their New Guinea impatiens. Offer cultural advice to ensure their success and satisfaction all season long (fig. 17.1). Finally, be sure that the price is obvious.

5. **Teach the use of color.** Create an educational display nearby that explains how to master using color. Help customers relate your plants to their color schemes. Color coordinate plantings and their surroundings. Display a color wheel and have a description of monochromatic, analogous, complementary, and polychromatic color schemes. The varieties chosen to create a flower bed or container garden should build upon the color scheme chosen for the entire landscape, including colors used for the house and trim work. Briefly, complementary colors exist opposite each other on the color wheel. Try orange New Guinea impatiens with blue pansies or browallia.

   New Guinea impatiens lend themselves well to monochromatic and analogous displays because of the large selection of pink, lavender, and violet colors available. Analogous colors are adjacent

| Your Company Logo | # New Guinea Impatiens
IN HANGING BASKETS |

OUTSTANDING FEATURES

Your hanging basket New Guinea impatiens will provide beautiful flowers all summer long and then may be enjoyed in early fall in a bright window or sun porch.

Choose a color that compliments the colors of your house, trim work, or patio furniture pattern. Select New Guinea impatiens with variegated or solid leaves.

We grow only from certified, disease-free stock to assure you the most vigorous plants possible.

GROWTH HABIT

You will enjoy fewer care chores with New Guinea impatiens. They are self-branching—**do not pinch!** The flowers are self-cleaning—no dead-heading! They are not heavy feeders—**less frequent fertilizing or use a weaker solution!**

From over 100 available varieties, we have selected the ones most suitable for hanging basket culture. Look for other varieties in our bedding plant display, too.

CULTURAL ADVICE

New Guinea impatiens enjoy bright light, but not scorching hot midday sun. We recommend choosing a 12-inch (30.5 cm) hanging basket for hot spots. The larger pot acts as a larger moisture reservoir. Considering that New Guinea impatiens are originally from a tropical climate with frequent soft rains, you can understand their natural desire for uniform and constant soil moisture.

Preferred temperatures are between 65F to 80F (18C to 27C).

Fertilize often, but every couple of weeks water thoroughly so as to leach the soil (let 50% of the water applied run out). Then be sure to let the soil dry down before watering again.

Cultural guides are available in our reference library.

$ Prices $

Fig. 17.1. *Handout to give customers to ensure their success with New Guinea impatiens hanging baskets.*

to each other on the color wheel. Monochromatic color schemes combine tints and shades of the same color. These schemes can be lots of fun to create when one variety is selected because the plants highlight one another, especially the many varieties with two-tone flowers.

A polychromatic display is all inclusive and provides a riot of color. New Guinea impatiens offer varieties with warm and cool colors. Suggest using the pink, lavender, and violets in a warm patio setting to visually cool down the setting. The warm red and orange colors stand out if used in a more distant flower bed or one that is a foreground to a spectacular view. Present these uses of color around your garden center and plant demonstration planters accordingly to finish off the display.

6. **Add a few nontraditional uses to the display.** Install a New Guinea impatiens in a planter of herbs. Perennial gardeners can add long-lasting color to their beds with New Guinea impatiens. Also provide New Guinea impatiens in decorative pots ready for the gift market, party decorations, or for "get well" wishes.

A pot size for every use

Promote the container size closest to the intended final container size needed by the customer. This will provide almost immediate color and success if consistent care instructions are included.

Basket packs. Basket packs are large packs with six 3-inch (9 cm) cells per pack and an attached handle that makes it easy to carry. Basket packs are sold as solid colors or as color blends that are preselected for different color schemes. This is a nice size for a border around a garden or along a walkway. Promote the price competitiveness of this size (fig. 17.2). This size is also proving popular with landscape contractors. Sell for a retail price of $5.99 to $7.99.

Large tubs. Eight- and 10-inch (20 and 25 cm) tubs provide instant color for larger containers, such as whiskey barrels or street planters. This is the size for the customer in a hurry. It's also perfect for instant party or summer home decorating. Plan ahead for these sales and build repeat business. Customers will be happy with the ease of care and the weeks of enjoyment they get from New Guinea impatiens. Retail prices—$9.99 to $19.99.

Moss baskets. Planted on the top and on the sides these become "Giant balls of color—with so little care!" (suggested signage phrase).

Blooming New Guinea impatiens ready for instant gardens for just about $1 each.

Fig. 17.2. Use signs to make customers aware of the many uses of New Guinea impatiens.

These are show pieces and are perfect for inns, restaurants, and other commercial establishments (CP 9.2). Prices range widely, often $50 to $75!

10-inch (25 cm) hanging garden. This is a plastic version of the moss basket. Plant the top and sides with New Guinea impatiens and suggest using it as either the intended hanging basket or remove the hanger and place it on the patio table for color that surrounds. Use this size to create a combination basket. Add some plants that vine, some with unusual foliage, and others with similar light requirements that build upon a color theme. Try using nierembergia, compact pansies, ivy and cascade geraniums, bright wax begonias, lantana, variegated zonal geraniums, and a host of others for a spectacular display of color and textures. Retail price—$19.99 to $24.

Basket buddy. A commercially available planter made of a 6-inch (15 cm) diameter tube, 14 inches (35 cm) long with holes in the sides for planting. The column effect of these planters makes it easy to suggest matching sets to accent doorways. Suggest a matched set for a "Two for $____" feature. Retail price—$24 to $29.99.

Wall pots. These are flat-sided for hanging against a wall. Wall pots are available in plastic or as coated wire with a fiber liner. They show an entirely different use for New Guinea impatiens. If your customer's site is too hot for a New Guinea impatiens hanging basket, try a wall pot that will be shaded and slightly cooler when used against a wall. Retail prices—$12.99 to $19.99.

12-inch (30 cm) hanging baskets. Offer a few of these for customers with hot locations. We have found the extra moisture reservoir allows us to grow hanging baskets in more heat and sun (CP 9.4, CP 9.5). Retail price—$25.

Preplanted window boxes and color bowls. These serve as both demonstration pieces and feature items for sale. Plant these up fresh continually through the season.

If your supplier does not grow these sizes, explain the increased volume potential you both could have if you offered these alternative sizes. Another suggestion is to purchase prefinished pots and plant your own unique containers.

Consider a trial garden

We have so many varieties now it would be valuable for us to put them all side by side and monitor their performance. If you do not have the room, consider letting your staff do the trials at home. Provide a selection for them to plant in their own beds and a data collection evaluation form for them to turn in at set intervals throughout the season. There is nothing like first-hand experience to provide a salesperson with the knowledge to satisfy a customer's needs. The top performers in such a trial earn a special place in our merchandising and pricing plans. We merchandise the top performers as our "Proven Performers" with blue ribbons custom-printed with our company name.

New Guinea impatiens offer a chance for creative promotion of your business and allow you to increase sales and profits. As new varieties are introduced, carefully evaluate their performance for their true merit, and discard older varieties that are less reliable. Finally, keep watch for new ways to use New Guinea impatiens. Develop communications with your customers to keep them informed and excited about your suggestions and advice.

CHAPTER 18

Production Costs

Robin G. Brumfield

Any time I am asked to discuss cost of production, I emphasize that every producer faces different costs. Nowhere is that more true than for producing New Guinea impatiens. Although they were introduced into the United States more than 20 years ago [11, 13], New Guinea impatiens are a relatively new crop for many growers. As a result, no consistent production method appears to exist for them.

New Guinea impatiens actually appear to be a very simple crop to produce with cropping schedules similar to geraniums. However, they require no pinching or growth regulator and need very little fertilizer and water at the beginning of the crop [1, 2, 10, 13, 15]. A producer not familiar with growing New Guinea impatiens can easily apply too much water, fertilizer, or growth regulator, thus increasing the crop time and therefore the production costs.

As with most floricultural crops, New Guinea impatiens are grown with tighter spacing and fewer cuttings per pot for the mass market than for the garden center market. Cropping times vary widely across geographic regions. Costs can also vary from firm to firm because of size, managerial practices, time of year, number of units produced, other options for greenhouse space, size of permanent work crew, availability of part-time labor, type of heating system, tightness of the greenhouse, sources of supplies, how quickly supplies are paid for, and the level of investment in overhead facilities. In today's competitive market, producers must know their costs and have an available market willing to purchase plants at a price that is higher than production costs.

Costs in general

The time from 1989-1994 has been a period of relatively low inflation. Thus, the cost of most inputs such as cuttings, pots, growing media, and fuel has been fairly stable. Costs of chemicals have been increasing more than other costs. Minimum wage has increased twice in the last five years, pushing production labor costs up. The stagnant economy has helped fuel the growth of the mass market's importance, which has in turn put downward pressure on retail plant prices in all markets.

As a result New Guinea impatiens' retail price has remained constant or even decreased in recent years. Most growers are faced with production costs that are increasing modestly and markets that offer little opportunity to raise prices. The bright spot for the moment is that New Guinea impatiens often command a higher price than other flowering annuals. My own limited survey found that prices growers receive for 4-inch (10 cm) New Guinea impatiens range from $1 per pot wholesale (in the mass market) to $4 per pot retail (in a garden center) with a mass market average of around $1.25. Mass market wholesale prices are about $4.50 to $5 for New Guinea impatiens in a 8-inch (20 cm) basket and $7 to $7.50 in a 10-inch (25 cm) basket.

As the mass market has become more mature, it has moved to a slightly higher quality product. The 36-cell flat is becoming the standard for bedding plants (not New Guinea impatiens) because it holds up longer, requires little watering, and offers instant color for consumers in the retail store. There is also a movement toward New Guinea impatiens in 10-inch (25 cm) hanging baskets or larger versus 8-inch (20 cm) baskets for the same reasons.

Costs of New Guinea impatiens produced in 4-inch (10 cm) pots and 8- and 10-inch (20 and 25 cm) hanging baskets are presented here because they are the most common plant sizes currently produced in the industry (tables 18.2–18.8). Vegetatively reproduced plants hold the major market share and are also analyzed. The costs to produce seed New Guinea impatiens (Spectra) in bedding plant flats are analyzed in tables 18.9–18.12.

Information provided in this chapter can be a guide in calculating costs for a specific greenhouse firm. It can also provide information on "average" costs that individual greenhouse managers can compare to their own particular operation, including costs of items that are low and can be used to their advantage and costs of items that are high and need to be reduced. But remember, looking at industry averages is no substitute for doing your own cost analysis. Every producer's costs are different! Do not assume that your costs are the same as those in the example presented here.

In the following tables each cost is categorized into overhead and variable types because these need to be treated differently. Variable costs vary as the number of units produced changes. Overhead costs don't vary directly with the number of units produced but are incurred regardless of output. Computer programs can make allocating costs to specific crops easier [4].

Overhead costs ⸻

Total overhead costs, or fixed costs, remain constant regardless of what crop or how many units are produced. On the other hand, overhead costs per unit decrease as more units are produced. Overhead costs include managerial salaries, depreciation, interest, insurance, repairs and other items which can't be easily allocated on a per unit basis to a particular crop. They must be allocated on some other basis, such as cost per square-foot-week of bench area. Other overhead costs include utilities, advertising, dues and subscriptions, travel and entertainment, office expenses, professional fees, truck expenses, land use cost, contributions, and bad debts.

Overhead costs presented here were derived by updating previous studies using Producer Price Indices and Employment Cost Indices [3, 5, 6, 7, 8, 9]. The example is a 20,000-square-foot (1,858 m²), double-layer, polyethylene greenhouse using 77% total floor area for production for mass market retailers (table 18.1).

Overhead costs per square-foot-week of bench space are calculated by dividing the total overhead costs by 52 weeks and dividing by 15,400 square feet (1,431 m²) (77% of the floor space) to determine a cost of $0.200 per square-foot-week of bench space for small firms. Overhead costs for medium and large firms were derived by multiplying $0.200 per square foot by 74% and 71% to obtain $0.148 and $0.142 for medium and large firms, respectively [7]. Medium firms are 100,000 square feet (9,290 m²), and large greenhouses are 400,000 square feet (37,160 m²) in size.

Overhead for hanging baskets

How should overhead costs be allocated to hanging baskets? Some managers argue that hanging baskets have no overhead costs, based on the assumption that overhead costs have already been allocated to other crops and that hanging baskets are an extra crop that only have to cover their variable costs of production. This argument has some validity, especially if hanging baskets are only a minor part of the product mix. If a manager is deciding to increase production, profits will continue to increase as long as marginal costs are covered. So to decide

TABLE 18.1

Overhead costs[a]

	Annual total	Cost per sq. ft./ week of bench area
Overhead labor & benefits	$63,000	$0.079
Utilities		
Heating fuel (13,420 gallons)	13,420	0.017
Electricity	1,935	0.002
Telephone	1,273	0.002
Depreciation	25,000	0.031
Interest	15,000	0.019
Insurance	4,852	0.006
Repairs	12,409	0.015
Property taxes	769	0.001
Advertising	716	0.001
Dues & subscriptions	344	0.000
Travel & entertainment	1,697	0.002
Office expenses	796	0.001
Professional fees	1,000	0.001
Truck expenses & equipment rental	14,000	0.017
Land rental	1,565	0.002
Contributions	400	0.000
Miscellaneous	2,800	0.003
Bad debts	700	0.001
Total	**$161,676**	**$0.200**

[a] 20,000-square-feet, double layer, polyethylene greenhouse.

whether it is profitable to grow one more hanging basket, a manager need only consider variable costs because the overhead costs have been allocated to other crops. Under this scenario, hanging baskets would probably be very profitable, and managers would look for mar-

TABLE 18.2

Labor inputs

	Time (seconds per pot)		
	4-inch pot (10 cm)	8-inch pot (20 cm)	10-inch basket (25 cm)
Transplant and move to greenhouse [a]	17.3	56.6	74.5
Water & fertilizer applications [b]	10.9	32.9	62.0
Treat for insect control [c]	9.8	40.0	49.2
Treat for disease control [d]	2.0	5.0	6.0
Harvest	23.7	90.0	97.8
Total seconds	**63.7**	**224.5**	**289.5**
Total labor cost @ $8/hr.	**$0.14**	**$0.49**	**$0.64**

[a] One rooted cutting per 4-inch (10 cm) pot, three per 8-inch (20 cm) basket, and five per 10-inch (25 cm) basket.

[b] Plants are watered once per week for the first four weeks with clear water and constant liquid feed at 200 ppm is applied five times per week for the remainder of the production period.

[c] Insecticide is applied three times for 4-inch (10 cm) pots and four times for hanging baskets.

[d] Fungicide is applied twice.

TABLE 18.3

Finished flat costs of producing 4-inch (10 cm) pots at three different-sized greenhouse firms

| | Greenhouse size | | |
Variable costs	Small	Medium	Large
Rooted cutting [a]	$0.42	$0.36	$0.34
Pot	0.07	0.06	0.06
Rooting medium	0.02	0.02	0.01
Labels	0.03	0.03	0.02
Fertilizer	0.02	0.01	0.01
Pesticide & fungicide	0.03	0.03	0.02
Labor	0.14	0.14	0.14
Interest on variable costs	0.03	0.03	0.03
Total variable costs	**$0.76**	**$0.68**	**$0.63**
Overhead costs [b]	0.41	0.30	0.29
Loss allocation	0.06	0.05	0.05
Total per pot	**$1.23**	**$1.03**	**$0.96**

[a] One cutting per pot.
[b] Overhead costs are calculated at $0.200, $0.148, and $0.142 per square-foot-bench-week for small (20,000 sq. ft.), medium (100,000 sq. ft.), large (400,000 sq. ft.) greenhouses respectively. The plants are grown for six weeks pot-to-pot and four weeks on 7-inch (17 cm) centers.

kets in which to sell as many units as possible. If this practice is carried to an extreme, however, hanging baskets would eventually shade the crop underneath to the point that the quality of the bench crops would suffer. Then the overhead cost is no longer free because of the increased costs the hanging baskets impose on the other crops.

Variable costs ───────────────────────

Variable costs, or direct costs, can be allocated to each unit produced based on information from invoices. Total variable costs are directly related to the number of units produced and increase as the number of units produced increases. However, the cost per unit stays the same except for quantity discounts. Material costs, which include the costs of containers, seedlings or cuttings, growing media, labels, and chemicals are direct costs and are among the easiest variable costs to allocate to each unit produced. Direct costs in this chapter were determined by contacting supply companies and commercial growers for 1994 costs (tables 18.2–18.12).

▰▰▰ TABLE 18.4 ▰▰▰

Costs of finishing in 4-inch (10 cm) pots based on crop time, pot spacing, and greenhouse size

Production time [b]	Final spacing	Greenhouse size [a] Small	Medium	Large
6 weeks	pot-to-pot	$0.94	$0.81	$0.76
	6-inch centers	1.12	0.94	0.88
	7-inch centers	1.23	1.03	0.96
	8-inch centers	1.36	1.13	1.05
	10-inch centers	1.68	1.36	1.28
8 weeks	pot-to-pot	0.99	0.85	0.79
	6-inch centers	1.05	0.89	0.83
	7-inch centers	1.09	0.92	0.86
	8-inch centers	1.13	0.95	0.89
	10-inch centers	1.24	1.03	0.96
10 weeks	pot-to-pot	1.04	0.88	0.82
	6-inch centers	1.15	0.97	0.90
	7-inch centers	1.23	1.03	0.96
	8-inch centers	1.32	1.09	1.02
	10-inch centers	1.53	1.25	1.17
12 weeks	pot-to-pot	1.08	0.92	0.85
	6-inch centers	1.26	1.05	0.98
	7-inch centers	1.37	1.13	1.06
	8-inch centers	1.50	1.23	1.15
	10-inch centers	1.82	1.46	1.38
14 weeks	pot-to-pot	1.13	0.93	0.89
	6-inch centers	1.36	1.13	1.05
	7-inch centers	1.52	1.24	1.16
	8-inch centers	1.69	1.37	1.29
	10-inch centers	2.11	1.68	1.59

[a] Overhead costs are calculated at $0.200, $0.148, and $0.142 per square-foot-bench-week for small (20,000 sq. ft.), medium (100,000 sq. ft.), large (400,000 sq. ft.) greenhouses respectively.
[b] Grown pot-to-pot for six weeks, remainder at final spacing.

Labor

Production labor is more difficult to allocate to each unit, but you can do it with some simple recordkeeping. Simply note the number of people performing the operation and when they start and finish. Then count the number of units they finish in that time period. The time per unit multiplied by the wage rate, including benefits, can be calculated to obtain the cost of that labor task per unit. Labor that is difficult to allocate to a specific crop can be included in overhead costs and allocated on a per-square-foot-per-week basis like all other nonallocated costs. Production labor inputs in the examples were derived from other studies [8, 12] (table 18.2).

Costs of finishing 8-inch (20 cm) baskets from cuttings at three different-sized greenhouse firms

	Greenhouse size		
Variable costs	Small	Medium	Large
Rooted cutting [a]	$1.26	$1.08	$1.02
Basket	0.61	0.53	0.49
Rooting medium	0.06	0.06	0.06
Labels	0.04	0.03	0.03
Fertilizer	0.09	0.08	0.07
Pesticide & fungicide	0.09	0.08	0.07
Labor	0.50	0.50	0.50
Interest on variable costs	0.12	0.11	0.10
Total variable costs	**$2.77**	**$2.47**	**$2.35**
Overhead costs [b]	2.33	1.73	1.66
Loss allocation	0.27	0.22	0.21
Total per pot	**$5.37**	**$4.41**	**$4.22**

[a] Three cuttings per pot.
[b] Overhead costs are calculated at $0.200, $0.148, and $0.142 per square-foot-bench-week for small (20,000 sq. ft.), medium (100,000 sq. ft.), large (400,000 sq. ft.) greenhouses respectively. The plants are grown for six weeks pot-to-pot and nine weeks on 12-inch (30 cm) centers.

Wages vary depending on the individual firm's labor policy and the type of labor performing a particular task. A wage rate of $6.50 per hour was used for the hourly labor in this analysis. Twenty-three percent was added to the base wage to cover benefits, bringing the total to $8 per hour. This hourly labor cost doesn't include overhead salaries paid to managers, growers, sales personnel, and office staff, which are included in overhead costs.

Interest

Interest on fixed assets, such as greenhouses, are included in overhead costs, but interest is also accrued on production expenses because supplies must be purchased and labor must be hired before plants are sold. The interest rate is assumed to be 9% for the example and is assumed to be required for six months.

Losses

Some of the crop will invariably not be sold due to production problems or inability of the marketing staff to sell all of the plants produced. To calculate the cost of losses, add all other costs per unit and multiply

TABLE 18.6

Total costs of finishing 8-inch (20 cm) pots based on crop time, pot spacing, and greenhouse size

Production time [b]	Final spacing	Greenhouse size [a]		
		Small	Medium	Large
8 weeks	12-inch centers	$3.90	$3.32	$3.17
	14-inch centers	4.05	3.44	3.28
	16-inch centers	4.22	3.57	3.41
	18-inch centers	4.42	3.71	3.55
	20-inch centers	4.65	3.88	3.70
10 weeks	12-inch centers	4.32	3.63	3.47
	14-inch centers	4.62	3.86	3.69
	16-inch centers	4.97	4.12	3.94
	18-inch centers	5.37	4.41	4.22
	20-inch centers	5.82	4.74	4.53
12 weeks	12-inch centers	4.74	3.95	3.77
	14-inch centers	5.20	4.28	4.09
	16-inch centers	5.72	4.67	4.47
	18-inch centers	6.32	5.11	4.89
	20-inch centers	6.99	5.61	5.36
14 weeks	12-inch centers	5.16	4.26	4.07
	14-inch centers	5.77	4.71	4.50
	16-inch centers	6.47	5.23	5.00
	18-inch centers	7.27	5.82	5.56
	20-inch centers	8.15	6.47	6.20
15 weeks	12-inch centers	5.37	4.41	4.22
	14-inch centers	6.06	4.92	4.70
	16-inch centers	6.84	5.50	5.27
	18-inch centers	7.74	6.17	5.90
	20-inch centers	8.74	6.91	6.61
16 weeks	12-inch centers	5.58	4.57	4.37
	14-inch centers	6.34	5.13	4.91
	16-inch centers	7.22	5.78	5.53
	18-inch centers	8.21	6.52	6.24
	20-inch centers	9.32	7.34	7.03

a Overhead costs are calculated at $0.200, $0.148, and $0.142 per square-foot-bench-week for small (20,000 sq. ft.), medium (100,000 sq. ft.), large (400,000 sq. ft.) greenhouses respectively.
b Grown pot-to-pot for six weeks, remainder at final spacing.

by the number of unsold units. Then divide by the number of plants sold to assign the cost of losses to each unit sold. The losses in these examples were assumed to be 5% of plants produced.

Producing 4-inch (10 cm) pots

Spacing and length of time on the bench for New Guinea impatiens varies regionally, by market channel, and by individual production sys-

TABLE 18.7

Costs of finishing 10-inch (25 cm) hanging baskets from cuttings at three different-sized greenhouse firms

| | Greenhouse size | | |
Variable costs	Small	Medium	Large
Rooted cutting [a]	$2.10	$1.80	$1.70
Basket	0.83	0.71	0.66
Rooting medium	0.14	0.14	0.13
Labels	0.04	0.03	0.03
Fertilizer	0.21	0.18	0.17
Pesticide & fungicide	0.14	0.12	0.11
Labor	0.64	0.64	0.64
Interest on variable costs	0.18	0.16	0.15
Total variable costs	**$4.28**	**$3.78**	**$3.59**
Overhead costs [b]	3.65	2.70	2.59
Loss allocation	0.42	0.34	0.33
Total per pot	**$8.35**	**$6.82**	**$6.51**

[a] Five cuttings per pot.

[b] Overhead costs are calculated at $0.200, $0.148, and $0.142 per square-foot-bench-week for small (20,000 sq. ft.), medium (100,000 sq. ft.), large (400,000 sq. ft.) greenhouses respectively. The plants are grown for six weeks pot-to-pot and nine weeks on 15-inch (38 cm) centers.

tems. Recommended spacing ranges from pot tight (all pots touching) for the entire crop to 10-inch (25 cm) centers [1, 2, 11, 13, personal communication with commercial growers]. Likewise the time on the bench varies from six to 14 weeks [1, 2, 11, 13, personal communication with commercial growers]. Pinching is not generally recommended [2], but some growers pinch lengthening production time by two to three weeks [15].

The plants in table 18.3 are grown pot-to-pot for the first six weeks and on 7-inch (17 cm) centers for four weeks. At a wholesale price of $1.25, the small firm (with overhead costs of $0.20 per square-foot-bench week) would not make much profit. The largest cost involved in producing New Guinea impatiens in 4-inch (10 cm) pots is the rooted cutting and the second largest is overhead. The rooted cuttings cost $0.37 each plus $0.05 for shipping and handling. Using seed New Guinea impatiens (Spectra), which cost only about $0.02 each, could lower production costs, providing overhead costs do not increase substantially.

Because bench spacing and production times vary, the costs for some of the alternatives are calculated in table 18.4. In each case, the plants are grown pot-to-pot for six weeks and then grown at final spacing for the remainder of the crop. If plants are grown at final spacing for the entire production period, costs would be even higher than those

TABLE 18.8

Costs of finishing 10-inch (25 cm) baskets based on crop time, pot spacing, and greenhouse size

Production time [b]	Final spacing	Greenhouse size [a]		
		Small	Medium	Large
8 weeks	15-inch centers	$6.05	$5.12	$4.87
	16-inch centers	6.14	5.19	4.94
	18-inch centers	6.33	5.33	5.08
	20-inch centers	6.56	5.50	5.24
10 weeks	15-inch centers	6.70	5.60	5.34
	16-inch centers	6.88	5.74	5.47
	18-inch centers	7.28	6.03	5.75
	20-inch centers	7.73	6.36	6.07
12 weeks	15-inch centers	7.36	6.09	5.81
	16-inch centers	7.63	6.29	6.00
	18-inch centers	8.23	6.73	6.42
	20-inch centers	8.90	7.23	6.90
14 weeks	15-inch centers	8.02	6.58	6.28
	16-inch centers	8.38	6.85	6.53
	18-inch centers	9.18	7.44	7.10
	20-inch centers	10.07	8.09	7.73
15 weeks	15-inch centers	8.35	6.82	6.51
	16-inch centers	8.76	7.12	6.80
	18-inch centers	9.65	7.79	7.43
	20-inch centers	10.65	8.53	8.14
16 weeks	15-inch centers	8.68	7.07	6.74
	16-inch centers	9.13	7.40	7.06
	18-inch centers	10.12	8.14	7.77
	20-inch centers	11.24	8.96	8.56

[a] Overhead costs are calculated at $0.200, $0.148, and $0.142 per square-foot-bench-week for small (20,000 sq. ft.), medium (100,000 sq. ft.), large (400,000 sq. ft.) greenhouses respectively.
[b] Grown pot-to-pot for six weeks, remainder at final spacing.

shown in table 18.4. Production costs vary from $0.76 per pot to $2.11 per pot based on the assumptions presented here. Variable costs for medium-sized greenhouses are assumed to be 86% of costs for the small size greenhouse, and the variable costs for the large size greenhouse are assumed to be 80% of those faced by the small size greenhouse. Because overhead cost is the second largest cost and becomes the largest as plants are given more space, consider growing plants without pinching to shorten production time. But weigh this against any reductions in uniformity and quality as the result of not pinching. The same is true for growing the crop on tighter spacing. Growing plants closer together reduces overhead costs per plant, but can adversely affect plant quality and therefore result in a lower price for the product.

TABLE 18.9

Labor inputs for seedling production at three different-sized greenhouse firms[a]

	Time (seconds per flat)						
	Bare rooted			Plug			
	Small	Medium	Large [a]	Small	Medium	Large	
Seedling state						Nonauto	Auto
Fill flat	35	37	22	24	49	47	47
Seed and move to germination area	144	162	85	103	140	81	81
Move to greenhouse	16	40	33	36	29	14	14
Irrigate [b]	14	14	6	14	7	5	5
Move to work area	40	30	67	46	51	25	25
Total	**249**	**283**	**213**	**223**	**276**	**172**	**172**
Finished flat stage							
Fill flat	45	120	35	36	44	66	4
Transplant and move to greenhouse	209	180	191	76	187	137	108
Irrigate	99	78	62	84	66	53	53
Spray growth regulator [c]	14	10	2	14	10	2	2
Spray pesticide [d]	14	2	2	14	2	2	2
Total	**381**	**390**	**292**	**224**	**309**	**260**	**169**

[a] Small greenhouses are 20,000 square feet, medium are 100,000 square feet and large are 400,00 square feet in size.

[b] Plants are hand watered an average of four times per week.

[c] Growth regulator is applied once.

[d] Pesticides area applied twice.

Producing hanging baskets

The spacing and length of production for hanging baskets varies greatly, similar to production in 4-inch (10 cm) pots [1, 2, 11, 13, 15, personal communication with growers]. One to three rooted cuttings are planted into an 8-inch (20 cm) hanging basket and baskets are spaced from 12- to 20-inch (30 to 50 cm) centers. Three to five cuttings are recommended for a 10-inch (25 cm) hanging basket, and baskets are spaced from 15- to 20-inch (38 to 50 cm) centers. Production time varies from eight to 16 weeks for both sizes.

Some growers say putting more cuttings per pot shortens production time and makes the basket fuller, while others say one plant per pot is adequate and does not lengthen production time. In these examples, each 8-inch (20 cm) basket has three cuttings and is grown pot-to-pot for six weeks and on 12-inch (30 cm) centers for nine weeks. Each 10-

TABLE 18.10

Bare rooted and plug seedling production costs at three different-sized greenhouse firms

	Bare rooted			Plug		
	Small	Medium	Large	Small	Medium	Large
Seeds [a]	$44.40	$36.08	$27.75	$23.04	$18.72	$14.40
Tray [b]	0.47	0.42	0.38	0.59	0.32	0.47
Growing medium	0.46	0.42	0.37	0.15	0.14	0.14
Labor	0.55	0.61	0.46	0.48	0.60	0.37
Interest on variable costs [c]	2.06	1.69	1.30	1.09	0.89	0.69
Overhead costs [d]	0.66	0.49	0.47	2.30	1.70	1.63
Total per flat	**$48.60**	**$39.71**	**$30.73**	**$27.65**	**$22.37**	**$17.70**
Total per seedling	**$0.10**	**$0.08**	**$0.06**	**$0.11**	**$0.09**	**$0.07**

[a] 555 seeds planted per conventional flat and 288 per plug flat. Germination rate is assumed to be 90%.
[b] Cost of tray, medium, and labor from Brumfield [3].
[c] Interest rate is assumed to be 9% for six months.
[d] Overhead costs are calculated using $0.200, $0.148, and $0.142 per square-foot-bench-week, respectively for small, medium, and large greenhouses. It is assumed that a flat uses 1.64 square feet (0.15 m^2) x two weeks for bare rooted seedling flats and seven weeks for plug flats.

inch (25 cm) hanging basket has five cuttings and is grown pot-to-pot for six weeks and on 15-inch (38 cm) centers for seven weeks.

A small firm producing a New Guinea impatiens in an 8-inch (20 cm) basket for $5.37 and selling it for $5 would lose money under this chapter's assumptions (table 18.5). Likewise, a small firm producing a New Guinea impatiens in a 10-inch (25 cm) basket under the assumptions presented in this chapter would lose money if the basket sells for $7.50 and costs $8.35 to produce (table 18.7). One way of reducing costs is to place only one cutting in an 8-inch (20 cm) basket and three cuttings in a 10-inch (25 cm) basket.

Growers need to experiment with their own production system to determine if this reduces plant quality and increases production time. They will also need to conduct their own cost analysis. A shorter production schedule reduces production costs (tables 18.6 and 18.8), but this may not be within the grower's control. Growing the plants at a wider spacing increases the costs (unless you believe that overhead costs are free!) and makes the product less profitable. However, a wider spacing may result in a higher quality plant that can command a premium price.

These costs are based on a specific set of conditions that will vary with each greenhouse firm. Managers should conduct their own cost analyses for information to make production and marketing decisions for their particular businesses.

Costs vary from one producer to another because of market conditions, labor supply, greenhouse age and condition, managerial skill,

TABLE 18.11

Finished flat production costs using grower produced bare rooted seedlings or plugs at three different-sized greenhouse firms

| | Bare rooted | | | Plug [e] | | | |
| | Small | Medium | Large | Small | Medium | Large | |
Variable costs						Nonauto	Auto
Seedlings [a]	$3.50	$2.86	$2.21	$3.84	$3.11	$2.46	$2.46
Flat [b]	0.47	0.42	0.38	0.47	0.42	0.38	0.38
Insert	0.29	0.25	0.23	0.29	0.25	0.23	0.23
Rooting medium	0.37	0.36	0.35	0.37	0.36	0.35	0.35
Label	0.15	0.13	0.12	0.15	0.13	0.12	0.12
Fertilizer	0.03	0.02	0.02	0.03	0.02	0.02	0.02
Pesticide	0.01	0.01	0.01	0.01	0.01	0.01	0.01
Labor	0.85	0.87	0.65	0.50	0.69	0.58	0.38
Interest on variable cost	0.26	0.22	0.18	0.25	0.22	0.19	0.18
Total variable costs	**$5.93**	**$5.14**	**$4.15**	**$5.91**	**$5.21**	**$4.34**	**$4.13**
Overhead costs [c]	3.61	2.67	2.56	1.97	1.46	1.40	1.40
Loss allocation [d]	0.50	0.41	0.35	0.41	0.35	0.30	0.29
Total per flat	**$10.04**	**$8.22**	**$7.06**	**$8.29**	**$7.02**	**$6.04**	**$5.82**

[a] 36 seedlings per finished flat.

[b] Costs other than seedlings were obtained from Brumfield [3].

[c] Overhead costs are calculated at $0.200, $0.148, and $0.142 per square-foot-bench-week for small, medium, and large greenhouses respectively. It is assumed that a flat uses 1.64 square feet of bench area per week and production takes 11 weeks for bare rooted flats and six weeks for plug flats.

[d] Based on a 5% loss.

[e] Produced in 288-cell tray.

and many other factors. The above examples can serve as a guide for the industry, but don't reflect the actual costs of any particular greenhouse. Compare your costs to these to determine your strengths and weaknesses, but doing your own cost accounting gives a true picture of your actual costs.

Growing seed New Guinea impatiens

Producing seedlings

While plug production has increased rapidly, some growers still use bare rooted seedlings for some or all of their bedding plant production. Production labor inputs for the seedling and finished flat stages for bare rooted seedlings and plugs were obtained from Jenkins' study [12] (table 18.9). In large automated greenhouses, transplanting takes place

TABLE 18.12

Finished flat production costs using purchased plugs [a] at three different-sized greenhouse firms

			Greenhouse size	
	Small	Medium	Large	
Variable costs			Nonauto	Auto
Seedlings [b]	$6.01	$5.19	$5.00	$5.00
Flat	0.47	0.42	0.38	0.38
Insert	0.29	0.25	0.23	0.23
Rooting medium	0.37	0.36	0.35	0.35
Labels	0.15	0.13	0.12	0.12
Fertilizer	0.03	0.02	0.02	0.02
Pesticide	0.01	0.01	0.01	0.01
Labor	0.50	0.69	0.58	0.38
Interest on variable costs	0.35	0.32	0.30	0.29
Total variable costs	**$8.18**	**$7.39**	**$6.99**	**$6.78**
Overhead costs [c]	1.97	1.46	1.40	1.40
Loss allocation [d]	0.53	0.47	0.44	0.43
Total per flat	**$10.68**	**$9.32**	**$8.83**	**$8.61**

[a] Plugs purchased in 288-cell tray.
[b] 36 seedlings per finished flat.
[c] Overhead costs are calculated at $0.200, $0.148, and $0.142 per square-foot-bench-week for small, medium, and large greenhouses, respectively. It is assumed that a flat uses 1.64 square feet of bench area per week and production takes six weeks for flats using plugs from a 288-cell tray.
[d] Based on a 5% loss.

on a conveyor belt and labor is considerably reduced. Some large greenhouses have switched to robotic transplanters, but their costs are not considered here.

A seedling flat occupies 1.64 square foot (0.15 m^2) of bench space and requires about 13 weeks from seeding until final sale. Seedlings are in a seedling flat for two weeks for bare rooted seedlings, and six to seven weeks for plug seedlings [12, personal communication with seed suppliers]. A germination rate of 90% is assumed, and 555 seeds are sown per conventional flat and 288 per plug flat. Seed cost is the largest cost in producing both bare rooted and plug seedlings (table 18.10). The cost per bare rooted seedling ranges from $0.06 to $0.10, while the cost for plugs ranges from $0.07 to $0.11.

Producing transplants from plugs

Most of the inputs involved in producing transplants from plugs are the same as those used to produce transplants from seedlings. However, the finished flats using plugs require only six weeks, while finished flats using bare rooted seedlings require 11 weeks. The other difference is that flats using plugs require less transplanting labor (table 18.9).

Unlike the seedling stage, production costs for a finished flat from plugs were lower than for a flat finished using barerooted seedlings. Costs in table 18.12 are the same as in table 18.11 except that in table 18.12, plugs are purchased rather than grower produced, and the costs of the finished flats are higher.

As the bedding plant industry becomes more competitive, producers will need to know their costs and be able to control them. Knowing the cost components for each crop produced will allow managers to adjust to changing market conditions by adjusting their production and marketing decisions to remain profitable.

References

[1] *Cultural requirements for Kientzler New Guinea impatiens*. 1993. Ecke Culture Guide.

[2] *New Guinea impatiens*. 1993. Ball Culture Advisor.

[3] Brumfield, R.G. 1994. Cost accounting. In *Bedding plants IV*. Batavia, Ill.: Ball Publishing.

[4] Brumfield, R.G. 1992. Greenhouse cost accounting: A computer program for making management decisions. *HortTechnology* 2(3):420-424.

[5] Brumfield, R.G. 1993. Production Costs. In *Geraniums IV*. Ed. J.W. White, Batavia, Ill.: Ball Publishing.

[6] Brumfield, R.G. 1991. Production costs. In *Tips on growing zonal geraniums*. 2d ed. Ohio State Coop. Ext. Serv.

[7] Brumfield, R.G., P.V. Nelson, A.J. Coutu, D.H. Willits, and R.S. Sowell. 1980. *Overhead costs of greenhouse firms differentiated by size of firm and market channel*. N.C. Agr. Res. Ser. Tech. Bul. 269.

[8] Brumfield, R.G., P.N. Walker, C.R. Jenkins, C.A. Frumento, L.R. Heard, and J.M. Carson. 1990. *Economic feasibility of conventional and reject water-heated greenhouses*. Rutgers Coop. Ext. Bul. E135.

[9] Bureau of Labor Statistics. U.S. Department of Labor. Producer Price Indices, Data for July 1979 to August 1993.

[10] Erwin, J. 1994. Asexually propagated bedding plants. In *Bedding plants IV*. Batavia, Ill.: Ball Publishing.

[11] Erwin, J., M. Ascerno, F. Pfleger, and R. Heins. 1992. *New Guinea impatiens production*. Minn. Commercial Flower Growers Assoc. Bul. 41(3):1-15.

[12] Jenkins, C.R. 1987. Economic analysis of Pennsylvania greenhouse production, bedding plant costs by firm size and production method: a linear programming model of output and income in a conventionally heated and a reject-water-heated greenhouse. Master's thesis, The Penn. State Univ.

[13] Kaczperski, M.P. and W. H. Carlson. 1989. *Producing New Guinea impatiens*. Mich. State Univ. Ext. Bul. E-2179.

[14] Konjoian, P.S. 1993. *New Guinea impatiens*. 1993 PPGA Conference. Duplicated.

[15] Myers, T. 1993. *Fundamentals of New Guinea impatiens production*. Duplicated.

[16] Nelson, P.V. and R.G. Brumfield. 1982. Production costs. In *Geraniums III*. Ed. J.W. Mastalerz and E.J. Holcomb. University Park, Penn.: Pennsylvania Flower Growers.

CHAPTER 19

Commercial Varieties

C. Anne Whealy

The number of commercial varieties of New Guinea impatiens offered in North America has increased from less than 60 in the late 1980s to almost 100. This proliferation of varieties is the result of new series and new varieties developed and introduced in the United States from domestic and foreign breeders (see Color Plate section, C.P. 19.1). Five breeding companies are responsible for seven series, ranging across a spectrum of 21 distinct flower colors. The series available in North America are as follows:

- Mikkel Sunshine Series, Mikkelsens, Inc., Ashtabula, Ohio USA
- Lasting Impressions Series, Mikkelsens, Inc., Ashtabula, Ohio USA
- Pure Beauty Series, Kientzler Jungpflanzen, Gensingen, Germany
- Paradise Series, Kientzler Jungpflanzen, Gensingen, Germany
- Celebration Series, Ball FloraPlant, West Chicago, Illinois USA
- Danziger Series, Dan Flower Farm, Beit Dagan, Israel
- Bull Series, Gartenbau Norbert Bull, Goennebek, Germany

The preferred New Guinea impatiens variety would provide uniformity, versatility, and exceptional performance for both the producer and the consumer. The most outstanding varieties are distinguished from other New Guinea impatiens varieties by their showy, flat, round flowers; continuous flowering and floriferousness; symmetrical and uniform plant habit; superior greenhouse and garden performance; and attractive foliage. The preferred and undesirable characteristics for New Guinea impatiens are listed in table 19.1.

The majority of New Guinea impatiens are finished in 4-inch (10 cm) pots, 6-inch (15 cm) pots, 8-inch (20 cm) hanging baskets, or 10-inch

Table 19.1

Preferred and undesirable characteristics for New Guinea impatiens varieties listed by plant part

Plant part	Preferred characteristics	Undesirable characteristics
Foliage	Nonvariegated or stable variegated foliage Shiny, dark green or bronze-red leaves Leaves held horizontally or upright Small to medium-sized leaves Smooth, nonrolling leaves	Unstable variegation Light green or dull-colored leaves Drooping leaves Large, grotesque leaves Puckered or curled leaves
Plant	Basally branching, does not require pinching Vigorous, but does not require growth retardants Symmetrical, mounded, and dense plant form Resistant and/or tolerant to insects and/or diseases	Poor branching Upright growth, requires growth retardants Nonsymmetrical, nonuniform plant habit Susceptibility to insects and/or diseases
Flowers	Large flower size, medium if floriferous Holds flowers above foliage Continues to flower over time, does not stall Floriferous Good flower to foliage color contrast Stable, nonfading, and clear flower color	Small flower size Flowers hidden underneath foliage Flowering stalls, does not continue to flower over time Not floriferous Unattractive flower to foliage color contrast Unstable flower color, faded or off-color flowers

(25 cm) hanging baskets. In general, varieties chosen for smaller pot production should be compact and for hanging baskets, varieties with spreading habits are recommended. For good landscape performance, good flower substance, larger foliage, and a more upright habit are desirable.

Purple, blue tones

Antares, Mikkel Sunshine, U.S. Plant Patent No. 7241
Foliage: Medium green leaves, variegated under high light
Plant: Compact to moderately vigorous with good mounded plant form
Flowers: Floriferous with white-eyed small flowers
Recommendation: Small pots, 4-inch (10 cm), and small hanging baskets, 8-inch (20 cm)

Aruba, Paradise, U.S. Plant Patent No. 8456
Foliage: Dark green, nonvariegated leaves
Plant: Compact plant habit
Flowers: Rounded, cupped flowers

Bora-Bora, Paradise, U.S. Plant Patent No. 8421 (see CP 19.2)
Foliage: Green, nonvariegated leaves

Plant: Compact to moderately vigorous; good mounded habit
Flowers: Large, rounded, flat flowers
Recommendation: Small pots, 4-inch (10 cm), and small hanging baskets, 8-inch (20 cm)

Purple, red tones

Apollon, Pure Beauty, U.S. Plant Patent No. 8429
Foliage: Dark green, nonvariegated leaves
Plant: Vigorous and upright
Flowers: Cupped flowers, sometimes hidden in foliage

Celebration Raspberry Rose, Celebration, U.S. Plant Patent Applied For (see CP 19.3)
Foliage: Medium green leaves, nonvariegated
Plant: Moderate vigor
Flowers: Large flowers, floriferous

Samba, Danziger, U.S. Plant Patent No. 8110
Foliage: Green, nonvariegated leaves
Plant: Moderately vigorous and upright plant habit
Flowers: Large, flat, rounded flowers

Danserra, Danziger, U.S. Plant Patent No. 8264
Foliage: Green, nonvariegated leaves
Plant: Compact to moderately vigorous, upright plant habit
Flowers: Lobed flowers hidden in foliage

Rhapsody, Lasting Impressions, U.S. Plant Patent No. 8396 (see CP 19.4)
Foliage: Green, nonvariegated leaves
Plant: Moderate to high vigor, spreading plant habit
Flowers: Large, flat, rounded flowers, very showy
Recommendation: Large pots, 6-inch (15 cm), and 10-inch (25 cm) hanging baskets

Papete, Paradise, U.S. Plant Patent No. 8457
Foliage: Green, nonvariegated leaves
Plant: Compact and upright
Flowers: Rounded, cupped flowers hidden in foliage

Purple bicolor

Sunregal, Mikkel Sunshine, U.S. Plant Patent No. 6389 (see CP 19.5)
Foliage: Dark green, nonvariegated leaves, good contrast
Plant: Compact to medium grower
Flowers: Small lobed flowers, but floriferous
Recommendation: Small pots, 4-inch (10 cm), and small hanging baskets, 8-inch (20 cm)

Octavia, Pure Beauty, U.S. Plant Patent No. 8430
 Foliage: Green, nonvariegated leaves
 Plant: Moderate to high vigor, upright plant habit
 Flowers: Cupped flowers

Shadow, Lasting Impressions, U.S. Plant Patent No. 8904
 Foliage: Dark green, nonvariegated leaves
 Plant: Moderately vigorous
 Flowers: Extremely large purple and red flowers, some flower
 form distortion

Lavender

Saturnia, Pure Beauty, U.S. Plant Patent No. 7839
 Foliage: Medium green, nonvariegated leaves
 Plant: Medium vigor
 Flowers: Cupped flowers

**Celebration Light Lavender II, Celebration, U.S. Plant Patent
Applied For** (see CP 19.6)
 Foliage: Medium green leaves, nonvariegated
 Plant: Moderate vigor
 Flowers: Large, flat flowers

Flamenco, Danziger, U.S. Plant Patent No. 8112 (see CP 19.7)
 Foliage: Green, nonvariegated leaves
 Plant: Moderate to high vigor, mounded plant habit, durable
 Flowers: Large, flat flowers, floriferous
 Recommendation: Large pots, 6-inch (15 cm), and hanging
 baskets, 8- and 10-inch (20- and 25 cm)

Heathermist, Lasting Impressions, U.S. Plant Patent No. 7797
 Foliage: Dark green, nonvariegated leaves
 Plant: Moderate vigor
 Flowers: Cupped flowers hidden in foliage

Serenade, Lasting Impressions, U.S. Plant Patent No. 8513
 Foliage: Dark green, nonvariegated leaves
 Plant: Moderate vigor, nice mounded plant habit
 Flowers: Round, flat flowers with white eye, floriferous
 Recommendation: Small and large pots, 4- or 6-inch (10- or
 15 cm), and large hanging baskets, 10-inch (25 cm)

Tonga, Paradise, U.S. Plant Patent No. 8408
 Foliage: Dark bronze, nonvariegated leaves
 Plant: Compact, upright plant habit
 Flowers: Cupped flowers hidden in foliage

White

Cirrus, Mikkel Sunshine, U.S. Plant Patent No. 6002
Foliage: Dull variegated leaves
Plant: Moderate to high vigor, upright plant habit
Flowers: Lobed flowers

Milky Way, Mikkel Sunshine, U.S. Plant Patent No. 5125
Foliage: Variegated leaves
Plant: Medium vigor
Flowers: Lobed flowers

Jasius, Pure Beauty, U.S. Plant Patent No. 7345
Foliage: Medium green, nonvariegated leaves
Plant: Compact to moderate vigor, uniform plant habit
Flowers: Clear white, lobed flowers that may pink under high light and high temperatures

Celebration Pure White, Celebration, U.S. Plant Patent No. 8410
(see CP 19.8)
Foliage: Medium green, shiny, nonvariegated leaves, good contrast
Plant: Moderately vigorous
Flowers: Rounded flowers, clean white color, no blushing
Recommendation: Small pots, 4-inch (10 cm), and small hanging baskets, 8-inch (20 cm)

Waltz, Danziger, U.S. Plant Patent No. 8109
Foliage: Medium green, nonvariegated leaves
Plant: Moderately vigorous and upright
Flowers: Lobed flowers hidden in foliage

Innocence, Lasting Impressions, U.S. Plant Patent No. 7789
Foliage: Medium green leaves that become variegated under high light
Plant: Medium vigor
Flowers: Small lobed flowers, but floriferous
Recommendation: Large pots, 6-inch (15 cm) and large hanging baskets, 10-inch (25 cm)

Moorea, Paradise, U.S. Plant Patent Applied For
Foliage: Medium green glossy leaves
Plant: Compact habit
Flowers: Clear white, large, and rounded flowers

Blush white

Celebration Blush White, Celebration, U.S. Plant Patent No. 8538
Foliage: Bronze, nonvariegated leaves that become lighter under high light

Plant: Habit is uniform and medium vigor
Flowers: White flowers with a medium pink eye

Samoa (Improved), Paradise, U.S. Plant Patent Applied For (see CP 19.9)
Foliage: Medium to dark green, nonvariegated leaves, good contrast
Plant: Moderately vigorous
Flowers: Large, round, flat flowers that are more white than original Samoa
Recommendation: Large pots, 6-inch (15 cm) and large hanging baskets, 10-inch (25 cm)

Light pink

Equinox, Mikkel Sunshine, U.S. Plant Patent No. 6297
Foliage: Dark green leaves that become red under high light, nice contrast
Plant: Medium vigor
Flowers: Floriferous, good flower form
Recommendation: Good for all sizes of pots and baskets, landscape

Tahiti, Paradise, U.S. Plant Patent No. 8601
Foliage: Green, nonvariegated leaves
Plant: Compact to moderately vigorous, upright plant habit
Flowers: Rounded flowers, sometimes hidden in foliage

Melanie, Bull, U.S. Plant Patent No. 8368
Foliage: Medium green, nonvariegated leaves
Plant: Moderately vigorous, upright plant habit
Flowers: Floriferous, but lobed flowers hidden in foliage

Medium pink

Gemini, Mikkel Sunshine, U.S. Plant Patent No. 5132
Foliage: Variegated foliage, long narrow leaves
Plant: Upright and vigorous habit, open plant form
Flowers: Gappy flowers, elongated peduncles

Delias, Pure Beauty, U.S. Plant Patent No. 7838
Foliage: Medium green, nonvariegated leaves
Plant: Compact, uniform and upright habit
Flowers: Cupped flowers sometimes hidden in foliage

Celebration Deep Pink, Celebration, U.S. Plant Patent No. 8409
Foliage: Dark green, nonvariegated leaves, excellent contrast
Plant: Uniform habit, moderately vigorous, free-branching
Flowers: Large, rounded flowers with dark pink eye, floriferous

Recommendation: Small pots, 4-inch (10 cm), and small hanging baskets, 8-inch (20 cm)

Rosetta, Lasting Impressions, U.S. Plant Patent No. 7791
Foliage: Bronze, nonvariegated leaves, nice contrast
Plant: Medium vigor
Flowers: Rose-pink lobed flowers that may fade under high light
Recommendation: Large pots, 6-inch (15 cm) and large hanging baskets, 10-inch (25 cm)

Pink bicolor

Celebration Candy Pink, Celebration, U.S. Plant Patent No. 7670
Foliage: Dark red-green, nonvariegated leaves
Plant: Uniform plant habit and medium vigor
Flowers: Large, rounded, flat flowers with dark pink radiating lines and eye
Recommendation: All sizes pots and baskets

Dark pink

Dark Delias, Pure Beauty, U.S. Plant Patent Applied For
Foliage: Medium green, nonvariegated leaves
Plant: Compact and uniform, upright habit
Flowers: Floriferous

Kallima, Pure Beauty, U.S. Plant Patent Applied For (see CP 19.10)
Foliage: Dark green leaves, excellent contrast
Plant: Medium vigor, upright
Flowers: Silvery pink flowers, floriferous

Dandin, Danziger, U.S. Plant Patent No. 8262
Foliage: Dark green, nonvariegated leaves
Plant: Moderate to high vigor, upright plant habit
Flowers: Large, lobed flowers that fade under high light

Impulse, Lasting Impressions, U.S. Plant Patent No. 8437 (see CP 19.11)
Foliage: Green, nonvariegated leaves
Plant: Moderately vigorous
Flowers: Lobed flowers, but floriferous
Recommendation: All sizes pots and baskets

Hot pink

Aglia, Pure Beauty, U.S. Plant Patent No. 6684 (see CP 19.12)
Foliage: Variegated leaves
Plant: Medium vigor, upright plant habit

Flowers: Large, lobed flowers, floriferous

Recommendation: Large pots, 6-inch (15 cm), and large hanging baskets, 10-inch (25 cm), landscape

Celebration Electric Pink, Celebration, U.S. Plant Patent No. 8399 (see CP 19.13)

Foliage: Dark green, shiny, nonvariegated leaves

Plant: Moderately vigorous with upright plant habit, good uniformity

Flowers: Extremely large, lobed flowers that are radiant

Recommendation: Large pots, 6-inch (15 cm), and large hanging baskets, 10-inch (25 cm), landscape

Dangal, Danziger, U.S. Plant Patent No. 8251

Foliage: Medium green, nonvariegated leaves

Plant: Moderately vigorous

Flowers: Cupped flowers sometimes hidden in foliage

Lambada, Danziger, U.S. Plant Patent Applied For

Foliage: Bronze, nonvariegated leaves

Plant: Compact to moderately vigorous, upright plant habit

Flowers: Lobed flowers hidden in foliage

Doerte, Bull, U.S. Plant Patent No. 8358

Foliage: Medium green, nonvariegated leaves

Plant: Moderately vigorous and upright plant habit

Flowers: Lobed flowers

Cherry red

Rondo, Danziger, U.S. Plant Patent No. 8111

Foliage: Medium green, nonvariegated leaves

Plant: Moderately vigorous and upright plant habit

Flowers: Cupped flowers hidden in foliage

Martinique, Paradise, U.S. Plant Patent Applied For (see CP 19.14)

Foliage: Green, nonvariegated leaves

Plant: Compact and upright

Flowers: Intense flower color

Anna, Bull, U.S. Plant Patent No. 8334

Foliage: Medium green, nonvariegated leaves

Plant: Moderately vigorous

Flowers: Lobed flowers hidden in foliage

Fuchsia

Pulsar, Mikkel Sunshine, U.S. Plant Patent No. 5783

Foliage: Dark variegated leaves

Plant: Medium vigor and upright plant habit
Flowers: Lobed flowers sometimes hidden in foliage

Red bicolor

Flambe, Pure Beauty, U.S. Plant Patent No. 7830
Foliage: Dull-colored, variegated leaves
Plant: Medium vigor and upright plant habit
Flowers: Large pink and red bicolor flowers

Celebration Cherry Star, Celebration, U.S. Plant Patent No. 8407
Foliage: Dark bronze, glossy, nonvariegated leaves, good contrast
Plant: Compact to moderately vigorous, uniform habit, excellent basal branching
Flowers: Large, flat, rounded flowers, distinct star pattern
Recommendation: Small pots, 4-inch (10 cm) and small hanging baskets, 8-inch (20 cm), landscape

Celebration Apple Star, Celebration, U.S. Plant Patent Applied For (see CP 19.15)
Foliage: Dark green leaves that are variegated under high light
Plant: Moderate to high vigor with upright plant habit
Flowers: Lobed red and white bicolor flowers

Danlight, Danziger, U.S. Plant Patent No. 8276
Foliage: Medium green, nonvariegated leaves
Plant: Moderate to high vigor, upright habit
Flowers: Rounded flowers

Ambience, Lasting Impressions, U.S. Plant Patent No. 8903 (see CP 19.16)
Foliage: Medium green, shiny, nonvariegated leaves, good contrast
Plant: Moderately vigorous, uniform habit
Flowers: Large, rounded, flat flowers
Recommendation: Large pots, 6-inch (15 cm) and large hanging baskets, 10-inch (25 cm), landscape

Pago Pago, Paradise, U.S. Plant Patent Applied For (see CP 19.17)
Foliage: Bronze, nonvariegated leaves
Plant: Compact
Flowers: Pink and red bicolor flowers

Red/scarlet

Mirach, Mikkel Sunshine, U.S. Plant Patent No. 6309
Foliage: Variegated leaves
Plant: Medium vigor, uniform habit
Flowers: Lobed flowers, good red color

Anaea, Pure Beauty, U.S. Plant Patent No. 7840
Foliage: Medium green, nonvariegated leaves
Plant: Medium vigor
Flowers: Cupped, lobed flowers

Prepona, Pure Beauty, U.S. Plant Patent Applied For (see CP 19.18)
Foliage: Medium green, nonvariegated leaves
Plant: Medium vigor
Flowers: Large, flat, rounded flowers

Celebration Bright Scarlet, Celebration, U.S. Plant Patent No. 8406
Foliage: Medium green, nonvariegated leaves
Plant: Compact to moderate vigor, good basal branching
Flowers: Large orange-scarlet flowers

Celebration Red, Celebration, U.S. Plant Patent Applied For (see CP 19.19)
Foliage: Medium green foliage, nonvariegated
Plant: Medium vigor
Flowers: Large, flat flowers

Danhill, Danziger, U.S. Plant Patent No. 8263
Foliage: Variegated leaves
Plant: Moderate to high vigor, upright plant habit
Flowers: Lobed bright red flowers, floriferous
Recommendation: Large hanging baskets, 10-inch (25 cm), landscape

Blazon, Lasting Impressions, U.S. Plant Patent No. 7793 (see CP 19.20)
Foliage: Medium green leaves that are variegated under high light
Plant: Moderately vigorous, upright plant habit
Flowers: Bright red flowers
Recommendation: Large pots, 6-inch (15 cm), and large hanging baskets, 10-inch (25 cm), landscape

Lanai, Paradise, U.S. Plant Patent No. 8397
Foliage: Medium green, nonvariegated leaves
Plant: Moderately vigorous and upright plant habit
Flowers: Good flower substance, but sometimes hidden in foliage
Recommendation: Small pots, 4-inch (10 cm), and small hanging baskets, 8-inch (20 cm)

Karina, Bull, U.S. Plant Patent Applied For (see CP 19.21)
Foliage: Medium green, nonvariegated leaves
Plant: Compact to moderate vigor, upright plant habit
Flowers: Cupped flowers hidden in foliage

Dark orange

Nova, Mikkel Sunshine, U.S. Plant Patent No. 6004
> Foliage: Dark variegated leaves
> Plant: Compact to moderate vigor
> Flowers: Large, lobed flowers

Marpesia, Pure Beauty, U.S. Plant Patent No. 8401
> Foliage: Dark bronze, nonvariegated leaves
> Plant: Moderately vigorous
> Flowers: Cupped flowers sometimes hidden in foliage

Celebration Bonfire Orange, Celebration, U.S. Plant Patent No. 8398
> Foliage: Dark bronze leaves, nice contrast
> Plant: Compact to moderate vigor, uniform plant habit
> Flowers: Floriferous, small, rounded flowers
> Recommendation: Small pots, 4-inch (10 cm) and small hanging baskets, 8-inch (20 cm), landscape

Ambrosia, Lasting Impressions, U.S. Plant Patent No. 7788 (see CP 19.22)
> Foliage: Dark bronze, nonvariegated leaves, good contrast
> Plant: Medium to high vigor, upright plant habit
> Flowers: Floriferous, cupped flowers
> Recommendation: Large pots, 6-inch (15 cm), landscape

Timor, Paradise, U.S. Plant Patent Applied For
> Foliage: Medium green nonvariegated leaves
> Plant: Compact and upright
> Flowers: Rounded electric orange flowers

Susanne, Bull, U.S. Plant Patent No. 8360
> Foliage: Medium green, nonvariegated leaves
> Plant: Moderate to high vigor, upright plant habit
> Flowers: Showy, large, cupped flowers

Orange

Zenith, Mikkel Sunshine, U.S. Plant Patent No. 5804
> Foliage: Variegated leaves
> Plant: Moderately vigorous
> Flowers: Floriferous
> Recommendation: Small pots, 4-inch (10 cm) and small hanging baskets, 8-inch (20 cm)

Nebulous, Mikkel Sunshine, U.S. Plant Patent No. 7097
> Foliage: Bronze, nonvariegated leaves
> Plant: Moderate to high vigor, upright plant habit

Flowers: Floriferous, showy

Recommendation: Large pots, 6-inch (15 cm), landscape

Escapade, Lasting Impressions, U.S. Plant Patent No. 8315

Foliage: Medium green, nonvariegated leaves

Plant: Moderately vigorous, uniform plant habit

Flowers: Large, flat, rounded flowers, bright flower color

Recommendation: Small pots, 4-inch (10 cm) and small hanging baskets, 8-inch (20 cm), landscape

Antigua, Paradise, U.S. Plant Patent No. 8283

Foliage: Medium green, nonvariegated leaves

Plant: Moderately vigorous, upright plant habit

Flowers: Bright flower color, good substance

Tanna, Paradise, U.S. Plant Patent Applied For

Foliage: Bronze, nonvariegated foliage

Plant: Compact habit

Flowers: Rounded flowers, floriferous

Mathilde, Bull, U.S. Plant Patent No. 8366

Foliage: Dark bronze, nonvariegated leaves

Plant: Moderately vigorous, upright plant habit

Flowers: Rounded small flowers

Salmon/dark coral

Melissa, Pure Beauty, U.S. Plant Patent No. 7837

Foliage: Dark green, nonvariegated leaves

Plant: Moderately vigorous, upright plant habit

Flowers: Rounded, cupped flowers

Celebration Deep Coral, Celebration, U.S. Plant Patent Applied For

(see CP 19.23)

Foliage: Bronze variegated leaves

Plant: Medium vigor

Flowers: Large flowers, vibrant color

Celebration Salmon, Celebration, U.S. Plant Patent No. 8870 (see CP 19.24)

Foliage: Variegated leaves

Plant: Moderately vigorous

Flowers: Large, round, flat flowers, floriferous

Recommendation: Small pots, 4-inch (10 cm), and small hanging baskets, 8-inch (20 cm), landscape

Charade, Lasting Impressions, U.S. Plant Patent No. 7787

Foliage: Dark bronze leaves that become variegated under high light

Plant: Compact to moderate vigor
Flowers: Lobed flowers, sometimes hidden in foliage

Bonaire, Paradise, U.S. Plant Patent Applied For (see CP 19.25)
Foliage: Dark reddish-green leaves
Plant: Compact and upright
Flowers: Lobed flowers, good substance

Inge, Bull, U.S. Plant Patent No. 8357
Foliage: Dark green, nonvariegated leaves
Plant: Compact to moderately vigorous, upright plant habit
Flowers: Cupped flowers hidden in foliage

Coral

Celebration Bright Coral, Celebration, U.S. Plant Patent No. 8848
Foliage: Medium green, nonvariegated leaves
Plant: Moderately vigorous, upright plant habit
Flowers: Large showy flowers

Illusion, Lasting Impressions, U.S. Plant Patent No. 7796
Foliage: Medium green, nonvariegated leaves
Plant: Medium to high vigor, upright plant habit
Flowers: Lobed, cupped flowers

Rosemarie, Bull, U.S. Plant Patent No. 8335
Foliage: Dark green, nonvariegated leaves
Plant: Moderately vigorous, upright plant habit
Flowers: Rounded flowers that fade under high light

Light salmon

Celebration Light Salmon, Celebration, U.S. Plant Patent Applied For
Foliage: Variegated medium green leaves
Plant: Moderately vigorous
Flowers: Large flowers, floriferous

Danshir, Danziger, U.S. Plant Patent No. 8252
Foliage: Dark green, nonvariegated leaves
Plant: Compact to moderately vigorous
Flowers: Cupped, lobed flowers

Cameo, Lasting Impressions, U.S. Plant Patent No. 8316 (see CP 19.26)
Foliage: Medium green leaves that are variegated under high light
Plant: Moderate to high vigor
Flowers: Large flowers, floriferous
Recommendation: Large pots, 6-inch (15 cm) and large hanging baskets, 10-inch (25 cm), landscape

Grenada, Paradise, U.S. Plant Patent Applied For
Foliage: Glossy bronze foliage
Plant: Compact
Flowers: Coral pink with dark eyed flowers

Orange bicolor

Twilight, Mikkel Sunshine, U.S. Plant Patent No. 5869
Foliage: Variegated dark green leaves
Plant: Moderately vigorous, upright plant habit
Flowers: Orange and white bicolor flowers, sometimes hidden in foliage

Danova, Danziger, U.S. Plant Patent No. 8275 (see CP 19.27)
Foliage: Dark bronze, nonvariegated leaves
Plant: Moderately vigorous, upright plant habit
Flowers: Cupped flowers sometimes hidden in foliage

Tempest, Lasting Impressions, U.S. Plant Patent No. 8938
Foliage: Variegated leaves
Plant: Moderately vigorous
Flowers: Unique reddish orange and white flowers

Editor's Note
An exciting characteristic—a double-flowered New Guinea impatiens—has been introduced recently by Mikkelsens in the Twice as Nice series. Further breeding should improve the double-flowered types and increase their commercial importance.

CHAPTER 20

Genetics

Mark Strefeler

Impatiens are distributed throughout tropical Africa, southwest Asia, and southern China. The greatest number of species are found in India [18]. A small number of species occur in northern temperate areas of Europe, China, North America, and the former Soviet Union [18].

New Guinea impatiens have increased in popularity since the release of the first cultivars in 1972. New Guinea impatiens' popularity is due to the large flowers and the wide range of flower colors and foliage types. An important characteristic of New Guinea impatiens is their tendency to self-branching [26, 31]. Improvements of New Guinea impatiens cultivars by plant breeders have resulted in compact, well-branched plants. Much has been accomplished in New Guinea impatiens breeding in the areas of new flower and foliage colors and types, but more work needs to be done to improve heat and drought tolerance and pest resistance.

New Guinea impatiens can also be used as potted flowering plants and in hanging baskets. Although cultural practices can remedy some problems associated with New Guinea impatiens production, the introduction of improved cultivars offers a long-term, economical solution. Current breeding programs have been successful in solving these problems over the last 20 years. These programs will continue to offer improved cultivars that are easier to grow, with better performance than those in existence today.

Botanical classification ──────────────

New Guinea impatiens, *Impatiens hawkeri*, belongs to the family Balsaminaceae, which consists of only two genera: *Impatiens*: with 850 to 900 species that are native to Eurasia and Africa, and five species that are native to North America (*I. capensis* Merrb., *I. pallida* Nutt., *I. noli-tangere* L., *I. ecalcaarata* Blankinship and *I. aurella* Rydb) [54]. The first two native North American *Impatiens* species are commonly named Spotted Touch-Me-Not and Pale Touch-Me-Not, respectively. The other member genus of the family is *Hydrocera*, which consists of only one species, native to Indomalaysia. Some authors recognize two other genera, *Impatientella* (one species in Madagascar) and *Seneiocardium* (one species in Indomalaysia) [23].

  Impatiens are annuals or perennial herbaceous plants with watery, translucent stems. Leaves are alternate or opposite, simple, and usually without stipules. Flowers are bisexual and irregular in form. The calyx consists of three, free, usually petaloid sepals, with the lower sepal spurred. Sometimes there may be two small additional sepals present on the flower. The corolla consists of five petals. The dorsal petal is free with the lateral petals fused in pairs (in *Hydrocera* all petals are free). There are five stamens with introrse anthers that are more or less fused and form a cap over the ovary. The ovary is superior, consisting of five fused carpels that contain numerous anatropous ovules on axil placentas. Stigmas are sessile, numbering one to five per flower. The fruit is an explosive capsule (in *Hydrocera*, fruit are indehiscent and berry-like). Seeds are without endosperm [23].

  The impatiens from New Guinea were initially split into 12 to 14 species [30] but according to Grey-Wilson [19] there was not enough evidence to separate the New Guinea *Impatiens* into different species. The earliest name for this taxon is *I. hawkeri* Bull, published in 1886. New Guinea impatiens, *I. hawkeri*, is probably a highly variable species. Grey-Wilson [19] was able to distinguish 15 groups within this species divided on a geographical basis, although these were not given a formal taxonomic rank. Two closely related species that have been used in cultivar improvement, *I. platypetala* and *I. aurantiaca*, are native to the islands of Java and Celebes, respectively.

Origin

New Guinea impatiens were first collected by J.D. Hawker. These plants were first cultivated at the Adelaide Botanic Garden and sent by Dr. Schomburgk in 1884 to Mr. Bull of Chelsea. The New Guinea impatiens was described as *Impatiens hawkeri* Bull, in *Bull's Catalogue* of 1886. Later in the same year a more detailed account, together with a fine illustration, appeared in the *Gardeners' Chronicle*. The first herbarium specimen was derived from these cultivated plants and was deposited at the Kew Herbarium. New Guinea impatiens were frequently seen in botanical gardens of Europe, mostly under the name of *Impatiens hawkeri*, but occasionally as *Impatiens herzogii* [19].

New Guinea impatiens were collected by H.F. Winters and J.J. Higgins in 1970 and brought to the United States. Plants originally identified as different species, *I. herzogii, I. schlecteri, I. linearifolia*, and *I. hawkeri*, are the progenitors of modern day commercial cultivars. The former three species are now all considered to be *I. hawkeri*.

New Guinea impatiens occur throughout the Island of New Guinea, except for the lowlands of the north and south. They are found from 660 to 10,400 feet (200 to 3,150 m). Their habitat is in the moist mountainous and submontane forests; rarely in the alpine region or at low altitudes. They usually grow in damp sites in full sunlight or partially shaded areas along the margins of streams and rivers, by roadsides and along tracks, in ravines and creeks and amongst moist rocks. The New Guinea *Impatiens* complex occurs on the Island of New Guinea and extends eastward into the Bismarck Archipelago and the Solomon Islands.

Taxonomy. The fact that the different groups of New Guinea impatiens easily cross with each other and produce fertile offspring supports the classification of New Guinea *Impatiens* as one variable species. In this chapter, the species *I. hawkeri* is implied when "New Guinea impatiens" is referred. New Guinea impatiens have also been able to hybridize with species from Java (*I. platypetala*; 2n = 16) and Celebes (*I. aurantiaca*; 2n = 8), but the offspring of these crosses are often sterile. Hybrids that were produced in the United States are known under a variety of specific and cultivar names, and the nomenclature and taxonomy of both these and the genus in the wild is needed to prevent further confusions and uncertainties [18, 19, 20, 37].

> *Impatiens hawkeri* Bull. First described in *Bull Catal* 8 (1886) & in Gard. Chron. (1886) 25: 760, fig. 168.
>
> Synonyms are:
> *Impatiens herzogii* K. Sch. (1888)
> *Impatiens herzogii* Hooker (1911)
> *Impatiens klossii* Ridley (1916)
> *Impatiens lauterbachii* Warburg (1905)
> *Impatiens linearifolia* Warburg (1905)
> *Impatiens mooreana* Schlechter (1913)
> *Impatiens nivea* Schlechter (1917)
> *Impatiens polyphylla* Warburg (1905)
> *Impatiens rodatzii* Warburg (1905)

Impatiens schlechteri Warburg (1905)
Impatiens schlechteri Grey-Wilson (1976)
Impatiens trichura Warburg (1905)

Anatomy

Description of *Impatiens hawkeri* Bull (from van Royen)[37]:

Herb, 10-110 cm high, simple or branched, solitary or in large groups. Stems usually green, but often wine red or purplish, often at first finely densely to sparsely pubescent, sometimes glabrescent, rarely entirely glabrous, decumbent to erect. Leaves 3-7 - whorled, 5-32 cm long, limb finely pubescent on either side or sometimes glabrous above, lighter and often grayish or silvery shiny below, often variegated, often along margin and nerves red, dark pink, white or green; ovate-elliptic, linear, linear-elliptic, elliptic, elliptic-oblong, oblong, or oblanceolate, 4-26 by 1-6.3 cm, tip acute to long-acuminate, base attenuate or cuneate, midrib flattened above, prominent below, lateral nerves 4-14 on either side of midrib; margin slightly crenate, the crenation's with scarcely developed filiform appendages, 1-2 mm long, sometimes finely to coarsely serrate or crenate-dentate and lower teeth terminating sometimes in filiform appendages, 3-5 mm long. Petioles often reddish, 0.5-6 cm long, glabrous. Pedicel's red, green, purplish brown, light to dark pink, orange or scarlet, 2-7 cm long. Calyx white, main nerves green or only tips green, lanceolate-linear, 4-15 by 1-6 mm, tips acute. Spur white, tip light green, 2.7-10 cm long. Corolla pink, very light lilac, purple, snow white, often tinged with pink on back, vermilion, orange, scarlet, salmon-pink, or bright orange. Lateral united petals 2-lobed, upper lobe broadly obovate to oblong, 1.9-4.2 cm long, tip obtuse or shortly 2-lobed, lower lobe broadly elliptic, apiculate to rounded, Upper petals suborbicular to quadrangular, 16-31 by 11-25 mm, slightly to deeply 2-lobed at tip and often apiculate between the lobes, anthers white, dark green at base, or red, 2-4 mm long. Ovary glabrous. Capsule ellipsoid to fusiform, 1.8-4 cm long. Pedicels elongate up to 12 cm.

Breeding history of New Guinea impatiens

New Guinea impatiens were first collected in 1884 and placed in cultivation at the Adelaide Botanic Garden. The first plants were described in 1886, and since that time have been distributed to botanic gardens, throughout Europe. Cultivation of New Guinea impatiens were restricted to the botanic gardens, and little attempt was made to commercialize this species during the 85 years following its initial introduction into Europe.

One of the main reasons New Guinea impatiens were not introduced to horticulture is that seeds are difficult to find and collect because of the way *Impatiens* disperse their seeds. The mature capsules explode at the slightest touch, scattering the seeds in all directions [51].

New Guinea impatiens have been cultivated widely in their land of origin: New Guinea; especially in the Western and Eastern Highlands and in the districts of Morobe and Madang. They are frequently planted around or within the confines of villages and along pathways. Many forms are grown, especially those with large, brightly colored, flowers and those with reddish, purple or variegated leaves [19].

New Guinea impatiens became important to Western horticulture only after a number of specimens were collected in 1970 and brought back to the United States. In 1970, H.F. Winters and J.J. Higgins of the Agricultural Research Service, U.S. Department of Agrigulture (USDA) went on a plant exploration to New Guinea to collect species of begonia, hoya, rhododendron, ferns, and other genera. The expedition was co-sponsored by the USDA and the Longwood Foundation. During their trip they noticed large numbers of different impatiens growing in the jungle. The collectors, with help of the natives, collected as many specimens as possible, and from these plants, 25 specimens survived the trip back to the United States [6, 14, 26, 30, 31, 51].

After nearly two years in quarantine, the USDA released cuttings from the New Guinea impatiens collection to research stations, commercial growers, and breeders [30, 31, and Appendix 1].

Prior to release by the USDA, Longwood Gardens had received propagules of the collected plants. The first breeding was already in progress under the supervision of R.J. Armstrong, and the first crosses were made during the winters of 1971-1972 and 1972-1973. The first 10 cultivars of New Guinea impatiens were released in 1972 as the Circus series. Many of these cultivars had variegated foliage. The primary use of these cultivars was as bedding plants in annual gardens and landscape plantings [14, 31, 51].

Dr. Toru Arisumi, plant geneticist at the Agricultural Research Center in Beltsville, Maryland, released a number of hybrids after he had intermated each of the collected plants with each other. These plants were again hybridized by other plant breeders [30] and serve as the germplasm base of nearly all the current cultivars.

In 1974 Iowa State University introduced the Cyclone Hybrids, also known as the Star series. They all have variegated leaves and deep violet flowers. These plants were obtained by Allen R. Beck and his staff, with support from the Society of Iowa Florists. The most praised cultivar from the Cyclone Hybrids was the cultivar Star Fire. It forms well-branched plants and flowers year-round. Most of these cultivars grow best in light shade [31, 55].

The California-Florida Corporation in Fremont, California, was successful with their American Indian Series named after Indian tribes. These cultivars all have large and abundant flowers.

In 1975 the Bicentennial series of New Guinea impatiens was released by Mikkelsens, Inc. of Ashtabula, Ohio. These cultivars represented a distinct stage of New Guinea impatiens development. Instead of resembling the original collections, which were spindly, weak, and poor blooming plants, these new cultivars were compact, floriferous, vigorous, and long-lasting plants. These cultivars were named after historical figures such as Betsy Ross. The Mikkelsens' new breeding goals were to develop cultivars with bicolor blossoms and highly variegated foliage. It did not take long before Mikkelsens, Inc. developed the Sunshine series, which truly outshone the Bicentennial series cultivars. The Sunshine series was characterized by cultivars that flowered abundantly in full sun and were quite striking because of their variegated leaves [30, 31].

The Longwood Gardens' breeding program issued a second set of hybrids in 1973. The new set had somewhat larger flowers and up to twice as many blossoms on each plant. [31].

A big breakthrough in breeding New Guinea impatiens occurred in 1987. Ludwig Kientzler of Kientzler Jungpflanzen in Germany introduced his Kientzler cultivars, which were named after French butterflies. His breeding goals were more focused on the European market, which preferred bright, fluorescent, single colored blossoms and very dark, single colored foliage. Later his selection criteria also included bicolor flowers and variegated foliage [30].

By 1984, New Guinea impatiens had become one of the most popular bedding plants in the United States because the new cultivars produced compact plants that were highly adaptable to a variety of light conditions—from full sun to partial shade—and came in a wide variety of colors ranging from white, pink, red and orange and several bicolor large flowers, which in some cultivars can be larger than 2 ¾ inches (7 cm) in diameter. These cultivars were attractive for their several foliage types that consisted of different forms—slightly rounded to lanceolate with smooth to serrated edges and the variety of leaf colors that ranged from green to burgundy or variegated.

The latest breakthroughs in New Guinea impatiens occurred in 1990 with the introduction of the first hybrid seed mix, Spectra, by PanAmerican Seed Company [1] (see Color Plate section, CP 20.1) and in 1992 with the development of the Twice as Nice series of double flowered New Guinea impatiens by Mikkelsens (CP 20.2).

New Guinea impatiens breeding ⎯⎯⎯

A great deal of progress has been made in New Guinea impatiens breeding. This rapid success can be attributed to the great diversity observed in progeny of crosses for flower and foliage color, size, and shape (CP 20.3). These highly diverse populations offer great potential for improving New Guinea impatiens and developing novel types for the market.

Most of the effort has been focused on qualitative traits, but current trends in the decreasing availability of pesticides and other agricultural chemicals for use during production, warrant a change in emphasis to breeding for tolerance of insect, disease, and environmental stresses.

Insects and mites can cause problems in growing New Guinea impatiens. The pest that causes the most problems is the two-spotted spider mite. During warm weather, spider mites can multiply quickly and devastate a crop of New Guinea impatiens. Variation in susceptibility to the two-spotted spider mite between different genotypes of New Guinea impatiens has been reported [38]. Resistance was significantly correlated with the cuticle content. Resistant plants all contained P.I. 354259 (P.I. = Plant Introduction) in their pedigree; probably P.I. 354259 contains a dominant resistant gene [38]. The cultivar Tangerine has been observed to be highly susceptible to the spider mite. Our own observations indicate that Tangerine is also highly susceptible to whitefly.

Due to high water demand, New Guinea impatiens are susceptible to several root rot diseases, including Rhizoctonia, Pythium, and Phytophthora. Botrytis is another major disease, occurring under cool, humid conditions, or when old flowers remain on the leaves [26, 30]. Breeding for low-water-requiring plants may reduce problems by allowing New Guinea impatiens to be grown under conditions less favorable for root rot organisms.

The University of Minnesota's New Guinea impatiens breeding program has focused on breeding for drought tolerance or reduced water requirements. Plants with improved drought tolerance would require less water and avoid some of the problems mentioned above. Crosses have been made among commercial cultivars, cultivars x species and cultivars x breeding lines. Drought tolerant plants have been selected based on leaf morphology and cuticular characteristics.

A study was conducted to evaluate the effectiveness of our selection methods and to assess the genetic variability for drought tolerance present in existing germplasm. In this study, six commercial cultivars (Anna, Aurore, Danhill, Danlight, Melanie and Thecla), one drought tolerant cultivar (Orangeade), nine breeding selections, and one check genotype of *I. hawkeri* Bull were evaluated for differences in drought tolerance based on water loss and time to wilt. The six commercially available cultivars had significantly higher average water loss than the breeding selections along with the drought tolerant cultivar Orangeade (table 20.1).

These cultivars wilted in 5.11 days versus 7.33 for Orangeade and 9.10 for the breeding selections. These results suggest that sufficient variability exists in New Guinea impatiens germplasm for the reduction of water loss to improve drought-tolerance. Regression analysis revealed that total transpirational water loss 96 hours after withholding water, was an excellent predictor of the time to wilting (a simple measure of drought tolerance) after water was withheld (r = 0.95). Thus, a simple, efficient and objective method for selection of drought-tolerant genotypes has been developed for New Guinea impatiens. A comparison of offspring to parental genotypes showed that after only one cycle of selection, water loss was significantly reduced by more than 30%. These results suggest that there is sufficient genetic variability present for the development of more drought tolerant cultivars.

Reproductive biology

The reproductive biology of impatiens species is highly uniform [18]. Protandry (maturation of the stamen before ripening of the pistil) promotes cross-pollination in many impatiens species [45]. In species native to temperate North America (*I. capensis* and *I. pallida*), cleistogamous (unexpanded, closed) flowers predominate and thus self-polli-

▮▮▮▮▮▮▮ TABLE 20.1 ▮▮▮▮▮▮▮

Average comparisons between cultivars, breeding selections, Orangeade, and control selections for water loss, leaf area, time to wilt, and transpiration rate

Group	Leaf area (cm^2)	Time to wilt (days)	Transpiration rate (mg/cm^2/hour)
Cultivars	116.8a	5.11a	6.68a
Control	93.3a	5.25a	8.36b
Orangeade	115.5a	7.33b	4.20c
Selections	84.1b	9.10c	4.58c

z Mean comparisons between groups were carried out using single degree of freedom contrasts.
Means with different numbers are significantly different at p = 0.01.

nation is the most common means of reproduction [39]. However, cleistogamy has not been observed in any tropical impatiens species, which are the predominant species in this genus [18].

Self-pollination can occur in the protandrus flowers of New Guinea impatiens. The pistil and stigma of these flowers are covered by a fused column of stamens, which act as a unit and a barrier between pollen and stigma. When the ovary begins to mature, the filaments of the stamen break at the base and the stamens fall off. If the stamens do not completely fall off the flower, self-pollination can occur. This situation is rare but has been observed in African species, *I. wallerana* and New Guinea impatiens [18].

Cytology and genetics

A number of people have conducted research on the cytology of *Impatiens* species, including New Guinea impatiens. A cytogeographical survey of a number of *Impatiens* species revealed that chromosome variation in the genus showed distinctive patterns of geographic and perhaps ecological distribution [24]. The Himalayan region represents the center of origin for the genus, since it is the richest in species. Cytological examination of species from this center of diversity showed that two basic chromosome numbers were found for these species (x = 7 and x = 10). Based on these findings, Jones and Smith [24] proposed that x = 7 was the base number for the genus and that evolution of *Impatiens* species has been primarily driven by an increase in chromosome number.

Chromosome number diverged from north to south with the *Impatiens* of Europe and America having a base number of 10 (x = 10), while the *Impatiens* of Africa and southeast Asia primarily having a base number of eight (x = 8). Chromosome counts of eight different plants from New Guinea revealed that six plants were tetraploids (2n = 32; x = 8); and two were hexaploids (*I. hawkeri*: 2n = 48; x = 8 and *I. mooreana*: 2n = 66; x = 11;). *Impatiens platypetala* from Java was a diploid (2n = 20; x = 10); while another collection of *I. platypetala* from Sarawak was a tetraploid (2n = 32; x = 8) [24].

Polyploid species

The high frequency of polyploid species in the New Guinea region formed a positive indication of hybridization's role in the evolution of species in *Impatiens* [24]. Southeast Asia forms a geographical boundary of the genus since no *Impatiens* are found in Australia. According to Jones and Smith [24], hybridization and polyploidization was of importance in extending the geographical boundaries of the genus.

Polyploid species, compared to diploid species, are thought to be more successful.

Polyploid species display a greater adaptability for vigor, thermal preadaptation, hardiness, tolerance to being water-logged, genetic discontinuity with related diploids, and a capacity to store variation. Probably the most important reason for their success is that polyploid species are of hybrid origin [24].

New Guinea impatiens are a highly variable species. This variability may be the result of polyploidy (tetra- or hexaploids), which may have developed from hybridization of different species. Another reason for the high variability may be that New Guinea impatiens are widespread on the island. New Guinea is 1,490 miles (2400 km) from end to end and over such a wide area, genetic isolation is bound to occur. The effects of altitude must also be taken into account. New Guinea *Impatiens* have reached a point in diversification in which groups are beginning to emerge as closely allied species [19].

Cytological research on the New Guinea impatiens collected by Winters and Higgins (USDA impatiens) showed 13 plants with 32 (2n = 32) and one plant with 64 (2n = 64) chromosomes. With some exceptions, the 32-chromosome plants were self- and cross-fertile. The plant with 64 chromosomes was self-fertile but did not set seed when crossed with 32-chromosome genotypes [3].

Chromosome numbers

Beck et al. [15] studied the breeding behavior and chromosome numbers among New Guinea *Impatiens* (P.I. 349586) and Java *Impatiens* (*I. platypetala*; P.I. 349629) species, the cultivar Tangerine (= *I. platypetala aurantiaca* Steen from Celebes) and cultivated varieties of *I. holstii* Engl. (= *I. wallerana* Hook.), which originates from East Africa, and their interspecific hybrids.

All crosses were successful except those made with *I. holstii*. The New Guinea impatiens (P.I. 349586) had a diploid chromosome number of 32. *Impatiens platypetala* (P.I. 349629), and *I. holstii* each had a diploid chromosome number of 16. Tangerine had a diploid chromosome number of 8, which indicated a new, lower base chromosome number of 4 (x = 4) for impatiens. Chromosome counts of the hybrids were midway between the respective parents. The chromosomes of Southeast Asian impatiens had similar chromosome morphology and size. The chromosomes of *I. holstii* were clearly different in morphology and size, which may be the reason why this parent did not cross with the other species.

Chromosome numbers of 44 taxa of *Impatiens* were reported to range from n = 4 to n = 24 (table 20.2) [58]. These results confirmed that the species from New Guinea (which were identified as *I. linearifo-*

lia and *I. schlechteri*) had 2n = 32 chromosomes. *Impatiens platypetala* ssp. *aurantiaca* from Celebes had a cytotype of 2n = 14, which confirmed the results of Khoshoo [27]. Arisumi [5] and Beck [15] discovered a chromosome number of 2n = 8 for the same species. Zinov'eva-Stahevitch and Grant [58] confirmed that Arisumi's [5] artificial interploid hybrid between *I. platypetala* ssp. *aurantiaca* (2n = 8) from Celebes and *I. platypetala* ssp. indeterminate (2n = 16) from Java, indeed had a chromosome number of 2n = 12. The karyotype consisted of four large and eight small chromosomes.

Genetic factors

Very little information has been published on the genetic control of factors affecting flowering and breeding strategies for increased flowering in New Guinea impatiens. Winters [52, 53] had limited success in improving flower production by selecting for random pedicel branching among various New Guinea plant introductions.

Seedlings selected after generations of crosses showed random pedicel branching. This resulted in predominantly one to three flowers per pedicel, but occasionally up to six flowers per pedicel were observed. Winters [52, 53] also observed a large amount of variability in the life of the flowers among plant introductions of New Guinea impatiens. Floral life ranged from five to 12 days after anthesis (flower expansion and anthers functional).

The original New Guinea hybrids were unable to flower until the plants were quite large and rarely flowered under hot, dry conditions. *Impatiens platypetala* from Java and *I. platypetala aurantiaca* (CP 21.1) from the Celebes did not possess either of these undesirable characteristics. Therefore, crosses between these species

▬▬▬▬▬▬▬▬ TABLE 20.2 ▬▬▬▬▬▬▬▬

Chromosome numbers of *Impatiens* spp. from New Guinea, Java, and Celebes

Species	Origin	Chromosome number
Impatiens hawkeri	New Guinea	2n = 32; 2n = 64
Impatiens platypetala (P.I. 349629)	Java	2n = 16
Impatiens platypetala aurantiaca cv. Tangerine	Celebes	2n = 8
Impatiens platypetala cv. Tangeglow	Java x Celebes	2n = 24

and the New Guinea *Impatiens* were made to improve the flowering characteristics of New Guinea impatiens. It was possible to make interspecific hybrids between diploid and tetraploid species from Celebes (2n = 8), Java (2n = 16) and New Guinea (2n = 32), indicating a relationship between these species [15, 4]. The chromosome numbers of the interspecific hybrids had the expected midparent values. The hybrid phenotypes were midparental for most traits and showed dosage effects in some traits.

Although different species had different chromosome numbers, the intra- and interploidy crosses functioned as diploids to each other. The diploid by tetraploid crosses produced little or no seed and nearly all triploid offspring were sterile. Amphidiploid and autotetraploid seedlings were pollen and seed fertile. Allotetraploids with four genomes were seed sterile. Some of these hybrids were considered ornamentally superior to their parents [4, 7] and had the ability to bloom under hot, dry conditions.

Sterility barriers

A problem with these interspecific hybrids is that most are sterile and cannot be used for further breeding purposes. This sterility barrier needed to be overcome since the New Guinea impatiens flower colors were recessive, and all hybrids had the flower colors of either their Java parent (magenta) or their Celebes parent [orange] [7]. The orange and yellow flower color of two Celebes impatiens (Tangerine and plant introduction (P.I. 366029) dominated in all hybrid crosses.

Most hybrid progeny of Java x New Guinea impatiens crosses inherited the magenta flower color of the Java parent species. Sixty percent of progeny from hybridizations involving Celebes impatiens had two or four purplish spots near the throat of the flower. The Celebes orange flower color was found to be completely dominant to the Java pigment [44]. Progeny of the second backcross from the non-orange, nonrecurrent parent did not produce any orange flowered offspring. This demonstrated that by using fertile interspecific hybrids, the dominant orange-flowering pigment could be deleted from inbreds of the original orange-flowered hybrids [44].

Studies of hybridizations between New Guinea and Indonesian (Java and Celebes) impatiens yielded important information regarding the inheritance of leaf variegation and flower color. Leaf variegation was found to be unstable in crosses between variegated and nonvariegated plants. Variegated seedlings from these crosses could produce nonvariegated shoots, and nonvariegated progeny could produce variegated shoots [8]. The instability of leaf variegation may be the result of transposable elements or jumping genes.

Overcoming sterility barriers

Methods of overcoming the interspecific sterility barriers are amphidiploid production, utilization of the random assortment principle, and naturally developing pollen fertility [35, 47]. Amphidiploid production is one method of restoring fertility. After treating impatiens cuttings and seeds with colchicine, Arisumi [2] obtained tetraploids and octoploids of New Guinea impatiens cultivars. These included two interspecific hybrids between New Guinea and Java species; two New Guinea hybrids; and two clones of a Java species. He compared these tetraploids with diploids for differences in morphology and fertility. The tetraploids were larger than the diploids and generally had a greater percentage of abortive pollen and less fertility than the diploids. A wild New Guinea impatiens specimen (New Guinea 13) with 2n = 64 did not cross with 2n = 32 plants, but did cross with the New Guinea hybrid tetraploids (2n = 64). This indicates that perhaps this specimen was a natural tetraploid. The octoploids were sterile and ornamentally inferior to diploids or tetraploids [3].

Amphidiploid production. Arisumi [5] phenotypically analyzed selfed and crossed progenies of colchicine induced and natural amphidiploid cultivars of New Guinea and Indonesian impatiens. The amphidiploids were comparable to inbreds. The seedlings within progenies were identical in nearly all of the floral, foliage, and plant characteristics. The most frequent variation occurred in patterns and intensity of flower colors. This lack of variability for many characters in the offspring of many doubled interspecific hybrids tends to hamper breeding progress. Arisumi [5] stated that the method of creating amphidiploids from diploids is useful when parental species or cultivars become sterile or difficult to breed after conversion into tetraploids [5].

The value of doubling interspecific hybrids can be improved by breeding and selection at the diploid level of each species. This would be followed by chromosome doubling and then crossing the two genetically distinct amphidiploids to create fertile and superior hybrids. This strategy alleviates the loss in variability and vigor often encountered in polyploidization by restoring heterozygosity via hybridization at the polyploid not diploid level.

Random principle. Random assortive mating is another technique to restore fertility to interspecific hybrids of *Impatiens* [33]. This technique involves making large numbers of crosses to find a random occurrence where all the cell's chromosomes, or all the chromosomes of either parental genome, migrate to one pole and form a stable gamete. Successful crosses were limited to the cross of the Celebes cultivar Tangerine, (2n = 8) with Java P.I. 349629 (2n = 16), yielding progeny (2n = 12) which appeared sterile. When a large number of crosses with these progeny were made with Tangeglow (a 24-chromosome amphidiploid produced by doubling a Java impatiens (P.I. 349629) and crossing it with the 8-chromosome Tangerine), numerous progeny resulted, some of which proved to be fertile in subsequent crosses. When it was backcrossed with Tangerine, only three progeny resulted with 2n = 8, 9 and 12. When backcrossed with the Java parent, five progeny resulted, all with 2n = 20. Use of random assortive mating becomes impractical when sterile hybrids of high chromosome number are used. This is because a large number of pollinations are required to form a single stable gamete [33, 34].

Natural pollen fertility. The most promising approach to overcome interspecific sterility is to look for naturally developing pollen fertility. Pasutti et al. [34] conducted a cytological study on the pollen-bearing clones and progeny of a number of Java x New Guinea impatiens interspecific crosses. Viable pollen-producing hybrids from these crosses were obtained and were crossed with a 24-chromosome amphidiploid Tangeglow resulting in 2n = 34-chromosome hybrids. One of these hybrids was again crossed with a Java impatiens (P.I. 349629) 2n = 16, producing two offspring, one with 2n = 24 chromosomes and one with 2n = 30 chromosomes. The 30-chromosome hybrid showed a continuing tendency for production of viable, partially unreduced gametes. Due to these fertile hybrids, it is now possible to transfer desirable characteristics, including precocious flowering under hot, dry conditions and the ability to flower when the plants are quite small, from the Java and Celebes species into the New Guinea material [34, 47].

Indian/African crosses

The species within the New Guinea-Indonesian group are much more closely related with one another than species within the Indian and African group. Intraspecific crosses within and between these groups showed that all of the 30 interspecific crosses of the New Guinea-Indonesian group were compatible, but none of the interspecific crosses of the Indian group and only four of the 72 crosses within the African group were compatible [9]. None of the between groups were shown to be compatible. These results suggest that from an evolutionary point of view, the African and Indian species are probably much older than the New Guinea-Indonesian species. The African and Indian species show wide morphological differences and strong barriers to crossability between most species.

Studies of New Guinea x Indonesian crosses suggested that ploidy level was an important factor affecting seed set among these crosses [7, 11, 47].

Interploidy crosses between New Guinea (4x = 64) x Java impatiens (4x = 32) set seed, but interploidy crosses of New Guinea (4x = 32) x Java (4x = 64) were sterile. The sterility was the result of unequal genomic combinations (CJJN; CJJJ; NNC; where letters refer to country of origin: N = New Guinea, J = Java and C = Celebes). All hybrids exhibited the expected chromosome number (i.e., 32 + 16 = 48) for these interploidy crosses.

The New Guinea-Indonesian species have many similar morphological traits and can cross easily among themselves regardless of differences in basic chromosome numbers. The seed capsules of incompatible crosses abscised within four to seven days (it takes 28 to 35 days for seeds to mature). In some incompatible crosses, however, the seed capsules were abscised after only seven to 14 days. This might be long enough to culture the embryos *in vitro*. *Impatiens flaccida alba* and *I. hookeriana* from India, and the African species *I. uguenensis* (= *I. sodenii*) were superior as seed parents to the New Guinea-Indonesian species [10].

Interspecific crosses

Arisumi [12] used ovule culture instead of embryo culture to obtain interspecific crosses. Ovules six to 11 days old usually had significantly higher germination rates than ovules three to five days old. The percentages of ovules ultimately recovered as established seedlings in soil ranged from 0 to 16.5%. A major cause of post-germination losses was the abnormal development of seedlings *in vitro*. About 75% of the seedlings were abnormal. Poor germination and abnormal development was probably caused by cultural as well as by genetic deficiencies. The hybrids showed morphological characteristics of both parents and were sterile [12]. Han and Stephens [22] reported that 16- to 20-day-old ovules germinated on Murashige and Skoog medium with 25 mM sucrose. A reduced inorganic concentration (30 mM), with a ratio of 10 mM ammonium to 20 mM nitrate, resulted in the best germination and percent normal seedling growth and development.

Arisumi [13] studied a number of interspecific hybrids obtained by conventional breeding methods and by ovule culture *in vitro*. The hybrids among African, Indian, and New Guinea impatiens were all euploids and sterile. Only a few of the hybrids developed into normal mature plants. Parental species, except for the New Guinea species, were homozygous for most traits. Seedlings of selfed New Guinea cultivars segregated for various plant, leaf, and floral traits. Flower color and flowering habit of the hybrid were intermediate to the parental species.

In overall size of plants, leaves, and flowers, the hybrids generally resembled the smaller parent. The following phylogenetic trends could have been conditioned by dominant or partially dominant genes: equal to unequal petals, flat to hooded dorsal petal, racemose to epedunculate inflorescence, nearly free to markedly fused lateral petals, and lower sepal and a filiform spur to bucciniform or saccate lower sepal. The spirally arranged leaf pattern was dominant over the whorled leaf pattern.

Progenies of *I. uguenensis* (= *I. sodenii*) were among the last plants to wilt when water was withheld for 12 to 24 hours. Two hybrids (*I. uguenensis* (= *I. sodenii*) x New Guinea or *I. flaccida*), were considered to be potentially useful for combining drought tolerance with other ornamental qualities. Other useful crosses in ornamental breeding were *I. auricoma* x *I. sultani* Elfin White or New Guinea species for yellow flowers and *I. flaccida* x for *I. repens* or Elfin White for double flowers [13].

Germplasm

Plant germplasm conservation has been a concern since the early 1960s, however, the conservation of ornamental genetic resources has been a low or nonpriority item as compared to food and fiber crops [16]. Government agencies involved in germplasm collection and preservation are primarily interested in the conservation of crops used for food, fiber, shelter, or pharmaceuticals. Thus, the burden of collecting and preserving ornamental germplasm must be shared by botanic gardens and arboreta as well as the ornamental industry. Boyle [16] and Raven [36] have discussed the vulnerability of important ornamental crop germplasm in South and Central America and the pressing need to collect and preserve this germplasm before it is lost with the destruction of rain forests.

The value of plant explorations to the ornamental industry is aptly demonstrated by the impact of New Guinea impatiens in the marketplace. The 1970 plant exploration expedition to New Guinea brought about the successful introduction of New Guinea impatiens as a commercially viable and profitable crop in the United States. In 1972, the USDA's New Crops Research Branch, which supervised the 1970 expedition, was discontinued and no further trips to New Guinea have been made.

Geographical distribution

The centers of origin or diversity of *Impatiens* have not been determined, but rather distinct geographical distributions have been proposed using chromosome numbers of 52 species of *Impatiens* [24]. Since India has the largest number of species and the greatest diversity of base chromosome numbers, Jones and Smith [24] proposed the Himalayan region to be the center of origin for the genus. These findings were confirmed by Grey-Wilson [18] and Zinov'era-Stahevitch [56]. Polyploidy in species of *Impatiens* were reported for Southeast Asia by

Jones and Smith [24]. They proposed that polyploidy and hybridization led to the spread of *Impatiens* into other geographic regions.

Hybrid complexes were observed in African and New Guinea impatiens as well and led Grey-Wilson [18, 19, 20] to support Jones and Smith's [24] conclusion that polyploidy and hybridization were responsible for the spread of the genus. Genetic diversity is generally greatest in areas of hybridization. Arisumi [2, 3, 7], Zinov'era-Stahevitch, and Grant [58] reported the hybrid nature and ploidy level of impatiens plants from wild populations. The center of diversity for temperate northern species is believed to be located in the Pacific Northwest region which includes Oregon, Washington, Idaho, Montana, and southern British Columbia [54].

The genetic base of cultivars developed from the plants collected during the 1970 expedition is very narrow and does not represent the true genetic diversity within New Guinea impatiens. New Guinea impatiens are a highly variable species [20] with many diverse groups. New Guinea is the second largest island in the world and has many high rugged mountain ranges which are very effective geographical barriers to the movement of man, plants, and animals. These barriers contribute to plant isolation which often leads to increased genetic diversity and possibly the evolution of new species.

Genetic diversity

The diversity of floral and leaf morphology is quite high in germplasm collections maintained at the University of Minnesota (CP 20.4a, CP 20.4b, and CP 20.5). However, it is not clear whether this diversity is indicative of the genetic diversity present in this collection. Genetic studies using isozymes or DNA markers will provide additional information on the genetic diversity of New Guinea impatiens germplasm. These studies will be important in determining the genetic vulnerability of commercial cultivars and the extent of new germplasm required to encompass and protect the diversity of genes in impatiens germplasm.

Genetic diversity of *Impatiens* germplasm was estimated for 49 accessions from Africa, New Guinea, Sri Lanka and Java/Celebes, a New Guinea breeding population and inter- and intracontinental interspecific hybrids [29]. Variability in two isoenzyme systems (peroxidase, PER, and aspartate amino transferase, AAT), 13 quantitative traits, and 19 qualitative traits were measured to estimate genetic diversity.

Lerch [29] reported that a high degree of genetic diversity (H') existed among accessions from the various geographic locations. This included higher genetic diversity in New Guinea inbreds for quantitative traits (mean H' of 0.86 and 0.85, respectively), with genetic diversity considerably lower for the qualitative traits (mean H' of 0.62 and 0.54, respectively).

Isozyme diversity differed considerably between these two groups.

The mean genetic diversity for geographic accessions was 0.88, whereas the mean for the New Guinea inbreds was 0.30. The reduced genetic diversity estimate for New Guinea inbreds was most likely due to the inbreeding and selection history of the plants examined. These results suggest that although genetic diversity is relatively high among *Impatiens* germplasm around the globe, genetic diversity within New Guinea impatiens is considerably lower.

The results of isozyme analysis of the inter- and intracontinental interspecific hybrids showed that the isoenzyme AAT was not useful in separating New Guinea/Java/Celebes crosses but had some utility in separating some of the inter- and intracontinental crosses [29]. The peroxidase enzyme system (PER) was able to separate all hybrids from their respective parents in the intercontinental and intracontinental group and three hybrids including two half-siblings from their respective parents in the New Guinea/Java/Celebes group. Several parental lines exhibited PER bands not visible in the hybrid offspring. This work suggests that isozymes may be useful in distinguishing hybrids and determining parentage of hybrids, but more work is needed to find biochemical markers for economically important traits in impatiens.

Germplasm collections

In light of their narrow genetic base (25 plant introductions) and increased loss of germplasm in New Guinea, the collection and conservation of the New Guinea impatiens germplasm (genetic diversity) should be a priority among floral crops. The Island of New Guinea does not have a germplasm conservation organization in place. Also there are no germplasm conservation efforts for ornamentals identified in Africa. Although India does have a National Bureau for Plant Genetic Resources that was established in 1976 [25], it is unclear what priority will be given to ornamental species.

The usefulness of germplasm collections is based on the collection, identification, description, characterization, preservation, management, and use of accessions. Phenotypic, genotypic, and biochemical descriptions of a collection are vital to the preservation and usefulness of the germplasm collection. Therefore, support for germplasm conservation must not end with collection of plant material but must continue to support research on the aspects listed above if the effort is to be successful and valuable to the plant breeder, industry, and consumer.

Final remarks —————————————

New Guinea impatiens are an important crop and will increase in importance as both a pot and bedding plant in the near future.

However, a lot of breeding work can still be done. In my opinion, the genetic base utilized by the plant breeders is much too small. All commercial cultivars trace back to those 25 plant introductions that were brought back from New Guinea by Winters and Higgins in 1970. Only one heterozygous genotype of *Impatiens platypetala* from Java (P.I. 349629) and one genotype from Celebes (the cv. Tangerine) are available to breeding programs in the United States. Weigle et al. [46] attempted to induce mutations in the Java genotype to obtain more genetic variety. After seeds were treated with 0.08M ethyl methanosulfonate (EMS), he found individuals in the M2 generation with a dwarf plant type. A genetic investigation indicated that this character was controlled by a single, recessive gene [46].

The Indonesia/New Guinea *Impatiens* are highly variable species. Therefore, it will be easier to increase genetic diversity by collecting more genotypes from these native areas than by any other strategy. I also believe that there are still unlimited ornamental and important horticultural characters available in the gene pool of the species in New Guinea which are just waiting to be utilized.

We should use different species from Africa such as *I. sodenii* or India (50% of the identified species grow in India) to find useful genes. This could include genes for tolerance to heat and drought required for outdoor plants or genes for tolerance to low levels of light and humidity required for indoor plants. Species on the other Indonesian islands, or islands around tropical India, might function as bridges between the New Guinea *Impatiens* and other species [7].

References

[1]   Decade opens with a burst of color. 1990. *Seed World* 128(2): 20-22.
[2]   Arisumi, T. 1973a. Morphology and breeding behavior of colchicine-induced polyploid *Impatiens* spp. *L. J. Amer. Soc. Hort. Sci.* 98(6): 599-601.
[3]   ———. 1973b. Chromosome numbers and interspecific hybrids among New Guinea impatiens species. *J. Heredity* 64(2): 77-79.
[4]   ———. 1974. Chromosome numbers and breeding behavior of hybrids among Celebes, Java, and New Guinea species of *Impatiens L. HortScience* 9(5): 478-479.
[5]   ———. 1975. Phenotypic analysis of progenies of artificial and natural amphidiploid cultivars of New Guinea and Indonesian species of *Impatiens L. J. Amer. Soc. Hort. Sci.* 100(4): 381-383.
[6]   Arisumi, T., and H.M. Cathey. 1976. The New Guinea impatiens. *HortScience* 11(1): 2.
[7]   Arisumi, T. 1978a. Hybridization among diploid and tetraploid forms of New Guinea, Java, and Celebes *Impatiens* spp. *L. J. Amer. Soc. Hort. Sci.* 103(3): 355-361.
[8]   ———.1978b. Somatic mutations affecting leaf characteristics of New Guinea *Impatiens. HortScience* 13(3 sect. 2): 350.

[9] ———. 1980a. Chromosome numbers and comparative breeding behavior of certain *Impatiens* from Africa, India, and New Guinea. *J. Amer. Soc. Hort. Sci.* 105(1): 99-102.

[10] ———. 1980b. *In vitro* culture of embryos and ovules of certain incompatible selfs and crosses among *Impatiens* species. *J. Amer. Soc. Hort. Sci.* 105(5): 629-631.

[11] ———. 1982. Endosperm balance numbers among New Guinea-Indonesian *Impatiens* species. *J. Heredity* 73: 240-242.

[12] ———. 1985. Rescuing abortive *Impatiens* hybrids through aseptic culture of ovules. *J. Amer. Soc. Hort. Sci.* 110(2): 273-276.

[13] ———. 1987. Cytology and morphology of ovule culture derived interspecific *Impatiens* hybrids. *J. Amer. Soc. Hort. Sci.* 112(6): 1026-1031.

[14] Armstrong, R.J. 1974. An *Impatiens* circus: the Longwood New Guinea hybrid *Impatiens*. *Am. Hort.* 53: 14-18.

[15] Beck, A.R., J.L. Weigle, and E.W. Kruger. 1974. Breeding behavior and chromosome numbers among New Guinea and Java species, cultivated varieties, and their interspecific hybrids. *Can. J. Bot.* 52: 923-925.

[16] Boyle, T.H. 1991. The genetic resources of Latin America's herbaceous ornamental crops—vital to commercial floriculture. *Diversity* 7(1&2): 50-51.

[17] Dostal, D.L., N.H. Agnew, R.J. Gladon, and J.L. Weigle,. 1991. Ethylene, simulated Shipping, STS, and AOA affect corolla abscission of New Guinea *Impatiens*. *HortScience* 26(1): 47-49.

[18] Grey-Wilson, C. 1980a. *Impatiens of Africa-morphology, pollination and pollinators, African species*. Rotterdam, Netherlands: A.A. Balkema.

[19] ———. 1980b. *Impatiens* in Papuasia. Studies in Balsaminaceae: *I. Kew Bull.* 34(4): 661-688.

[20] ———. 1980c. *Impatiens of Africa*. Rotterdam: A.A. Balkena.

[21] Grueber, G. 1989. Neu-Guinea *Impatiens* trends und tendenzen. *Gaertnerboerse und Gartenwelt* 89(5): 231-233.

[22] Han, K., and L.C. Stephens. 1992. Carbohydrate and nitrogen sources affect *in vitro* germination of two interspecific *Impatiens* hybrids. *Sci. Hort.* 32: 307-313.

[23] Hickey, M., and C. King. 1981. *100 families of flowering plants*. 2nd ed. New York: Cambridge University Press.

[24] Jones, K., and J.B. Smith. 1966. The cytogeography of *Impatiens L. (Balsaminaceae)*. *Kew Bull.* 20: 63-71.

[25] Jones, Q., R.S. Paroda, and J.A. Pinto. 1987. India develops major national program in plant genetic resources. *Diversity* 12: 14-16.

[26] Kaczperski, M.P., and W.H. Carlson. 1989. *Producing New Guinea impatiens. A commercial grower's guide*. Michigan State University Extension Bulletin E-2179: 1-4.

[27] Khoshoo, T.N. 1957. Cytology of some *Impatiens* species. *Caryologia* 10: 55-75.

[28] Koenigsberg, S., and R. Langhans. 1976. Tissue culture studies with the New Guinea-Java hybrid *Impatiens*. *HortScience* 11(3): 37.

[29] Lerch, V. 1992. Phenotypic and isozyme diversity in an *Impatiens* germplasm collection. Ph.D. diss., University of Maryland.

[30] Mack, C. 1989. Spring showcase. *California grower* 13: 20-22.

[31] Martin, T. 1984. New Guinea *Impatiens*. *Horticulture* 63(8): 32-36.

[32] Merlin, C.M., and W.F. Grant. 1985. Hybridization studies in the genus *Impatiens*. *Can. J. Bot.* 64: 1069-1074.

[33] Pasutti, D.W., J.L. Weigle, and A.R. Beck. 1976. Cytology and breeding behavior of some *Impatiens* hybrids and their backcross progeny. *Can. J. Bot.* 55: 296-300.

[34] Pasutti, D.W., and J.L. Weigle. 1977. Pollen fertility in Java x New Guinea *Impatiens* hybrids. *Can. J. Bot.* 58: 384-387.

[35] Pasutti, D.W., and J.L. Weigle. 1980. Growth-regulator effect on New Guinea *Impatiens* hybrids. *Scientia Horticulturae* 12(1980): 293-298.

[36] Raven, P.R. 1976. Ethics and attitudes. In *Conservation of threatened plants*. Ed. J.B. Simmonds, et al. New York: Plenum Press.

[37] Royen, P. van. 1982. The Alpine flora of New Guinea. Vol. 3 of *Taxonomic part winteraceae to polygonaceae*. Vaduz, Liechtenstein: J. Cramer.

[38] Sabri, H., A. Abbasi, and J.L. Weigle. 1982. Resistance in New Guinea *Impatiens* species and hybrids to the two-spotted spider mite. *HortScience* 17(1): 47-48.

[39] Schemske, D.W. 1978. Evolution or reproductive characteristics in *Impatiens* (Balsaminaceae): The significance of cleistogamy and chasmogamy. *Ecology* 59: 596-613.

[40] Simmonds, J. 1982. Temperature and photoperiodic of flower initiation in a New Guinea *Impatiens* hybrid. *Can. J. Bot.* 60: 320-324.

[41] ———. 1985. The effect of photoperiod on axillary branch development and flower production of a New Guinea *Impatiens* hybrid. *Can. J. Plant. Sci.* 65: 995-1000.

[42] Smith, F.H. 1938. Reduction divisions in triploid *Impatiens*. *Amer. J. Bot.* 25: 651-654.

[43] Stephens, L.C., S.L. Krell,and J.L. Weigle. 1985. In vitro propagation of Java, New Guinea, and Java x New Guinea *Impatiens*. *HortScience* 20(3): 362-363.

[44] Stephens, L.C., J.L. Weigle and S.L. Krell. 1988. Flower color inheritance in inbred progenies of *Impatiens* interspecific hybrids. *J. Heredity* 79(2): 136-137.

[45] Vogel, S., and A. Cocucci. 1988. Pollen threads in *Impatiens*: their nature and function. *Beitin. Biol. Pflanzen* 63: 271-287.

[46] Weigle, J.L., and J.K. Butler. 1983. Induced dwarf mutant in *Impatiens platypetala*. J. Heredity 74: 200.

[47] Weigle, J.L., and D.W. Pasutti. 1976. Approaches to transfer of characteristics between ploidy levels in New Guinea *Impatiens*. *Acta Horticulturae* 63: 109-112.

[48] Weigle, J.L., and D.W. Pasutti. 1979. Blue Moon *Impatiens*. *HortScience* 14(6): 766.

[49] ———. 1979. Tropical Sunset *Impatiens*. *HortScience* 14(6): 767.

[50] ———. 1979. Burgundy *Impatiens*. *HortScience* 14(6): 768.

[51] Winters, H.F. 1973. New *Impatiens* from New Guinea. *Am. Hort.* 52: 16-22.

[52] ———. 1977. Flower longevity in New Guinea *Impatiens*. *HortScience* 12: 261-263.

[53] ———. 1982. Branched pedicels in New Guinea *Impatiens*. *HortScience* 17: 340-341.

[54] Wood Jr., C.E. 1975. The Balsaminaceae in the southeastern United States. *J. Arnold Arboretum* 56: 426-513.

[55] Woodroffe, F.B. 1975. Cyclone hybrids *Impatiens* take hurdles of heat sun shade. *Am. Hortic.* 54: 22-23.

[56] Zinov'eva-Stahevitch, A.E. 1981. Systematic studies in the Balsaminaceae. Ph.D. diss., MacDonald College of McGill University, Montreal.

[57] ———. 1984. Chromosome numbers in *Impatiens* (Balsaminaceae). *Can. J. Bot.* 62: 2630-2635.

[58] Zinov'eva-Stahevitch, A.E., and A.E. Grant. 1984. Chromosome numbers in *Impatiens* (Balsaminaceae). *Can. J. Bot.* 62: 2630-2635.

CHAPTER 21

Breeding for the Future

Scott Trees

The challenge ─────────────

New Guinea impatiens have become stars in their own right as part of the bedding plant mix of the 90s. The highly variegated, small flowered, gangly plant has been refined. Today's varieties are fairly uniform as a series and much more compact and basal branching than their ancestors. A wider color range with larger and more numerous flowers make New Guinea impatiens popular. The majority of the current varieties have little or no variegated foliage and are better adapted to pot, basket, or landscape use than the first introductions.

Some might say, "Why put any more effort into breeding? What more can be done with New Guinea impatiens?" But there are the visionaries who wonder what the next impatiens will be for the bedding plant industry. This author falls into the latter group. There clearly exists unlimited potential in the future breeding and development of not only New Guinea impatiens but other impatiens species as well.

In this chapter we will examine the breeding potential for New Guinea impatiens in particular, using traditional and nontraditional breeding methods. In addition, leading commercial breeders' and researchers' perspectives on future breeding of New Guinea impatiens will be included. The challenge to breeders is to incorporate, as efficiently as possible, the wealth of germplasm available in the genus *Impatiens* into commercial products that fill market needs.

249

The opportunity————————————————————

Even though some of the photos in this book capture what may seem to be near perfection in New Guinea impatiens, there is room for improvement. Although not inclusive, the following topics are areas where definite improvements can be made through breeding and product development.

Drought tolerance

Unlike other bedding plant superstars (i.e., petunias, geraniums, or vinca), impatiens are much less forgiving if rain is lacking or one forgets to water the flower bed. Under dry conditions, New Guinea impatiens may perform slightly better than their *Impatiens wallerana* cousins, but both classes could benefit from less demands for water. Burt Andrews [1] of Ball Seed Company lists drought tolerance as one of his top three most desired characteristics for future improvement in New Guinea impatiens. He is not alone.

Dr. John Erwin [7] at the University of Minnesota and Dr. Loren Stephens [2] at Iowa State University both feel that drought tolerance is a problem with a solution. The late Dr. T. Arisumi [5] of the USDA Beltsville, Maryland, noted apparent differences in germplasm for drought tolerance. Dr. Arisumi recommended two species that may contribute genes for drought (and/or heat) tolerance including *I. mirabilis*, a succulent type plant from Malaysia and *I. niamniamensis* from East Africa.

A personal observation is that *I. balsamina* from India, which is used widely as an ornamental, appears to have more drought and heat tolerance than New Guinea impatiens. Arisumi [5] also recommended making use of *I. uguenensis* to incorporate drought tolerance into cultivated varieties. Arisumi reported in the same article interspecific hybrids between *I. uguenensis* and a New Guinea impatiens cultivar (*I. hawkeri*) as well as between *I. uguenensis* and *I. flaccida*. Both interspecific hybrids were reported to have potential horticultural traits including large flowers and long blooming times.

Soon, by using genetic engineering techniques [20], it will be possible to bring specific genes in from unrelated species. *Tortula ruralis* (star moss), grows in Alaska and has been shown to recover from nearly complete desiccation. This could be a possible source of drought-tolerant genes.

Heat tolerance

Heat tolerance is most likely a separate component in the physiological puzzle that controls flowering in New Guinea impatiens. Iowa State University has led the way in recognizing and describing the problem of so-called "heat stall" in New Guinea impatiens. Dr. Loren

Stephens [18] at Iowa State has proposed using the Java (*I. platypetala*) and/or Celebes (*I. platypetala aurantiaca*) (see Color Plate section CP 21.1) impatiens, making interspecies crosses with New Guinea impatiens (*I. hawkeri*). By a series of backcrosses, Stephens proposes incorporating the heat-tolerant genes from the Java types into New Guinea impatiens. Stephens [17] also believes *I. platypetala* may contribute wind tolerance to these interspecies hybrids. Dr. John Erwin working with Dr. Mark Strefeler at the University of Minnesota is also looking at incorporating heat resistance into New Guinea impatiens [7].

Pasutti and others [12, 13] showed that it is possible to find fertile progeny from such interspecies crosses that will allow for continued recombinant breeding. A need exists for more trialing and selection by commercial breeders in environments like the U.S. Midwest and Southeast where high night temperature causes heat stall in many commercial varieties. Noticeable differences seem to exist among varieties for this trait as witnessed in my own trials in these warmer areas.

Disease/insect resistance

One characteristic that makes New Guinea impatiens so popular is the relative lack of problems caused by diseases and insects. Nevertheless, under certain circumstances, diseases or insects can become a major problem for commercial growers and the homeowner.

What are some of the important insect problems? Can one breed for disease or insect resistance/tolerance? (For a complete discussion on New Guinea impatiens pests, see Chapters 12, 13, and 14.)

Impatiens necrotic spot virus (INSV)/tomato spotted wilt virus (TSWV). The biggest challenge that New Guinea impatiens breeders will face is the developing of varieties resistant to impatiens necrotic spot virus (INSV) and tomato spotted wilt virus (TSWV) or to its vector, the western flower thrips. At this time, there is no reported resistance to thrips in impatiens although it may exist. A more likely approach to solving this problem may come via biotechnology. Genes for resistance to INSV and TSWV are available in nonrelated crops (i.e., lettuce). Insertion of viral-coat protein genes may offer a means of suppressing infection by INSV/TSWV. (See Chapter 12 for more details on thrips and INSV/TSWV.) Resistance to thrips, as the vector of INSV and TSWV, may also be possible using genes from the soil bacterium *Bacillus thuringiensis* (Bt technology).

Fungal disease. Fungal diseases caused by *Rhizoctonia solani* and *Pythium ultimum* (see Chapter 13) can attack New Guinea impatiens.

Castillo and Peterson [6] screened commercial varieties of New Guinea impatiens for resistance to these two diseases and found a range of resistance among the varieties indicating a genetic component. The variety Milky Way showed the best resistance. Breeders may choose to screen their segregating populations for such disease resistance.

Another important pathogen, *Botrytis cinerea*, can cause leaf spots, dieback, and flower petal damage under the right conditions. There does appear to be inherent variability among existing commercial varieties. Standard recombinant breeding methods and proper selection pressure should lead to improvement for Botrytis tolerance/resistance in New Guinea impatiens. If the traditional approach fails, New Guinea impatiens resistant to bacterial and fungal diseases may be developed utilizing biotechnology.

Mite resistance. Sabri, Abbasi, and Weigle [12] reported finding differences among New Guinea impatiens and interspecies hybrid genotypes for resistance to spider mite. The resistance was associated with cuticle content and a dominant resistance gene was postulated. This resistance may carry over against other insects.

Flower color

Is the gardening public ready for a large flowered yellow or even a blue flowered New Guinea impatiens? It has been the dream of many breeders and marketing organizations for years. It may soon be reality. There are many yellow flowered species among the 850 to 1,000 species [9] believed to make up the genus *Impatiens* (table 21.1).

Arisumi [5] showed that crosses were possible between two yellow species, *I. auricoma* (2n = 16) and *I. repens* (2n = 14), and several other species (See table 21.2). He obtained crosses between *I. auricoma* and both New Guinea impatiens (*I. hawkeri*) and *I. wallerana* and also crossed *I. repens* with *I. flaccida* and *I. uguenensis*.

By making use of bridge crosses it may be possible to transfer the yellow color from the less domesticated species into New Guinea impatiens and *I. wallerana*. *Impatiens uguenensis* (2n = 16) (syn *I. sodenii*) crosses with both *I. auricoma* (CP 21.2) and *I. hawkeri* (2n = 32)(CP 21.3). Bridges between New Guinea impatiens and other species could possibly exist among Indonesian, Indian, and Sri Lankan species [15].

Biotechnology may offer the fastest route to new flower colors in New Guinea impatiens with the incorporation of genes associated with the flavonoid pathway (yellow flowers) or the blue gene touted by several biotech enterprises as a source for blue flowers [16].

TABLE 21.1

Yellow flowered impatiens species as possible sources of germplasm for breeding

Species	Geographic origin
I. auricoma	Comoro Islands
I. oncidioides	Malaysia
I. repens	India, Sri Lanka
I. scabrida	Kashmir to Bhutan
I. cristata	India
I. sulcata	Himalaya
I. stenantha	Himalaya
I. urticifolia	Himalaya
I. calcycina	Himalaya
I. longicornu	Himalaya
I. grandis *	Sri Lanka
I. mirabilis	Malaysia
I. parviflora	Europe
I. gomphophylla	Africa
I. omeiana	China

* See CP 21.4.

Interspecies hybridization ———

With almost 1,000 species of impatiens scattered throughout many climates of the world, the question arises as to why more use has not been made of this variable gene pool. Unfortunately viable seedlings from interspecific hybrid crosses are difficult to obtain. Embryo rescue offers some opportunity for overcoming this barrier, but often the hybrids, when obtained, are sterile and present a roadblock to future traditional breeding.

Toru Arisumi was a pioneer in this work at the USDA. He outlined procedures for rescuing fertile embryos of divergent species crosses [4]. Arisumi was very successful in creating interspecies hybrids [5] (see table 21.2). Specifically with New Guinea impatiens (*I. hawkeri*), he was able to achieve crosses with *I. auricoma*, *I. niamniamensis*, and *I. wallerana* (*I. sultani* in his publications) [3].

TABLE 21.2

Cytogenetic results of work done by Tori Arisumi [5] with various *Impatiens* species and interspecies hybrids

Species and hybrids	Number of plants sampled	Number of somatic chromosomes
African species		
I. auricoma Baill P.I. 380525	1	16
I. epiphytica G.M. Schulze P.I. 404257	1	16
I. niamniamensis Gilg P.I. 404262	1	32
* *I. sultani* Hook. Elfin White	1	16
** *I. uguenensis* Ward P.I. 366034	1	16
Indian species		
I. campanulata Wight P.I. 404255	1	18
I. flaccida Arn. P.I. 366028	1	14
I. hookeriana Arn. P.I. 404260	1	36
I. repens Moon P.I. 404266	1	14
I. verticillata Wight (from Longwood Gardens)	1	14
New Guinea-Indonesian species		
C6 (identified Celebes species)	1	12
C35 (*I. platypetala aurantiaca* Steen Tangerine	1	8
N cvs (unnamed New Guinea cultivars)	7	32
Hybrids among African species		
I. auricoma x *sultani* Elfin White	1	16
I. auricoma x *niamniamensis*	1	24
I. sultani Elfin White x *I. auricoma*	3	16
I. sultani Elfin White x *I. epiphytica*	4	16
I. sultani Elfin White x *I. niamniamensis*	7	24
I. uguenensis x *I. auricoma*	—	—
I. uguenensis x *I. epiphytica*	3	16
I. uguenensis x *I. niamniamensis*	1	24
I. uguenensis x *I. sultani* Elfin White	3	16
Hybrids among Indian species		
I. flaccida x *I. repens*	10	14
I. hookeriana x *I. campanulata*	5	27

—   Plants died before chromosome numbers could be determined.
*   Now referred to as *I. wallerana*.
**   *I. uguenensis* Warb (syn. for *I. sodenii*) [10].

TABLE 21.2. continued

Species and hybrids	Number of plants sampled	Number of somatic chromosomes
Hybrids among African and Indian species		
I. flaccida x *I. sultani* Elfin White	6	15
I. uguenensis x *I. campanulata*	4	17
I. uguenensis x *I. flaccida*	10	15
I. uguenensis x *I. repens*	10	15˙
I. uguenensis x *I. verticillata*	3	15
Hybrids between African and New Guinea-Indonesian species		
N cv x *I. auricoma*	2	24
N cv x *I. niamniamensis*	1	32
I. sultani Elfin White x C6	2	14
I. sultani Elfin White x N cvs	—	—
I. uguenensis x C6	3	14
I. uguenensis x C35	3	12, 16
I. uguenensis x N cvs	5	24

— Plants died before chromosome numbers could be determined.

* Now referred to as *I. wallerana.*

** *I. uguenensis* Warb (syn. for *I. sodenii*) [10].

Again, the use of bridge crosses can be postulated as a means of overcoming crossing barriers among impatiens species in order to obtain new flower colors [15]. Gager [8] in his thesis on interspecific hybridization proposed that sporophytic incompatibility may have led to the inability to obtain hybrids among impatiens species with which he worked. Arisumi [2] illustrated in his 1973 work with colchicine-induced amphidiploids, that fertility restoration of sterile interspecies hybrids was possible. Merlin and Grant [10] demonstrated the possibility of crossing *I. wallerana* (syn. *I. sultani*) with *I. gordonii* (syn. *I. Thomasetti* Hook.) and *I. uguenensis* (syn. *I. sodenii*). The hybrids showed fairly normal meiotic behavior and were fertile. Again the possibility of using bridge crosses as proposed by Arisumi [5] showed that New Guinea impatiens (*I. hawkeri*) would cross with *I. uguenensis* as well as *I. wallerana* (syn. *I. sultani*). The use of interspecies hybrids will eventually lead to cultivars with new flower colors, habits, flower forms, wider adaptability, and a host of other desirable traits in the future.

Professor Ron Parker [11] at the University of Connecticut has spear-headed the use of more divergent germplasm resources in the breeding of both impatiens and catharanthus. No one can deny his success.

Dr. Parker's enthusiasm is contagious as he talks of a very bright future for use of interspecies hybrids in impatiens. *He predicts new flower forms, flower colors, flower petal patterns, new leaf shapes, leaf and stem pigments, new landscape and pot uses, better sun tolerance, drought tolerance, and possibly even fragrance as a result of incorporating more exotic germplasm into current breeding programs through interspecies hybridization.* The possibilities are only limited by the breeder's imagination.

Other areas for improvement

The following list identifies other areas where breeders could possibly focus more efforts.

1. Adaptation to cooler greenhouse conditions.
2. Adaptation to full sun garden conditions.
3. Adaptation to indoor pot plant use (postharvest qualities).
4. Better shipping qualities.
5. Better uniformity within series.
6. Higher production of cuttings.
7. High uniformity of seed lines (see chapter 13).

Additional techniques such as somaclonal variation and mutation breeding could possibly be used to obtain the desired characteristics listed above.

Future breeding in New Guinea impatiens

Dr. Loren Stephens of Iowa State University was asked to give feedback on several questions dealing with the subject of breeding for the future. Here are some of his comments:

Q. What characteristics should be improved in existing lines? What new traits can you visualize in New Guinea impatiens?

A. This question is probably best answered by commercial breeders who maintain a closer tie with their customers (commercial greenhouses and ultimately, consumers). However, as an amateur gardener who uses New Guinea impatiens, I would certainly like to see a New Guinea impatiens cultivar that is more summer-hardy, especially in the Midwest.

Q. Will we be able to transfer genes from related species to do this?

A. This really depends on overcoming sterility and the development of a workable back-crossing strategy. Interspecific hybrids between Indonesian and New Guinea *Impatiens* can be made easily, even between species of different ploidies. We showed [*J. Hered.* 79:136] that it is possible to use complex hybridization and back-crossing using 2n gametes [manuscript in review, *J. Hered.*]. Using this approach, one could develop separate lines, using independent Java x New Guinea hybrids that produced 2n gametes. I am guessing that a couple of lines would be needed because of probable inbreeding depression.

Collection of other "wild" germplasm that are crossable to New Guinea impatiens would probably be a good idea. This is especially true with accessions growing in ecological niches that are similar to the environment of temperate regions in the United States.

Q. How will biotechnology impact the breeding of New Guinea impatiens?

A. We need to develop a transformation system. We have found that Impatiens are transformable with *Agrobacterium* [unpublished data], but transgenic plants cannot be produced by the commonly used leaf-disc method. Alternate procedures that we are considering are meristem transformation and the particle gun system. Some practical reasons for developing a transformation method are:

1. To introduce TSWV coat protein-mediated resistance into New Guinea impatiens. This could reduce production costs for propagators and growers, especially if impatiens could be propagated without an expensive clean stock program.

2. To introduce different flower colors (ones not normally found in New Guinea impatiens) into New Guinea impatiens by blocking endogenous pigments with anti-sense and/or adding new colors (new pathways). One problem with this idea is that a cDNA library of New Guinea impatiens is needed so specific genes (e.g., flower color pigment genes) could be utilized.

Q. **What about breeding for more disease/insect resistance?**

A. Thrips are the major pest in Iowa and are especially dangerous in the greenhouse because they carry TSWV. Unfortunately, we have found that hybrids involving New Guinea impatiens, Java, and Celebes genomes are susceptible [unpublished data]. Either a new source of resistance is needed, or New Guinea impatiens need to be genetically engineered to resist TSWV.

Viewpoints of other breeders/researchers

New Guinea impatiens commercial breeders from North America and Europe were asked to give their outlook on the subject "Breeding for the Future." The following are comments by those who responded (arranged alphabetically by the company that the breeder represents):

1. Norbert Bull Gartenbau (Norbert and Hartwig Bull, breeders)
2. Dummen Jungpflanzenkulturen (Benno Bohn, breeder)
3. Kientzler KG (Ludwig Kientzler, breeder)
4. Mikkelsens, Inc. (Lyndon Drewlow, breeder)

Norbert and Hartwig Bull of Norbert Bull Gartenbau

New Guinea impatiens breeding has improved the last 10 years. New Guinea impatiens are now one of the most popular pot plants worldwide. In the early 1980s N. Bull recognized the potential for New Guinea impatiens and started breeding.

New colors and new types were developed by Bull leading to a full line in this class. The varieties with variegated leaves were soon replaced by nonvariegated varieties. Here in Europe there is only a demand for green, red, or bronze-leaved varieties. There is already a large variety assortment in the common colors, so breeding goals for the future include new color combinations, better foliage and flowers. Because New Guinea impatiens are so important worldwide, it is also important to breed varieties that perform well under different temperature conditions.

Under all environments, they should maintain good growth habits, remain floriferous, have good flower color, flower size, and be able to withstand unfavorable weather conditions.

Resistance against pests and diseases is also important. Today, only half of the existing varieties meet these standards. Many varieties are only adapted to the region in which they were bred. In other climates they fail. Bull's goal is to improve the already existing good habits so worldwide production of New Guinea impatiens can be increased. After breeding, climatic adaptation has to be guaranteed through an extensive testing period. Recently the market has developed around two different size plants:

1. A pot plant 1 to 4 inches (4 to 10 cms), which is popular in Europe. This requires compact plants that can be grown at high densities. These plants are used on windowsills as well as outdoors in gardens, balconies, and cemeteries.
2. Hanging baskets, which are more important in North America than in Europe.

The breeder of New Guinea impatiens is faced with requirements from the young plant producer, the young plant buyer, and the final consumer. Bull's main breeding goals are: short production time, weather resistance, early flowering and large flowers, good shipping performance, fast and compact growth, disease and pest resistance.

Benno Bohn of Dummen Jungpflanzenkulturen

Propagator/young plant producer. A new variety must have good branching in order to produce a high number of cuttings per plant every week. Subsequently, the quick and easy rooting of the cuttings is also of great economical importance.

Young plant buyer and final consumer. A new variety must also fulfill the different requirements of the grower/young plant buyer and the final consumer. Therefore, the breeder has to consider further plant characteristics that can be classified in two groups.

1. **Flower and leaf characteristics.** Early flowering, number, and size of flowers, as well as shape and color are characteristics that can be easily selected. The breeder must provide varieties with bright as well as pastel colors, big as well as smaller flowers, and the color of the leaves, whether green or red, must fit the color of the flower. Breeding to obtain good weather resistance is very difficult and requires field trials.
2. **Characteristics of plant habit.** At Jungpflanzenkulturen, we developed two series with different growth habits (a compact and medium-sized series), in order to fulfill the different requirements of growers according to their specific culture conditions and their final products. Plant habit is a very important selection parameter and decisive for a high propagation rate and the shape of the plant.

Future breeding. In the near future, the most important fields of application will be clonal propagation and the production of disease-free plants. If the problematic nature of TSWV increases in Europe, we will need an efficient means of control.

Embryo rescue would be useful if you wanted to transfer characteristics from related species (wide hybridization). Beyond that, it is also imaginable that biotechnology could be used for *in vitro* selection, the production of haploids to receive homozygous, diploid plants after doubling the chromosome number and, at least, genetic engineering as a means to transfer foreign genes for resistance to disease and insects.

Ludwig Kientzler of Kientzler KG

The idea to start a breeding program with New Guinea impatiens occurred to us shortly after we started producing this crop as a propagator/distributor in the early 1980s. I had the impression that the varieties that were on the market at the time were not all uniform. The variance in flower size, color, and shape as well as the diversity in foliage coloration were evidence that there was much room for improvement through intensive breeding. Once the seedlings from the first crosses flowered, it was surprising to see what a tremendous genetic potential could be found in this material. The intensive breeding efforts quickly resulted in the first marketable Kientzler varieties, which were introduced to the market in 1985.

The distinct characteristics of the first Kientzler cultivars were not only new, intensive colors, but also floriferousness and less leaf variegation. The market acceptance was extremely good from the start. Although New Guinea impatiens are mainly used for bedding purposes in Europe, they are also quite important as a basket plant. The trend towards mixed window boxes also helped promote the rise of this crop.

Vast quantities of New Guinea impatiens are planted every year to decorate graves, especially in the German speaking parts of Europe. The growing conditions are excellent for New Guinea impatiens there, since they are watered regularly and usually have some shade. Another use for New Guinea impatiens is employing them as a flowering indoor pot plant for the windowsill.

Breeding for the mass market. To meet mass market needs and mechanized production, the growers needed a uniform group of cultivars with a full color range. The breeding and selection efforts at Kientzler concentrated mainly on fulfilling the requirements of the market, however, without neglecting the other breeding goals. The most important breeding goals in the past few years have been: compact growth habit, good branching habit, quick and easy to grow, small, tough foliage, many plants per square feet in production, large, round flowers held over the foliage canopy, resistance to insects and diseases, good contrast between flowers and foliage and significant improvement over existing cultivars.

Breeding for the future. The currently available Paradise series fulfills virtually all of these requirements. The original breeding goals are still valid in principle although they continually have to be adjusted to the current needs of the market. The keeping qualities of the flowers under shipping conditions and under low light conditions, increased tolerance to full sun conditions and to drought are just a few of the characteristics that still need to be improved. These breeding goals can be achieved by use of conventional breeding techniques. Other breeding goals, such as virus resistance or disease resistance in general, can only be brought about by use of biotechnological methods.

Inducing mutations through irradiation or other means does not make much sense, since the genetic variability of New Guinea hybrids is extremely broad. Interspecific crosses are often impossible due to the differences in chromosome counts. Biotechnology could be of some assistance here. Even though the color range of New Guinea impatiens is quite broad, true yellow would be a very welcome addition and is therefore the "holy grail" of many breeders. Indeed, there are many unrelated Impatiens species that have this flower color, so there is hope.

Breeding for the grower. The most important tool of the breeder is self-restraint. Under consideration of the differing market requirements in various parts of the world and in view of the many ways that this crop is used, one quickly comes up with a large assortment of varieties that are likely to confuse most growers. However, if one considers that there is a need for an assortment of basket cultivars, an assortment for the production of flowering pot plants, and an assortment for window boxes and bedding purposes, a full range of solid colors, plus various bicolors, then it is not difficult to come up with at least 50 varieties. The importance of this crop justifies such diversity.

Mini New Guineas. In the past few years, in the course of our breeding program, several extremely compact, miniature genotypes occurred, many of which had very small leaves and flowers. These were treated as a distinct group of cultivars and improved through further breeding efforts. These tiny new cultivars are not related to the Chico mini-mini series (*I. wallerana*) bred by PanAmerican Seed; they are indeed miniature New Guinea impatiens (*I. hawkeri*). They are excellent for small pots, as a border plant, and for color bowls. These new cultivars are virtually marketable and will be introduced soon.

Room for more introductions. The changing tastes of consumers alone will ensure that the assortment of varieties on the market will be in constant motion. In addition, the needs and requirements of the growers, who have to constantly react to the changing conditions on the market and in production, will demand new, improved varieties. There are still many years of work left in this crop. Novel breeding techniques may help us attain these goals more quickly. Some of these techniques may, in fact, be necessary in order to develop disease-resistant varieties. The career of New Guinea impatiens on the international market has been like a comet, and the tail end is still nowhere in sight!

Lyndon Drewlow of Mikkelsens, Inc.

Jim Mikkelsen received and sold progeny of the original collection of plants as well as early cultivars developed by Longwood and USDA. Jim saw potential in the New Guinea impatiens. A breeding program was started to develop compact floriferous plants. Early on many people dropped out of New Guinea impatiens breeding as they felt it would be too difficult to control propagation of plants as New Guinea impatiens are easy to grow from cuttings. Plant patents were not widely used yet on flowering pot crops. Mikkelsens had seven cultivars ready for release in 1975, with a second group of 10 cultivars ready for release as the American Heritage series for the Bicentennial in 1976.

In 1978 the first cultivars of the Sunshine series were released using names from the solar system such as Meteor, Galaxy, and Constellation. The first bicolor New Guinea impatiens were released in the mid-1980s in this series under the names Sunregal, Sunburst, Sunglow, and Sundazzle. Cultivars continued to be released under the Sunshine Series name until 1988 with Radiance, Antares, and Nebulous being the last cultivars in this series.

In 1990 the first seven cultivars in the Lasting Impressions series were released. This series was bred for earlier flowering, numerous large flowers, highly self branched and superior outdoor performance under a wide range of conditions.

The double-flowered series. The work to develop the double-flowered New Guinea impatiens began in August of 1983 when Jim Mikkelsen found a seedling line in the breeding population that had a partial extra petal on approximately 20% of the flowers. The individual was selfed, but no viable seeds were ever obtained, probably because of the severe inbreeding depression that exists in New Guinea impatiens. The individual was also crossed to other breeding lines, which was the beginning of many generations of recurrent selection where progeny with increased doubleness were selected and incorporated into the breeding program. Backcrossing to the original parent and other superior double plants was carried out as well as sib-mating.

In the spring of 1990 we saw the first seedling populations where most of the seedlings from a double times double cross were double. At this time, it was finally possible to put strong selection pressure on plant habit, vigor, flower size and number, and outdoor performance. This selection pressure resulted in the release of the Twice As Nice series in January of 1993 with the six cultivars, Allegro, Minuet, Largo, Canon, Baroque, and Sonata. Work is continuing to improve flower size and number on plants, outdoor performance, increased number of petals, and other characteristics.

Plant breeders, including Jim Mikkelsen, who have worked at Mikkelsens, Inc. on the development of New Guinea impatiens were John Ryan, Cornelius Van Den Berg, and Lyndon Drewlow.

Improvements for future New Guinea impatiens. As work continues on New Guinea impatiens, the following improvements are important:
- Improved outdoor performance—more tolerance of low humidity and high temperatures; reduced transpiration so varieties can tolerate windy sites; more efficient root systems to improve plant performance in a range of soil types and moisture conditions; increased tolerance to low temperatures especially during the spring sales period.
- Reduced water requirement of plants.
- Earlier flowering and more numerous flowers.
- Indoor pot plant types.
- Improved shelf life and shipping characteristics.
- Reduced ethylene production in plants.
- New flower forms and colors.
- New foliage types on plants.
- Disease and insect resistance.

Sources of traits in related species.
- It is possible to obtain F1 hybrid plants between New Guinea impatiens and the Celebes and Java (*I. platypetala*) types with Claude Hope developing Tangeglow from a Celebes cross with New Guinea impatiens.
- Work of Dr. Arisumi of USDA and Dr. Loren Stephens at Iowa State suggests that interspecific crosses may be possible if embryo rescue and correct growing media are used to grow the embryo into a plant.
- It is just a matter of time before genetic engineering will let us use genes from one species in another.

Breeding for disease/insect resistance. Disease resistance such as for Rhizoctonia can be selected in seedling populations. For example, in the red flowered group, there are individuals that are very susceptible to Rhizoctonia and others that are very resistant. It should be possible to select for resistance or tolerance for other fungal diseases. Insect resistance probably will be more difficult to attain in a breeding program with the exception of red spider mites. Red spider mites usually do not like to feed on hirsute (with coarse hairs) leaves, a trait that exists in New Guinea impatiens.

Biotechnology. Biotechnology will probably not play a major role in the near future until procedures, cost reductions, and regulation problems are worked out on this crop. At this time, I see tissue culture as the main tool for such things as embryo rescue from wide crosses and holding disease-free plants in a protected environment. Biotechnology's role in developing virus resistance in plants will be important in developing INSV/TSWV-resistant cultivars.

Utility patent. Protection of the double-flowered characteristic in the New Guinea impatiens is being sought as a utility patent. Utility patents protect the characteristic or trait, not just the individual plants as in the traditional plant patent systems. This choice was made because of the time and cost of development of the double-flowered characteristic and the need to recover development costs.

It will also allow us to offer our customers new, improved cultivars as they are developed. We also will not need to go through the plant patent process with each variety since they will already be protected under the utility patent. The utility patent differs from the regular plant patent in that it prohibits other individuals from using the plants in a breeding program unless they have a signed agreement with the holder of the utility patent to use the characteristic in breeding.

Conclusion

Breeders of New Guinea impatiens have made tremendous strides in improving the wild jungle plants that became available for breeding in the early 1970s. Now that New Guinea impatiens play a major role in the bedding plant business, breeders have even bigger challenges in the future to improve this crop. I hope that this chapter has stimulated new thinking among breeders as to the challenges and opportunities that exist for improving New Guinea impatiens.

References ─────────────────────────

[1]   Andrews, B. New product development manager. Ball Seed Co., West Chicago, Ill. Personal communication.

[2]   Arisumi, T. 1973. Morphologhy and breeding behavior of colchicine-induced polyploid *Impatiens* spp. L. *J. Amer. Soc. Hort. Sci.* 98 (6): 599-601.

[3]   ———. 1974. Chromosome numbers and breeding behavior of hybrids among Celebes, Java, and New Guinea species of *Impatiens* L. *HortScience* 9 (5): 478-479

[4]   ———. 1980. *In vitro* culture of embryos and ovules of certain incompatible selfs and crosses among *Impatiens* species. *J. Amer. Soc. Hort. Sci.* 105 (5): 629-631

[5]   ———. 1987. Cytology and morphology of ovule culture-derived interspecific impatiens hybrids. *J. Amer. Soc. Hort. Sci.* 112 (6): 1026-1031.

[6]   Castillio, S., and J.L. Peterson. 1990. Cause and control of crown rot of New Guinea impatiens. *Plant Disease* 74: 77-79

[7]   Erwin, John. University of Minnesota. Personal communication.

[8]   Gager, C.F. 1987. Interspecific hybridization in the genus *Impatiens.* Master's thesis, Univ. of Connecticut.

[9]   Grey-Wilson, C. 1980. *Impatiens of Africa.* Rotterdam: A.A. Balkema.

[10]   Merlin, C.A., and W.F. Grant. 1986. Hybridization studies in the genus *Impatiens. Can. J. Bot.* 64:1069-1074.

[11]   Parker, R. University of Connecticut. Personal communication.

[12]   Pasutti, D.W., J.L. Weigle, and A.R. Beck. 1977. Cytology and breeding behavior of some impatiens hybrids and their backcross progeny. *Can. J. Botany* 55:296-300.

[13]   Pusutti, D.W., and J.L. Weigle. 1980. Pollen fertility in Java New Guinea impatiens interspecific hybrids. *Can J. Bot.* 58: 384-387.

[14]   Pennisi, E. 1992. True blue—molecules stack up to color flowers. *Science News* 142 (12): 184-186.

[15]   Quene, R.-J. W., and M.S. Strefeler. *A review of the literature on New Guinea impatiens.* 1992. Minnesota Flower Growers Bulletin 41 (3) 16-27.

[16]   Sabri, H., A. Abbasi, and J.L. Weigle. 1982. Resistance in New Guinea *Impatiens* species and hybrids to the two-spotted spider mite. *Hortscience* 17 (1): 47-48.

[17]   Pasutti, D.W., J.L. Weigle and A.R. Beck, 1977. Cytology and breeding behavior of some impatiens hybrids and their backcross progeny. *Can. J. Botany.* 55: 296-300

[18]   Stephens, L., and R. Fruth. July 1992. *Breeding of heat-tolerant New Guinea impatiens using interspecific hybridization.* Bedding Plants Foundation, Inc. No. F-054.

[19]   Stephens, L. Iowa State University. Personal communications.

[20]   U.S.D.A. Agriculture Dept. awards $10.5 million for plant genome research. *Genetic Engineering News.* June 15, 1992.

APPENDIX I

United States Department of Agriculture
Agriculture Research Service
Plant Science Research Division
Beltsville, Maryland 20705

Notice to Plant Breeders and Nurserymen Relative to the Release of 23 Impatiens Introductions

The Plant Science Research Division of the U.S. Department of Agriculture hereby releases 23 introductions of *Impatiens* for scientific study, use by plant breeders and for propagation and sale by nurserymen. The introductions were collected in the highlands of New Guinea and Java by the 1970 Expedition sponsored jointly by ARS and Longwood Gardens of Kennett Square, Pennsylvania. They represent a wealth of genetic material totally unlike commercial varieties now grown in the United States.

All of the *Impatiens* introductions are distinctive for flower size or color, for leaf size, shape or color or for plant size. Flower diameter in some of the introductions has attained 7 cm with spurs of equal length. Flower colors range from pure white through pastel shades of lavender and pink, and from pale orange to dark vermillion or scarlet. Leaf and stem color varies from green to intense dark red and in some introductions the leaves are beautifully variegated with white, yellow or pink. Although not completely identified they are directly suitable for cultivation as foliage or flowering varieties. The heaviest flowering occurs during winter and early spring on mature plants but some flowers are produced throughout the year. All are easily propagated by cuttings and some by seed. Preliminary tests indicate their suitability for summer planting outdoors in moist semi-shaded locations. They tolerate now more cold than older varieties. The 23 varieties are hereby named and released. The names are derived either from place names or descriptive terms in Pidgin English, the lingua franca of Australian Papua and New Guinea.

New Guinea Collections

Impatiens hawkeri, 'New Guinea Giants' — P.I. 354251, 354252, 354253.

> Tall, vigorous plants with thick fleshy stems, some marked with red. Leaves green. Flowers flat, 5-6 cm by 4-5.5 cm, spurs to 6 cm long, pastel shades of lavender, pink or white.

Impatiens herzogii, 'Daulo Pass' — P.I. 349584.

> Plants low growing, well branched. Foliage bronze-green. Flowers 3.5 cm by 3.5 cm, pale orange with white eye.

Impatiens linearifolia, 'Longpela Lip' [1] — P.I. 354263.

> Plants medium tall. Stems swollen at nodes, red at base. Leaves very narrow, wider at tips of branches, to 18 cm long, undersurface red, metallic green above with red mid-rib and petiole. Flower 5 cm by 5 cm, narrow petals, light pink with dark pink eye.

Impatiens linearifolia, 'Liklik Susa' [1] — P.I. 354266, 354267.

> Semi-dwarf to tall. Stem fleshy, tinted red at swollen basal nodes, light red above. Leaves long strap-shaped at lower nodes, long-lanceolate at branch tips, dark green variegated with yellow along mid-rib. Flower round in outline, 3.3 cm by 3.1 cm, pale pinkish salmon, small violet eye.

Impatiens schlechteri, 'Pikinini' [1] — P.I. 354258.

> Dwarf. Stems with short internodes, fleshy, light red. Leaves medium green with mid-rib and petiole pink. Flower size medium, petals medium wide, dark vermilion with darker eye. Spur 5 cm long.

Impatiens schlechteri, 'Naispela' [1] — P.I. 354259.

> Semi-dwarf. Stem fleshy with short internodes, medium red. Leaves dark green with red veins. Flower round, 4 cm, dark vermilion, dorsal sepal strongly keeled on reverse.

---

[1] In pronunciation Pidgin English resembles British English except that "a" is always pronounced ah, "e" as in pen, "i" as ee, and "u" as in put. It is unaccented.

Impatiens schlechteri, 'Luluai' [1] — P.I. 354262.

Semi-dwarf. Stem fleshy with short internodes, reddish. Leaves light green. Petioles pink. Flowers 5 cm by 4.5 cm bright vermilion. Petals medium width, notched at tip.

Impatiens sp., 'Aiyura' — P.I. 349582.

Tall. Stems fleshy, usually showing red. Leaves large, green. Flowers 5.0 by 4.0 cm, shades of bright magenta with white eye. Petals narrow to broad. Spurs white, to 5 cm long.

Impatiens sp., 'Kassam' — P.I. 349583.

Tall. Stems somewhat fleshy, red. Flowers 5 cm by 4.6 cm, light pink with darker pink outlining white eye zone. Petals notched at tip. Spur 6 cm long, pink.

Impatiens sp., 'Patep II' — P.I. 349586.

Medium tall. Stem fleshy, reddish below. Leaves green. Flowers 4 cm by 4 cm in shades of bright magenta. Spur greenish white, pubescent, 4.5 cm long.

Impatiens sp., 'Mindik' — P.I. 349588.

Tall. Stem fleshy, reddish to green below and at nodes. All parts free of pubescence. Leaves green. Flowers 5 cm by 4.5 cm, white to pale pink. Spur 5.5 cm long.

Impatiens sp., 'Kundiawa' — P.I. 354254.

Medium height. Stem slightly reddish. Leaves green. Flowers 5 cm, round, flat, intense vermilion with white to pale lavender eye. Spur 5 cm.

Impatiens sp., 'Mt. Kum' — P.I. 354255.

Tall. Stem less fleshy than others, dark red on lower part. Leaves dark green, irregular surface. Petiole red. Flower 4 cm by 4 cm, round with widely overlapping petals, bright orange red with small violet eye. Spur slender 5.5 cm long, red.

Impatiens sp., 'Korn Farm' — P.I. 354256, 354260.

Tall. Stem swollen at nodes, very dark red. Upper surface of leaves dark metallic reddish green, lower surface and petiole dark red. Flower round, flat, 6 cm by 5.5 cm, light vermilion red with violet eye. Spur dark red, slender, 7 cm long.

Impatiens sp., 'Redpela' [1] — P.I. 354257.
> Tall. All plant parts very dark red. Flowers 4 cm by 3.8 cm dark red with orange overlay, dark violet eye, petals medium wide. Spur 6 cm long, red.

Impatiens sp., 'Mt. Hagen' — P.I. 354261.
> Medium height. Stem fleshy, red at the nodes. Leaves whorled, green with white variegation along with mid-rib. Flowers round, 4 cm by 4 cm, petals wide, overlapping, medium salmon red with pinkish tones, pale lavender eye. Spur 4.5 cm.

Impatiens sp., 'Masta Mausgras' [1] — P.I. 354264.
> Tall, vigorous. Dark red stems and petioles. Leaves large, glossy, reddish green, mid-rib pink, bordered with irregular yellowish variegations on upper leaves. Flower dull scarlet, 5 cm by 5 cm not opening flat. Spur slender, 5.3 cm long.

Impatiens sp., 'Plaua Misis' [1] — P.I. 354265.
> Semi-dwarf. Stem thick with short internodes, red. Leaves large, dark green to reddish, irregularly variegated white to pale pink. Flower 7 cm by 6.5 cm, salmon pink shading lighter toward base of petals, dark eye zone. Petals somewhat reflexed with age. Spur 6 cm long.

Java Collection

Impatiens platypetala, 'Tjibodas' — P.I. 349629.
> Somewhat procumbent to medium tall. Stems more slender than in New Guinea collections, green to red. Internodes short at base becoming longer on upright stems. Leaves green. Flowers light to dark magenta with darker markings on basal petals, 3.2-4.5 cm by 2.0-4.0 cm. Spur white or pale magenta, 3.6-4.5 cm long.

The Plant Science Research Division has none of these plants for sale. Limited quantities of cuttings will be available to qualified nurserymen and plant breeders during the late spring of 1972. Requests should be sent in writing to the U.S. Plant Introduction Station, Glenn Dale, Maryland 20769.

Hugo O. Graumann
Director
Plant Science Research Division
Date: Feb. 23, 1972

[1] CP refers to the photo number in the Color Plate Section.

[1] CP refers to the photo number in the Color Plate Section.

[1] CP refers to the photo number in the Color Plate Section.

[1] CP refers to the photo number in the Color Plate Section.

T

taxonomy, 12, 15, 229–230
temperature
    carbon partitioning, 48, 51
    development rate, 43–45
    DIF, 46–47, 51, 53, 84
    dry weight, 49, 51
    finishing, 52, 95, 98, CP [1] 5.3
    flower size, 48, CP 5.2
    garden, 115
    and IPM, 172
    leaf area, 48
    leaf dry weight, 51
    leaf number, 48
    optimum range, 45, CP 5.1
    rooting, 83
    seed plants, 108
    stem caliber, 47
    stem elongation, 45, 46–47, 53
    stock plants, 70
tissue culture, disease, 57
transplanting. *See* cuttings,
    transplanting

U

United States Department of
    Agriculture, 4, 11, 13, 16, 231
uses
    European, 9
    garden, 104
    general, 2, 4, 9, 227

V

viruses. *See* diseases

---

[1] CP refers to the photo number in the Color Plate Section.

ABOUT THE EDITORS

Warren Banner is General Manager of Ball FloraPlant in West Chicago, Ill. His responsibilities encompass Ball FloraPlant's breeding direction, disease-free certification, production, and marketing. Warren is a graduate of the University of Tennessee with a B.A. degree in botany and an M.S. degree in plant physiology. He served as operations manager with Phyton Technologies Inc. from 1982 to 1984 and is the author of a chapter on tissue culture for the *Ball RedBook*.

Michael J. Klopmeyer is the Pathology Group Manager for Ball FloraPlant, West Chicago, Ill. He manages the clean stock program (Ball Certified Plants) and production planning for Ball FloraPlant and supervises the plant pathology research program. Mike received a B.S. degree in botany and zoology and an M.S. degree in botany from Eastern Illinois University. His Ph.D. degree in plant pathology is from the University of Illinois. Mike is a member of the American Phytopathological Society. He has written chapters for the *Ball Guide to New Guinea Impatiens, Ball RedBook, Geraniums IV,* and *Proceedings* of the 3rd International Geranium Conference.